THE
MAVERICKS
American Engravers

THE
MAVERICKS

American Engravers

By

Stephen DeWitt Stephens

RUTGERS UNIVERSITY PRESS

NEW BRUNSWICK, NEW JERSEY

1950

Preface

FOR SOME TIME before his death in 1939, Mr. William South-
worth Hunt of Newark, New Jersey, had been collecting notes
and materials which were intended to serve as the basis for a book on
Peter Maverick, with special regard to the period from 1809 to 1820
when Maverick lived and worked in Newark. After Mr. Hunt's death,
Mrs. Hunt offered his materials to his friends in the hope that one of
them would carry on the task. Eventually these materials reached me.

As my work progressed, I found I could not write of the life and
career of Peter without a glance also at the lives and careers of other
Mavericks whose names are found on engravings and lithographs of
his time — the father who trained him, the two brothers who learned
their trades beside him in his father's shop, the one son and the several
daughters whom he himself trained, the son of one brother who
carried on lithography to the end of the century, and the son of the
other brother who did engraving and printing and who gave the name
of Maverick to a girl who had learned the craft under the tutelage of
another great engraver of the time, her father Alexander Anderson.

The history of the family was in utter confusion, but in the
meager records available the family stood forth as one marked by an
independence, industry, and initiative which made their struggle for
success an interesting part of the history of America as well as of the

history of engraving and lithography. This family built no great corporation with massive factories, but only a series of little shops in which
they worked throughout the half century following the founding of
the United States of America. But these little shops, with a few apprentices and helpers, turned out copperplate and lithographic prints
for a varied trade, and those who worked in the shops laid foundations
for developments which even Mavericks of the most vivid imagination
could scarcely have foreseen.

But the story still remains chiefly the story of the Peter Maverick
who was born in 1780 and died in 1831. The works which I have found
bearing his signature far exceed in number those of all the other Mavericks combined; and a study of his work shows, further, that it sur-
passes that of his family not only in quantity but also in quality.
Although it is true that Peter could turn out from his shop an inex-
pensive and perfunctory plate and often did so, even his run-of-the-
mill work shows the firm hand of a workman proud of his work; the
plate that was a real challenge to his skill would bear comparison with
the best.

In writing about this little-known man * more than a century
after his death, I have had to call upon a great number of institutions ** and public agencies whose records might help to reconstruct
the successes and failures, the business transactions, the engraving tasks,
the hopes and aspirations of Peter Maverick. My original plan was to
record by name the helpers in these places who gave of their time and
their skill to set me on the right track or to lead me further along it,
but that plan I soon gave up, for their number, or their preference for
anonymity, would make any such list unjust. Without their aid, however, this study would have been far more unworthy than it is, and the
work far less pleasant as a memory.

Many persons, however, have helped me in ways which can be

---

* The longest biography of Peter
Maverick in print, and the only one of
any value, is the half-page sketch by Mr.
Frank Weitenkampf in the *Dictionary of
American Biography*.
** See page 183.

acknowledged only individually. Mr. Manton Maverick, though he knew little about his grandfather Peter, was most patient with my attempts to probe his memory; in a letter shortly before his death he urged me to hurry along any further questions lest they come too late. The Misses Harriet M. and Grace E. Parkes, great-granddaughters of Samuel Maverick, have copied records, searched through diaries and scrapbooks, and listed family heirlooms which might be of assistance, as they very often were. Charles E. Townsend, great-great-grandson of Peter, who learned of my search from a newspaper story, lent me family scrapbooks (since purchased by the Newark Public Library) and restored to public record the Neagle portrait of his ancestor, which I had vainly sought for years.

Private collectors have been generous with their treasures. Dr. Walter Haushalter sent me his collection of some five hundred Maverick items for my leisurely study. Mr. Walter Davenport checked his collection and furnished me with detailed descriptions of some engravings that I had not seen. Mr. J. N. Spiro combed his rich collection of bank notes for those engraved by the Mavericks, and has aided me in other ways. Mr. W. H. Dillistin has not only helped me by his publications on New Jersey banks and their currency, but also by information from his own Maverick bank notes.

To Dr. Lester Cappon I am indebted for digging out the details of Maverick's work for Thomas Jefferson in making a plan for the University of Virginia, after I had all but given up the search. To Dr. H. E. Dickson I owe gratitude for many helpful suggestions, and for the use in manuscript of his extensive study of the life of John Wesley Jarvis. Mrs. Walter McGee, the owner of Jarvis's portrait of Peter's sister Rebecca, has been most generous in giving me access to that portrait and in sharing her photographs of other Maverick portraits. Miss Marguerite Lynch, at work on a life of John Neagle, gleaned from his papers the circumstances surrounding his painting of Peter Maverick's portrait in 1826.

To Miss Helen Knubel I owe special thanks, for in her study of the life and work of Alexander Anderson she has indexed many notes about the Mavericks, and these she has graciously passed on to me. Without her help I should probably never have pieced together my notes about the daughter of Anderson who married a Maverick and engraved under that name.

Dealers and their representatives have allowed me many privileges, sometimes even the free run of their stores. In New York, I am indebted to Mr. Harry Shaw Newman of the Old Print Shop, to Mr. Robert Fridenberg, to the Kennedy Galleries, to Messrs. Harry Bland and Harry F. Stone. In Boston, the Print Department at Goodspeed's and Holman's Print Shop have been helpful in many ways. And nearer home, Mr. Malcolm Stone of West Englewood, New Jersey, has lent me items from his stock which I have seen nowhere else, and so opened up several new avenues of research.

In preparing this material for publication, my most difficult problem concerned the presentation of the biographical material. To tell the story baldly, demanding that the reader believe in my omniscience regarding this engraver who died more than a century ago, would obviously not be playing fair. But, since a plan of documentation would have required a footnote for nearly every sentence, with several for some, I have chosen instead to discuss now and then with the reader my problems of research, and to submit, in addition to known facts, speculations concerning the Mavericks which resulted from my increasing awareness of their character. But, lest I leave some future student of this family to guess at my authority (as I have had to guess at the authority behind the statements of Cummings or Dunlap or Sumner), I shall deposit with the Rutgers University Library, the American Antiquarian Society, the Library of Congress, and the New York Historical Society a typescript containing line-by-line documentation, which will be indexed according to the pages and lines of this printed volume. For the general reader, however, I have included a discussion of bibliographical sources in the Appendix.

PREFACE

One final word. I am well aware of the possibility of errors of commission and omission. It has been my purpose to include in this volume all that is known of this family of master craftsmen; I would, therefore, welcome knowledge of any additional material that may have escaped my attention, or the correction of any inadvertent errors.

STEPHEN DeWITT STEPHENS

RUTGERS UNIVERSITY
THE NEWARK COLLEGE OF ARTS AND SCIENCES
NOVEMBER, 1949

Contents

I

PETER MAVERICK AND HIS FAMILY

II

MAVERICK ENGRAVINGS AND LITHOGRAPHS

CONTENTS

CONTENTS

XV

List of Illustrations

On Engraving in Metal

TO TEST your feeling in this matter accurately, here is a manuscript book written with pen and ink, and illustrated with flourishes and vignettes.

I imagine that most of my pupils would think me very tyrannical if I requested them to do anything of the kind themselves. And yet, when you see in the shop windows a line engraving, you never say "how wonderful" that is, nor consider how you would like to have to live, by producing anything of the same kind yourselves.

Yet you cannot suppose it is in reality easier to draw a line with a cutting point, not seeing the effect at all, or, if any effect, seeing a gleam of light instead of darkness, than to draw your black line at once on the white paper? You cannot really think that there is something complacent, sympathetic, and helpful in the nature of steel; so that while a pen-and-ink sketch may always be considered an achievement proving cleverness in the sketcher, a sketch on steel comes out by a mere favour of the indulgent metal; or that the plate is woven like a piece of pattern silk, and the pattern is developed by pasteboard cards punched full of holes? Not so. Look close at this engraving, or take a smaller and simpler one, Turner's Mercury and Argus,—imagine it to be a drawing in pen and ink, and yourself required similarly to produce its parallel! True, the steel point has the one advantage of not blotting, but it has tenfold or twentyfold disadvantage, in that you cannot slur, nor efface, except in a very resolute and laborious way, nor play with it, nor even see what you are doing with it at the moment, far less the effect that is to be. You must feel what you are doing with it, and know precisely what you have got to do; how deep, how broad, how far apart your lines must be, etc. and etc., (a couple of lines of etceteras would not be enough to imply all you must know). But suppose the plate were only a pen drawing: take your pen—your finest—and just try to copy the leaves that entangle the head of Io, and her head itself; remembering always that the kind of work required here is mere child's play compared to that of fine figure engraving. Nevertheless, take a small magnifying glass to this—count the dots and lines that graduate the nostrils and the edges of the facial bone; notice how the light is left on the top of the head by the stopping, at its outline, of the coarse touches which form the shadows under the leaves; examine it well, and then—I humbly ask of you—try to do a piece of it yourself! You clever sketcher—you young lady or gentleman of genius—you eye-glassed dilettante—you current writer of criticism royally plural,—I beseech you,—do it yourself; do the merely etched outline yourself, if no more. Look you,—you hold your etching needle this way, as you would a pencil, nearly; and then,—you scratch with it! it is as easy as lying. Or if you think that too difficult, take an easier piece; —take either of the light sprays of foliage that rise against the fortress on the right, pass your lens over them—look how their fine outline is first drawn, leaf by leaf; then how the distant rock is put in between, with broken lines, mostly stopping before they touch the leaf-outline; and again, I pray you, do it yourself,—if not on that scale, on a larger. Go on into the hollows of the distant rock,—traverse its thickets,—number its towers;—count how many lines there are in a laurel bush —in an arch—in a casement; some hundred and fifty, or two hundred, deliberately drawn lines, you will find, in every square quarter of an inch;—say three thousand to the inch,—each, with skilful intent, put in its place! and then consider what the ordinary sketcher's work must appear, to the men who have been trained to do this!

—JOHN RUSKIN in *Ariadne Florentina*, 1872

[I]

PETER MAVERICK

& HIS FAMILY

ONE

No. 3, Crown Street

LIBERTY STREET in lower Manhattan Island in the late eight-eenth century — before the new American consciousness had turned to the task of purging the nation of inappropriate geographical terms — was named in proper loyalty Crown Street. At No. 3, near the eastern end where it meets Maiden Lane, soon after these newly united states had set up their first offices and installed their first president in the refitted municipal building on Wall Street a few blocks south, a nine-year-old boy was busy in the shop of his father. Before him on his bench was a printing block. To it had been transferred a drawing — a small simple drawing of a tree and a serpent and a man and a woman, the age-old picture of Adam and Eve (page 5). Under the boy's hand was an engraver's burin, a steel tool with a point like a tiny plow, which can turn up a curl of soft metal or end-grain wood in strokes light or heavy as the engraver's hand and wrist may direct. With this tool the boy was at work preparing the block for printing, cutting from its surface all that which should be white in the final picture, and leaving untouched the other parts, the lines and dots and dark areas which should press the ink upon the paper in the final printing.

3

The proprietor of the shop came from time to time to encourage his son, leaving for a moment the copperplate which he himself was preparing. Copperplate work, with which the shop was chiefly concerned, involved a quite different process from that in which the boy was engaged, and a more difficult one, but one by which the boy was destined to make his fame. Sometimes, too, the father's assistant, perhaps a relative,* or an apprentice who had been indentured for training in the craft of engraving or silversmithing, would look with half condescension and half awe at this child whose hand seemed already almost skillful, whose discrimination seemed already almost sure.

It was a good shop. Here were to be found copperplates and type-metal blocks, and burins and supplies of all sorts for professional or amateur engravers. To this shop, after studying art in the studios of Europe, had come the actor and painter, William Dunlap, to learn the "theory and practice of etching," and to etch and print the frontispiece for a dramatic publication then occupying his mind. Years later this versatile artist made special mention of the adequacy of the shop, and his opinion was that of a discriminating judge. Here too, to echo newspaper announcements of the owner, men came to have their coats of arms engraved, and women to have their tea-table silver decorated, and all would be done as well, said the shopmaster in his enthusiasm for the new nation, as could be done in Europe. With what pride the maker of that boast must have received, the year before, the order from James Duane to provide a silver seal for the new United States District Court and to engrave on it the figure of Liberty, or the order from a neighboring institu-

* The U.S. census of 1790 records one man as a member of the household who was not listed as an employee nor as a member of the immediate family.

4

tion of learning to remove the name of King's College from its seal and inlay a plate with the name Columbia.*

The boy had already cut carefully around the outline of his design and had routed out enough of his large white areas to know which of the remaining areas were trees and hills and figures. The large central tree offered an attractive task. Holding the tool with a light steady pressure, he moved tool and block in a circular movement to outline the apples, and then, as his father had instructed him, he covered the curved surfaces of the apples with short rounded strokes, varying the direction that the apples might not seem to blend too much with the foliage. The foliage itself was easy, for after the edge of the area had

Now the serpent was more subtile than any beast of the field which the LORD GOD had made. And he said unto the woman,. Yea, hath God said, Ye shall not eat of every tree of the garden?

And the woman said unto the serpent, We may eat of the fruit of the trees of the garden?

Genesis iii. 1—2.

been cut like the edge of a saw, he had merely to repeat over and over again the quick curved stroke that suggested leaf shapes. In the part of the tree above Eve he seems to have become careless, or perhaps his hands became tired of repeating the same stroke, but just above Adam his burin again moved

* Bills for the Court seal and the Columbia inlay are among the papers of the N.Y. Historical Society and the Columbia archives, respectively.

NOTE: The Adam and Eve print [349] is reproduced with the permission of the N.Y. Public Library.

with sureness, for the lines are clean and firm. Let us hope that his father praised him a little for that spot of clean cutting! *

But the tree trunk and the serpent were left, and both were cylindrical objects. So the boy, according to his instructions, cut strokes across each, strokes with a slight curve to suggest the surface, strokes minutely drawn from the top of the trunk to the spreading root, from the head of the snake to the curiously broken tip of its tail. But what happened to that tail? Did a routing tool slip while the white area was being cleared, and thus suddenly change the tail's direction?

The background demanded only variations of the techniques required for the tree; the strokes for the foliage, of course, were smaller and lighter. When the effect seemed too much like that of a single tree on each side of the central group, a few vertical strokes of the burin separated the trees and moved them back to where they belonged. To keep them there, the boy accentuated the rolling hills in front of the woods, varying the direction of the curving strokes to mark each rise. But Adam and Eve are standing on no such varied surfaces; here the strokes are straight, with a change of their direction as the foreground approaches the eye of the spectator.

Of course the boy did not learn how to do all this as he cut this particular block. Under his father's direction he had been drawing pictures and cutting practice blocks for a long time, studying especially how to establish this or that effect with black pencil lines on white paper. In this engraving he treated the hills and the foreground in much the same way as he had learned to produce such an effect with a pencil; as long as he was

---

* It is, of course, possible that it was the father who cut the spot in showing the boy how to do it.

dealing with close parallel lines, it mattered little whether he drew the black lines or cut out the white ones.

But the human figures presented problems. Here his tool must leave the black surface untouched, and the strokes of its cutting edge must be made where the final picture was to be white. The surfaces on body and limbs and face which were in shadow had to be left untouched, the areas in full light had to be cut away. The boy took no chances with the faces; except for suggesting a little stubble on Adam's cheek and chin, he shows the features in outline only, and in the noses of Adam and Eve the outline reaches a minimum which might be called perfection. The boy's hand must have moved carefully to leave these shaped dots untouched on the surface.

But he was not satisfied to make of the whole picture a mere outline drawing; after clearly marking off bodies and arms and legs (notice the knees) he worked for highlights and shadows. With Eve he adopted the traditional source of light, a point above and to the left of the picture, and he shaded consistently. With Adam, however, his sense of symmetry and balance must have overcome his feeling for the source of light, and he shaded as if the light were coming from the center of the picture, from the tree or—as some of the devout who were shocked by his father's religious views might have been glad to say—from the serpent. Whatever the source, Adam's right leg, from the knee down, is unrecipient to that light, and has a source of its own somewhere over at the left.

With these problems met, and the shadows softened with light strokes to relieve their blackness, the bowknots of fig leaves—or whatever their substance is—were carefully cut. One speculates as to where the boy found a model for those garments, for they are strangely reminiscent of the garments worn by two figures in a bookplate which his father had recently made for P. J. Van Berckell.

On an untouched strip which remained at the bottom, the boy cut the signature which he was later to learn to cut with confidence and skill in plates of many kinds. On the straight lines he cut boldly, varying the broad and the narrow strokes according to intention. The initial *P* is accomplished, the *M* is well passed, the *A* is fumbled a little at the top but the *V* redeems it, and the *E* deserves praise. The *R* demanded curves, however, and although they are executed with a fine sweep, the lines are weak; perhaps he decided not to fatten them and risk a worse flaw. The *I* and *C* and *K* go swimmingly, although the curves of *C* appear to have presented some hazards. But on the small *Sct.*, written as his father wrote it with the *t* raised above the line, his boldness evidently waned; the curves are cut with a hesitant hand, with the surface of the block scratched scarcely enough to show in the print.

Confidence seems to have returned with the capital letters in the linked *Æ* and to remain with him for the most part in the word *YEARS*, carrying him fairly well through the curves of *R* but failing him on the tricky *S* at the end. But immediately after the *Æ* (which his father had explained was the abbreviation of the Latin for *aged*, as *Sct.* was for *engraved*), in cutting the figure 9 his confidence deserted him completely; he seems first to have scratched in a hasty figure, and then to have tried to correct it by scratching again, as if stricken with a sudden shock at his own presumption in preparing a cut for publication at such an age.

But it *was* published. With an ornamental border of type

and with an explanatory quotation from Genesis below it, it had the place of honor as the frontispiece of *The Holy Bible Abridged*, published by Hodge, Allen, and Campbell in New York in 1790. We have evidence that the father and master of the shop, Peter Rushton Maverick, was proud of his promising son and pupil. The boy's mother had died three years before, but his new stepmother, his mother's sister, probably also approved the youngster's progress and wished the like, or better, for her own baby Samuel. Seven-year-old Andrew and five-year-old Maria perhaps realized little what the excitement meant, but big sisters Sarah and Rebecca and Ann could have appreciated his work and given the oldest of their brothers the praise that was due him, for there are many evidences of close and friendly family ties.

It was a humble family, and none of its members recorded for posterity its thoughts, opinions, or deeds. The very few letters that exist today were kept chiefly because they were written *to* prominent people, not because they were *from* people that were worth remembering. The only record of their births was in the family Bible and perhaps in the baptismal record of some church. When they married, the Bible and the civil and church records again recorded the fact. At their deaths the newspapers ran no obituary, but listed as briefly as possible the age, the cause of death, and the hour and place of the funeral services. They were businessmen and craftsmen in a large city which did not find in an industrious worker in his craft a person of special importance.

But the family was proud of itself and kept a record of its members. Moreover, these members left records when they bought land and sold it, or gave mortgages and had them foreclosed. They qualified as freemen of the city and served in the militia. They joined churches and lodges and reform and mutual-aid societies; they signed petitions; they made contracts and wills; they testified in court proceedings. And they made engravings—for all kinds of purposes—to which they proudly attached their signatures. These engravings, hundreds of them, tell a story of the development of an American family and its craftsmanship which is as valid as if documented throughout by contemporary written opinion.

It was from such source materials as these that this biographical sketch has been built, and from them we know that between October 22, 1789, and the same date in 1790, the childhood triumph related above took place at No. 3, Crown Street.

TWO

The Early Mavericks

PETER MAVERICK, the young boy in the shop, bore a surname which had long been a part of America's history, although there is little reason to believe that he was aware of the fact. His children and nephews a generation later apparently had a vague and completely erroneous idea that their grandfather Maverick had come "to this country from England (probably from the county of Kent), about the year 1774, when but eight or ten years of age." They suspected that the New York Mavericks had some connection with the Boston Mavericks but they could not establish the link, even when they understood that a legacy in the Bank of England was somehow at stake. Sometime later, in 1894, a report in the *New England Historical and Genealogical Register* proved their suspicions to be correct; records published by the same journal in 1942 and 1943 for the first time made generally available the genealogical ramifications of the Massachusetts Maverick family.

The known genealogical line begins with a certain Robert Maverick of Devonshire who had a son Peter, a clergyman who flourished in the early years of Elizabeth's reign. Among his children was a Reverend John Maverick, baptized November

28, 1578, who went to Exeter College at Oxford in 1595, receiving his degree of Bachelor of Arts in 1599 and Master of Arts in 1603. He served his church in Devonshire for years, and then in 1630 sailed with several of his family for Massachusetts, arriving at Hull on May 30 and proceeding thence to Dorchester. A year later he took the freeman's oath, and he lived as a colonist and leader of his church until his death in 1637, to be followed in that leadership by Richard, the first of the Mathers.

Although Reverend John Maverick was the founder of the family in America, he was not the first of that family to arrive in this country. His young son Samuel had left England six years earlier and had settled on an island in Massachusetts Bay. In the new country he began a stormy career as a defender of the British crown against colonial discontent, a career which gave him the title of Loyalist, brought him an appointment as King's Commissioner, and earned him finally a royal gift of a house and lot at what is now 50 Broadway in New York.

There may have been another son of John, bearing his father's name, who went to the Barbadoes and later in life to the colony of Carolina, there to found the American family of Mavericks who have long been prominent in the South. That this John was a son of Reverend John, and a brother of Samuel the Loyalist, is entirely plausible, but careful genealogists seem unwilling to say that the link is established.

But our chief concern is with Elias, another son of Reverend John. Elias' marriage to Anne Harris in 1633 brought him five sons and six daughters. Paul, one of these children, married Jemimah, the daughter of Lieutenant John Smith. Paul and Jemimah were the parents of the John Maverick who became an importer of hard woods in Middle (now Hanover) Street in Boston, at the sign of the Cabinet and Chest of Drawers. Probably the most famous Boston Maverick was Samuel, the grandson of this John, who as a boy was killed in the Boston massacre. But it is John's son Andrew, the father of Peter Rushton Maverick, who attracts our particular attention.

Andrew was born in Boston February 4, 1729, and baptized five days later. How and where he spent the first twenty-four years of his life is unknown, but in 1753 we find him in New York City, where on July 17 he was admitted as a freeman. On March 28 of the following year he married eighteen-year-old Sarah Rushton, the daughter of the prosperous mason Peter Rushton, and four years later, on March 13, 1759, he joined Captain Tobias Van Zandt's company of New York militia. His occupation has been given by one writer as "painter," by another "artist," but when he was admitted as a freeman and when he joined the militia, he himself designated his occupation as "painter." Except for a self-portrait which has been mentioned as his work, there appears to be little reason to consider him a worker in the fine arts.

There is one more record of Andrew before he slips from view in the obscurity of the scarce and poorly kept pre-Revolutionary records. In 1760, after George the Second died in England, the American colony elected a new assembly to represent the people to his young successor, George the Third. In New York city there were six candidates, two of whom, James DeLancey and William Bayard, were eager to give the young king the same loyalty that they had given so profitably to his predecessor, while the other four, who were of the Whig or Patriot Party, represented the fast-growing national sentiment

13

that was to bring revolt fifteen years later. During the three days of polling, in February of 1761, Andrew Maverick recorded his vote for the Patriots, Philip Livingston, William Cruger, John M. Scott, and Leonard Lispenard. Although Andrew did not live to see his only son, Peter Rushton Maverick, grow up, he left him this and other examples of independent thinking which the son was to follow energetically.

The early years of Peter Rushton Maverick are little illuminated by records, beyond that of his birth on April 11, 1755, and the death of his mother four years later. When the boy was ten, his grandfather Rushton made a will in which he left all his estate, including "houses, lands, bonds, slaves," to his wife Bethiah during her widowhood, but after her death the whole was to go to "my grandson Peter Rushton Maverick." From this and other provisions in the will it appears that Peter was not only an only child of his parents but also an only grandchild of the Rushtons, and the fact that no mention was made of Andrew may be the basis for the belief that he died before Peter's tenth birthday.

Two years after making this will the grandfather died. Bethiah lived on for twenty-three years longer, to see her grandson well established as an engraver and her great-grandson beginning his young apprenticeship. There appears to be no further record of the transfer of the family property to Maverick. Years afterward, however, when he sold the Rushton Liberty Street lot to the Quakers for a meeting house, he claimed his title to it as the "grandson and only heir" of Peter Rushton.

On July 4, 1772, the day not yet being a national holiday, seventeen-year-old Peter Rushton Maverick and nineteen-year-old Ann Reynolds posted bond with the secretary of the Province of New York and received a license to wed. Three years later, on Sunday, April 23, 1775, word of the battles of Concord and Lexington reached New York late in the day. Within forty-eight hours the royal arsenal had been sacked by the revolutionary mob and arms distributed among the revolutionary citizens. Peter, now a father as well as a husband, received a firelock, bayonet, belt, and other equipment; when he signed the receipt he wrote, as if in realization of the importance of the occasion, his full name, "Peter Rushton Maverick."

By midsummer, apparently to equip an organized body of militia, the weapons issued to the willing young men were recalled; and Maverick, described as a silversmith of Batteau (Dey) Street, was credited with Musket No. 543. This record gives us two bits of knowledge. It gives us Maverick's address nine years before the announcement in 1784 of his business in Crown Street. More important, it proves that Maverick was already established in his craft before the Revolution. The knowledge is not surprising, for an apt young man was scarcely likely to have been untrained at twenty, and he was, moreover, a man of family — baby Sarah was now a year and a half old, and another child was expected in the approaching winter.

Nearly a century ago the story was first recorded in print, without documentation, that by August of 1775 he was an ensign in Captain M. Minthorn's company of John Jay's Second Regiment of New York Militia, but there appears to be no official record. However, in 1789 after the Revolution had ended and the new nation had begun, the somewhat more mature Peter Rushton Maverick was listed as an ensign in Lieutenant Colonel James Alner's regiment, and four years later, in 1793, his title had become lieutenant.

15

It would be of interest to know how and where Peter Rushton Maverick got his training as a silversmith. Silversmithing leads naturally to engraving, for cutting a design on a silver teapot is little different from cutting it on a flat copperplate, and the taking of an impression on paper follows easily. Sometimes the elder Maverick has been called the first engraver in New York City; he is said also to have educated himself in the arts. Though he may have been first in importance (though some may dispute that), he was preceded in time by others who were called engravers; and though he may have been self-taught in that he was not bound out by formal indenture, yet he would scarcely have developed even the moderate proficiency which he shows in the 1780's if he had not had experience in a shop where work was going on with silver tableware and copperplates for printing.

We know of a few masters under whom he may have worked, for announcements of their business can be found in contemporary newspapers. In 1768, when this Maverick was thirteen, Charles Shipman advertised himself as a silversmith in the New York *Mercury*, and two years later in the same journal we find Charles O. Bruff setting himself forth as a goldsmith and jeweler, while in the *Journal* John Anthony Beau is announced as an "engraver and chaser," suggesting again the joint nature of the silversmith's and engraver's work. A fourth possible employer is Henry Pursell, who in 1775 announced a change of address for his engraving business. In 1771 Elisha Gallaudet was active in New York, and two years later John Hutt "from London" solicited the trade of the public. A Joseph Simons from Berlin announced his business in the New York *Gazetteer* of May 9, 1763, with this closing sentence: "Those

Gentlemen and Ladies that please to send their Escutcheons, may depend upon having them done after the Manner of the Herald's office, and as neat as in England." The final phrase is so similar to that used by Maverick in his announcements two decades later that we cannot help wondering whether this was his teacher, though at the date of the announcement Maverick was too young to be an apprentice.

That there were other silversmiths or allied tradesmen of the time in New York is known to us because they, like Maverick, signed their names and indicated their occupations when they took British muskets in April, 1775, and again when they returned them in July. One was John Burger of Maiden Lane, later to be prominent in the Society of Mechanics and Tradesmen. Another was Yellis Mandeville, identified as "with John Leary, Broadway," who may have been a young employee himself. There was William Smith of Crown Street, and there was Barthalemus Stakes of the same street as Maverick. Perhaps it was one of these who was Maverick's teacher.

When Rebecca, the second daughter of the Peter Rushton Mavericks, was born on January 8, 1776, New York was in constant threat of attack by the British. By 1778, the city was in the hands of the British Army, and about half of the population had fled to the Jerseys or to that part of New York above the Harlem River. Some of those who remained in the city stayed because they could not get away; many others stayed because their sympathies were with the established government. Did the Mavericks flee from New York at the threat of British attack? No record tells us, but, with a wife and two children to care for, it is hardly likely that Maverick would remain and risk British captivity.

Although three children were born to the Mavericks before the British evacuated New York in 1783, their places of birth are not recorded, and thus we have little or no clue as to the whereabouts of the family. We do know that a girl Ann was born on December 3, 1778, that a boy Peter * was born on October 22, 1780, and another boy Andrew on May 26, 1782. If the Mavericks were among the refugees from New York, then they must have returned very soon after the British left; the birthplace of a sixth child, Maria, who was born on January 14, 1784, can probably be assigned with reasonable certainty to that city.

It could not have been long after the British left the city that Maverick opened his shop in Crown Street, for on July 12, 1784, the following announcement appeared in *The New York Packet and the American Advertiser:*

Peter Maverick, *Engraver*,

Takes this method to inform the public, that he takes in Engraving at No. 3, Crown-street, next to the old Quaker-Meeting, where gentlemen may have their coats of arms, crests or cyphers done in the neatest manner. Ladies may have their tea-table plate ornamented in the newest fashion, with elegance and dispatch, by applying to their humble servant

Peter Maverick **

The service of the shop is set forth also on March 16, 1786, when in the *Packet* appears the following:

* Peter's birthplace was given on his death certificate a half century later as New York State. Since many of his Reynolds relatives lived in upstate New York, it is possible that the Maverick family went to one of their homes during the occupation.

** P. R. Maverick seldom used his middle initial in this early period.

The Subscriber, ever willing to serve the public, respectfully informs them that he carries on engraving seal-
sinking and copperplate printing at No. 3 Crown Street,
where ladies may have their tea-table ware engraved in
the most elegant manner and in the newest fashion, resembling the flat chasing, as neat as in Europe.

By their humble servant,

Peter Maverick

The shop must have prospered, for considerable dated
work for magazines and books falls within this period, and
much of the undated material so resembles this in technique or
in the signature that it may well have also been done at this
time. The bulk of the work was most prosaic and practical; it
must be remembered that the Mavericks served a trade which
wanted reproductions of pictures, and that, at the time, the way
to reproduce a picture was to carve a wooden or soft metal block
for relief printing with type, or to incise a plate for intaglio
printing. Hand-engraving, on wood or metal, is now a medium
for an artist seeking a multiplication of a personal artistic product, but in Maverick's time it was primarily a method of commercial reproduction.

With the Mavericks there was no line of separation in
their work between the art and the craft; the shop of the 1780's
did what it was called upon to do. It made pictures for encyclo-
pedias and for books on medicine; it made magazine illustrations of a new dock-cleaning machine or of Indian pipes of
peace. It engraved a fire-fighting scene for an insurance company, certificates of membership for a militia company or a society library, and a diploma for a medical society. It reproduced
ball tickets, business cards, and maps. But along with these, and
with no thought of a difference, it made pictures for magazines,

19

frontispieces for books, and bookplates. These last, because they have attracted the attention of collectors, have done much to keep the Maverick name alive, for the new America, although it had so recently renounced the foppery of a foreign aristocratic system, rushed to Crown Street to have its coats of arms engraved on bookplates. And Maverick did his part, not only to engrave the arms but to relieve them of the taint of aristocratic austerity. He festooned ropes of flowers about them, or he set flowers and grasses beside the central shield. He embellished the plate of a military figure with cannon and flags, the plate of a lawyer with a shelf of books. Typically he drew beneath and beside the shield a bit of landscape — water, shrubbery, trees, and distant hills. Apparently he pleased his trade, for his customers were many.

In such a business, in the shops at No. 3 and for a time No. 5 Crown Street, the son Peter Maverick grew up. Before he made the cut of Adam and Eve at the age of nine he must have watched and tried many things about the shop: he must have handled a graver in many simple tasks or in the simpler parts of his father's work, and he must have printed blocks on his father's press or taken off proofs from copperplates. Since these skills do not spring fully developed from anyone's head or hand, he must have been already experimenting in August of 1787 when, soon after the birth of another sister Elizabeth, his mother died. When the next year his father married his mother's sister, Aunt Rebecca, he must have been already adept, and when Samuel, the other engraver-to-be of the family,* was born on June 5, 1789, young Peter was ready to produce his initial work, the

* Andrew did printing of copperplates, but apparently no engraving.

Adam and Eve engraving. He was to work with his father for many years, doing part or perhaps all of many things which would be signed with his father's name or with the single family name, but this relief block marks a significant point of beginning.

THREE

The Young Engraver

ONE SMALL indication that Peter Maverick was recognized as an engraver in his own right very soon after the publication of his Adam and Eve engraving is to be found in his father's change in signature about this time. In his early work in the 1780's, Peter Rushton Maverick most commonly signed his engravings merely "Maverick," but in the dated work of the 1790's we frequently find "P. R." or "Peter R. Maverick," as if he had begun to recognize that he should leave the simple "Peter Maverick" for the son who had no middle name. The same tendency to include the use of his middle initial is also evident in early city directories and in advertisements. From the first directory in 1786 to that of 1792, he uses the signature "Peter Maverick," but from 1793 to his death he added his middle initial. The intent seems clear: a recognition that his twelve-year-old son should have the distinction of a separate nomenclatural niche.

The work of young Peter in the Adam and Eve picture was quite different from the type of work which was to make him famous; the early work was a relief block, in which the surface not intended for printing was carved away, but his fame as a craftsman depends on his intaglio work, where the design to be printed was cut on a polished copperplate, and the parts to be white in the finished print were left untouched. Since the Maverick shop was not seriously concerned with relief blocks, we may be sure that a nine-year-old boy so familiar with the burin must have begun very early to work on copper.

Probably one of the first tasks undertaken by Peter was that of polishing plates. Perhaps no better training could be devised to impress the beginner with a respect for the prepared plate than to require him to prepare his own. Not only must the polisher rub the plate with pumice or a fine abrasive until it is clean, shiny, and mirror-like, he must make it so smooth that not the slightest bit of sticky oily ink can resist being wiped away, so smooth that uncut parts of the plate, after inking and wiping, will not soil white paper. Occasional dabblers in engraving would have this done by a silversmith's assistant who did polishing in his spare time. One such man, mentioned in Alexander Anderson's diary and known to us only as "a Swede," received $1.15 for the labor alone of polishing a plate about six inches square, and $1.35 for one slightly larger. Considering the price of labor at that time, it must have been slow, tedious work to command such amounts. But considering also the type of father Peter had, we can scarcely believe that the boy did not polish many plates before he had an assistant to do it for him.

When the plate was properly polished, it was ready for the transfer of the design and for cutting. The burin (in one of its various forms) which was used in cutting the relief block was also used to produce the intaglio plate, but in the case of the relief block it was used to cut away *all but* the lines of the design, whereas in the case of the intaglio plate it was used to cut the lines; for it is the furrow which the tiny plow cuts, or which the acid eats, that is printed in this latter method, not the metal between. Peter also had to learn that in intaglio work he could not print a black surface as he had in the background of his signature in the Adam and Eve print. In line engraving there is no such thing as a plain black surface; if an area of metal were to be cut away, the ink would fill it but the wiping would empty it, and the print would show only the edges. So Peter had to learn to think of his dark areas in the picture as lines — lines spaced very close and yet not merging, or lines crossed at various angles — and his lighter areas as lighter lines or more widely spaced lines, or both.* The control of these factors, the spacing of the lines and the thickness of the line itself, continued to be a part of Peter's learning during his whole career. Though mechanical devices were later developed to make this control more exact, yet his eye and hand, and the brain where even manual skill resides, never surrendered to a machine.

We may be sure that Peter also learned very early to print his plates, for this shop was equipped to do so, though it was the custom for some engravers to employ other shops for their printing, or simply to furnish the plate to the customer, who would then find his own printer. The process of printing is essentially simple, but like many other simple processes demands that much be mastered before an expert product results. Peter had to learn how to spread an oily ink over the whole surface with a dauber, which must then be wiped off — at least all that would wipe off — first with a cloth and then with the whiting-

* Some of these statements do not apply to stipple work, which Peter did masterfully, but the nature of engraving will perhaps be better understood if one process is considered at a time.

covered palm of the hand, leaving ink only in the lines cut into the polished surface. He then had to warm the plate sufficiently to ensure the softening of the ink in all the lines, place it face up on the bed of his press, place over it a sheet of paper (dampened so that pressure would force it down into the grooves to receive the ink), and squeeze paper and plate under powerful rollers turned by long spoke-like handles. To turn the wheel, if the press was tight or the padding over the plate was thick, the boy must have had to climb those spokes like a monkey.* But when the powerful pressure had pushed the softened paper into every channel of ink, no matter how delicate the line, the sheet of paper which Peter peeled off the copper surface must have seemed worth the labor. Something, at least, must have kept him at it through years of drudgery, and the skill which his first signed work shows, ten years later, would indicate that one force that kept him at work was his own successful progress.

The engraving of the shop during this period of Peter's youth continued to be various, and it appears that at about this time a new type of work was added which was to become of great importance. This was bank-note engraving. Early paper money was commonly printed from type, and depended commonly for its safety upon the rarity of printing equipment, upon elaborate type designs, and upon such warnings as "Death to counterfeit" printed upon it. But as printing presses and capable printers became more common, and the threat of death proved too weak a deterrent, a premium was placed on devices to make harder the task of the unauthorized reproducer of currency. The skillful engraver had a powerful device in his own skill, of course, and as time went on he added elements to his pattern to increase the

* This type of press is shown on the Samuel Maverick trade card engraved (1813–1817) by Peter and reproduced herein following page 76.

25

challenge to the copyist. We find these elements in the earliest notes bearing the Maverick name. These early notes contained, in their simplest form, the elaborately lettered promise of the bank to pay either a stated amount or an amount to be inserted in ink, spaces for signatures, and pictorial designs related to the history or the location or the name of the bank. In some also we find the early use of panels containing the engraved or inserted figures for the denomination of the note. These panels were blocks of parallel lines, serving much the same purpose as devices for check protection serve today. As machine controls were created, the lines were more accurately spaced, or the variations in spacing achieved an effect resembling moire silk.

But a craftsman's shop was not only a business establishment, it was also a training school. At No. 3 Crown Street and at No. 65 Liberty Street,* where the Mavericks moved in 1794, Peter must have been in daily contact with many whose names were to become important ones in the graphic arts. One of these was William Dunlap, painter, theatrical producer, and historian of both arts, who in 1787–88 put himself under Peter Rushton Maverick's tutelage to learn "the theory and practice of etching." ** Many persons consider it also likely that Benjamin R. Tanner, later prominent in Philadelphia, learned his engraving under Maverick. Francis Kearny, who was to fol-

* The name Crown Street finally gave way to the new name Liberty Street. Tradition persists that the elder Maverick was a chief factor in the change of name, that he even offered to pay out of his own pocket the expense of changing the street signs.

** I have avoided, throughout this volume, the use of the word "etching," since it is perhaps best reserved for the complete wax-and-acid methods. Alexander Anderson, in the 1790's, records the following formula for etching varnish: "wax, black pitch, and Burgundy pitch," and that of one of the Tiebouts as "wax and rosin." Although Peter Maverick used acid for stipple and for etching in the rotary lathe engraving processes developed by him and the Durands in Newark, the inventory of his richly stocked shop at the time of his death shows no wax, acid, or other material that would indicate his use of acid for cutting line.

low Tanner to Philadelphia after beginning his famous career in New York, is recorded as Maverick's apprentice from 1798 on. Kearny was near Peter Maverick's age, and the two young men worked together for years. And there must have been many others whose training, or partial training, touched this shop in Crown or Liberty Street. In the next quarter of a century five copperplate printers by the name of Reynolds were in New York at various times; it would be strange if some of them were not maternal relatives of Peter's who had learned the trade in the elder Maverick's shop.

A more important possibility flickers enticingly through the mist of a century and a half: Alexander Anderson may well have got his start as an engraver from his contacts with Maverick; a formal apprenticeship seems unlikely, for he was first apprenticed, against his will, to a doctor. In his old age, Anderson said that in the procession to honor the adoption of the new federal constitution, on July 23, 1788, he walked with the elder Maverick, and that Maverick was then the only engraver in New York. This is a long-remembered detail; it is incorrect at least in respect to Maverick's uniqueness in the field, but it may point to an early Maverick inspiration if not specific instruction. Anderson was thirteen at the time; seven years later he was a licensed physician in charge of Bellevue Hospital during a yellow-fever epidemic, but shortly afterward he renounced medicine for the stronger claim of engraving, an art which was to bring him a long career and the title of America's first engraver in wood.

Another influence which was strong in this decade in the Maverick shop and residence was Peter Rushton Maverick's ardor for the new nation and for the opportunity it gave for

27

new freedom of thought. Very early, however, and probably from the beginning, his enthusiasm was not of a piece with that of some of the new American aristocrats who brought him their coats of arms to engrave. It went further than theirs, and embraced the hopes of the group calling themselves Republicans, who shortly accepted the leadership of Thomas Jefferson, refused to take too seriously the many loud and sweeping denunciations of the French Revolution, looked to reason as a worthy source of enlightenment, and fought everything, fundamental or trivial, that smacked of aristocracy and monarchy. For the Republican Society of this time Maverick made a bookplate, and its motto, "Mutual Improvement," epitomizes this new belief that the mass of mankind could lift itself by its own collective bootstraps instead of waiting until someone might think to throw down a rope.

Peter R. Maverick's espousal of this attitude in political matters was only a moderately bold act, but in respect to religious questions he went still further, as he sought to find the answers in intellect and reason. His most public manifestation of this quest was in his association with the poet Freneau and with John Lamb in the interests of deism. When this group sponsored an address by Elihu Palmer, the deist leader, and petitioned the Common Council for the use of the City Hall courtroom on July 4, 1797, the petition was rejected, and alongside Palmer's name a clerk inserted the label "infidel." Three years later the group gave support to a short-lived weekly *The Temple of Reason*, which stirred the opposition of the devout and which embarrassed Jefferson's Republicans by forcing them to defend themselves against charges of enmity to religion.

Maverick's position in respect to political and religious

thinking brought him into contact with the aged Thomas Paine, when that patriot, after defending humanity's cause as a citizen in three great nations, came back to die in the land of his last remaining citizenship, only to see that citizenship revoked and the masses for whom he had labored turn against him. A letter pasted in a scrapbook by Maverick's grandson nearly a century ago and recently discovered by two great-great-granddaughters gives evidence of Thomas Paine's straits, and of Peter Rushton Maverick's attempts to help. It reads:

Tuesday

Friend Maverick

I send the dollar I owe you and am much obliged to you. I will return your bed and pillows. They are both on my cot. John sleeps on my own bed in the passage. I did not know that the straw bed was destroyed. When I fixed up my cot, the straw bed made it too high which was the reason it was put away and no care, I find, was taken of it.

Thomas Paine

I am going tomorrow to look at some rooms at Mr. Jervis [sic] *the painter as Hitt's rooms are not yet ready.**

But where young Peter stood on these matters of politics and religion we cannot say, for he held himself close to his engraving business. His name is not to be found tied to any causes; he is not listed in church or lodge records. His father, and later his brother Samuel, were active Masons; his father and later his two brothers were active as volunteer firemen; his grandfather,

* Paine, after leaving William Carver's on November 3, went to live with John Wesley Jarvis in early November of 1806, and the letter was apparently written just before this time. Hitt is probably John Hitt, the baker in Broome Street from whom Paine later rented a room. As to John who slept in the passage, I know of no clues that will warrant anything weightier than a guess, but it is a pleasant guess that friendly John Fellows had given temporary shelter in his own lodgings to the old Patriot, and that Maverick had aided in the emergency with the loan of his pillows and mattresses, and the dollar.

father, and his brother Andrew joined the militia; and his father, brother, and nephew were members of the Society of Mechanics and Tradesmen. But Peter's name does not appear in connection with any of these organizations; it would seem that he was only interested in those directly connected with his professional life.

We know little of Peter's own mother, Ann Maverick, who died in 1787. Her place was taken the next year by her sister Rebecca, who lived long and has left a fairly clear impression of what she must have been like as a mother to Samuel and stepmother to Sarah, Rebecca, Ann, Peter, Andrew, and Maria.* She it was who during the British occupation of New York City was pursued across Kingsbridge by Tory guerrillas. From her later business career as a widow she seems to have been shrewd, practical, and somewhat domineering. She dressed smartly and, so her children and grandchildren sometimes thought, a little garishly. She was "always a very devout person," said one who knew her from the beginning of her widowhood. The most educated, perhaps, of all the people of her acquaintance considered her "a person not endowed with a very high order of intellect," but several less literate observers spoke of her brilliance, her keen interest in history and current happenings, her ability to converse about literature. She must have been a force in the family during her husband's life, for she obviously held the reins in her hands through her long widowhood, in spite of the fact that she could read only a little and could not write even her name.

The first of the children to leave home was Sarah, who on May 10, 1792, at the age of eighteen, married Benjamin Mon-

* Elizabeth, Ann's seventh child, apparently did not survive infancy.

tanye, son of Peter Montanye, in the Reformed Protestant Dutch Church of New York City. On May 27, five years later, in the same church, Rebecca, aged twenty-one, married James Woodham, and Ann, aged eighteen, became the wife of Patrick Munn. Peter was now the oldest child left at home with Andrew and Maria and his half-brother Samuel. Andrew was old enough to be helping in the shop, and Samuel was probably around the shop as something less than a help.

Soon after these marriages, the family was again forced to flee for refuge outside the city, this time before a force more terrible than the invading British Army, the deadly yellow fever. Several times during the 1790's it struck; at one time a crude quarantine was enforced by a board fence across the island of Manhattan on the line of Liberty Street. Pedlars drove through the streets crying their wares, "Coffins! All sizes of coffins!" All who could escape from the pest-ridden city did so, and many a shop was left in charge of a single employee to serve what little business there was.

At 65 Liberty Street one young man was so left in the great epidemic which began in the summer of 1798. Carrying on the work of the shop, he also helped nurse a sick friend, only to be stricken with the fever himself and to lie sick and alone. Many years later, Grant Thorburn, brother of the sick friend, told of making the rounds of all the young men who had fallen ill while befriending his brother. He reported that all of these men, stricken in late August, "had got better or died" by September 22, but he gave no clue as to which fate befell the young man at 65 Liberty Street, or who the young man was. He may have been a hired employee, perhaps the anonymous "male adult" listed as a member of the household in the 1790 census.

Or he may have been a member of the immediate family, and, if so, he may have been the eldest boy, Peter, a competent workman and manager by this time.

Though the toll of yellow fever was heavy, all the Mavericks appear to have escaped its fatal consequences. The work of the shop flourished once again, and in 1802, at the age of twenty-one, Peter married Mary Griffin, daughter of Timothy and Catharine Griffin of New Providence, New Jersey. Mary's maternal grandfather, Isaac Sayre, had moved out to Jersey from Southampton, Long Island, long before the Revolution, and later, in the tavern he kept at Summit, Isaac had been host to George Washington. Mary was nineteen when she married Peter on May 15; they moved to a new home a few blocks north of Liberty Street at 68 Beekman Street and established their own shop there. Marriage not only marked the beginning of Peter's independent personal life, it also marked the end of his professional preparation. Although he continued his association with his father's shop, the period of apprenticeship had given way to the beginning of his independent career as an engraver.

FOUR

The Independent Engraver

THOUGH Peter Maverick's independent career as an engraver may be justifiably dated from the time of his marriage and his departure from home, he had produced some signed and dated work a year or two before his marriage, and some of his signed but undated engravings may have been done then also. There exists a trade card of "Peter Maverick, 65 Liberty Street," which is quite likely that of the young engraver, indicating his ability to take independent commissions; of course it is conceivable that this was the card of the elder Peter, but from the time the shop moved to 65 Liberty Street the latter consistently included his middle initial in his signature. Engraving partnerships of the time were often generously loose, even among workers with no ties of kinship; furthermore, the elder Maverick's relations with all his sons give no suggestion that he ever tried to exploit them.

The new shop and home must have soon become a busy place. Peter was aggressive and industrious; moreover he was a good engraver. Some of his father's business must have come to him in natural course, and since it seems likely that the father, though only in his forties, was failing in health, the transfer of

33

business was perhaps greater for that reason. The variety of work continued in accordance with the needs of the trade for pictorial reproduction. Bookplates seem to have been a smaller part of Peter's work than of his father's; perhaps a bookplate was becoming less the thing to have, perhaps those who wanted their coats of arms engraved had already been served. Those bookplates which Peter did, however, he did well, eschewing the festoons and the posies and the landscapes, and cutting the arms and formal designs with a distinction of which his father was scarcely capable.

But bookplates were not his chief product. An important part of a good engraver's work was the copying of engravings in foreign books which were being reproduced in America for the American trade. Since American copyright laws offered little protection to foreign publishers, popular foreign books were reproduced freely in America; the sheets of the text were sent to the printer to be set in type and the illustrations to the engraver to be reproduced in new plates. It is sometimes said that certain publishers voluntarily paid royalties to the foreign author; but whether or not the foreign illustrator was ever paid seems not a matter of record. The American publishers were not infrequently accused of piracy, but Peter Maverick was not acting as a publisher; he was simply a craftsman who had been engaged by the publisher to use his skill in reproducing a work of graphic art. An engraver may be an artist in a very real sense and still not be guilty of plagiarism when he uses his skill to reproduce the art signed by another. To suggest that he is guilty is like suggesting that the actor playing Hamlet is plagiarizing Shakespeare.

In this work Peter's skill showed itself sometimes superior

to that of the original foreign engraver, and sometimes it did not, for he was pitted against eminent workmen. In respect to design, he held his work close to the original — so close that some of the crudities of drawing sometimes attributed to him are merely the results of his truthfulness to his copy. But his handling of the line that achieved his effect shows his mastery. In the original, the lines of shading may be blotched and merging; Peter Maverick drew them clear and separate, and yet by infinitely small gradations he gives us an interesting play of light over the surface. An original may be flat and pale, but in Maverick's copy the high lights are kept clean, and the shadows are graded deeper. With nothing but black lines on white paper he struggled to reproduce the texture of a linen tablecloth, the streaks of light and shadow on the surface of a quiet lake, the play of subdued light over a face, the curl and froth of a breaking wave, or the dim form of a distant hill.

In addition to book illustration, he was also early called upon to engrave maps. A little work with maps had been done in his father's shop, but Peter's clean line and his accurate transfer of the originals served quickly to build his reputation. The maps were of various kinds: a private map of a large tract of land in Pennsylvania, a mariners' map of Long Island Sound, a map of Caracas, two maps of New York City, and several simple charts for books of travels. Peter was beginning to be known.

In spite of the demands of his work, Peter and Mary did not remain long at any one address: during seven years we have seven different recorded addresses, the first on Beekman Street, the last on Frankfort Street, and the others on Nassau. Presumably shop and family moved together. Why they moved so frequently is not clear; perhaps the cause was simply restlessness, perhaps it was the rapidly increasing size of his family. The long list of Peter's children began a few weeks before the first wedding anniversary with the birth of Emily on April 3, 1803. Two days after Emily's first birthday a boy was born and named William Munn, the middle name being surely a salute to Sister Ann's husband. William lived less than a year, but two months after his death Maria Ann was born on her parents' third wedding anniversary. In the spring of 1806, on April 28, another boy was born and named William Henry. He, too, did not survive infancy; he died in June of the next year, shortly after the birth of a sister Lavinia on May 4. The next year, on May 26, a sixth child Cornelia was born. Exactly a year and five months later a third boy, the only boy who was to survive his mother, was born and called Peter.

During this period the rest of the Mavericks were growing up, or growing old. Although old Peter was to live four years longer, in 1807 he made his will. He began it with the invocation "In the Name of God, Amen," a manner of speaking which was not inconsistent with his deism, but which would have surprised those who ten years before had classed him with infidels.

Andrew, only two years Peter's junior, married on June 2, 1804 and moved from his father's home, where he had already begun his life's work of copperplate printing. He took his bride, who had been Catherine Dow, to his new home on Fair (now Fulton) Street, and the next year established his independent printing shop.

Samuel seemed destined for a trade unrelated to copperplate when on June 5, 1804, his fifteenth birthday, he was apprenticed for six years to his brother-in-law, James Woodham, to "learn the art, trade, and mystery of a mariner." How long he followed this art, trade, and mystery is not known,* but his marriage to Mary Howell, daughter of the merchant Aaron Howell, on October 8, 1808, gives evidence that the apprenticeship was not completed, and suggests the reason. In the following year he was listed in the city directory at his father's address, and in 1810 he had a copperplate establishment of his own.

Peter's sister Rebecca died on July 4, 1809, and her husband James took as his second wife the remaining unmarried sister, Maria.

More and more the work of the elder Maverick receded into the background as his place in the craft was taken over by his three sons. In 1809 there were three Maverick establishments in Liberty Street, but in the fall of that year Peter moved his family and shop to a farm in New Jersey which he had purchased from a New York coachmaker. Perhaps he was prompted to make this move because of his realization of the profits in taking apprentices — profits to be derived both from their fees and the benefits of their work. The prospect of establishing a shop and training school where the cost of board and lodging could be kept low might well have been very attractive to the ambitious Peter. But this was scarcely his sole motive; the desire to own land of his own and to give his family the benefits of country living may well have influenced the decision which brought the family to the little farm near Newark between the Newark-Belleville road and the Passaic River.

* Stauffer says he began as copperplate printer in 1805, but gives no documentation for the date.

FIVE

Country Squire and Teacher

NEWARK in 1809 was a busy and optimistic town of eight thousand people situated between the swamps called the Newark Meadows and the hills called the Newark Mountains. A traveler went there from New York by a plank road across the cedar swamps to what is now Bridge Street, or by boat through the bay and up the Passaic River to the public dock. The town clustered around the old common which had been used as a military training ground during the Revolution, and around the intersection of Broad and Market Streets. At the north end of the common was Trinity Church, just being rebuilt around the sixty-year-old spire of the first structure. South along Broad Street were the homes and shops of townsfolk, some of them with the names of the original settlers who had come by boat from Connecticut and landed a century and a half before at a point on the Passaic banks not far from Trinity. Intersecting Broad Street was Market, which ran west up the hill toward Orange and east into the marshes. From Newark's center a walk of only a few minutes in any direction brought one to the woods and open fields.

But Peter Maverick had not come to Newark to live in

town. A mile and a half north of Trinity Church were Peter's twenty acres; on the east side of the road to Belleville were fourteen acres of fertile land, stretching level from the road until it descended sharply to the Passaic, and on the west side of the road were six acres of woodlot.* An occasional cart passed on the road, and an occasional boat on the river. Cattle wandered freely and grazed on the roadside; violets grew on the river bank for the girls to pick in the spring.

Now, nearly a century and a half later, Maverick's name is not among those attached to the land. A few rods south of the site of the farm is Gouverneur Street, commemorating Samuel Gouverneur. The nearby Kemble estate, originally the property of Gouverneur, was occupied in Maverick's time by his grandson, Gouverneur Kemble. It was here that Kemble entertained Washington Irving during the summer months, and it was Irving who named the house Cockloft Hall. To the north of Peter's farm a little gully ran to the river, and along it a lane called Gully Road (now Herbert Place). Years after Maverick had left New Jersey, the eccentric Henry William Herbert was to make his home at the lower end of the road and to write books under his own name and his pen name of Frank Forester. Just north of Gully Road, descending the hill to the river, there was once, so it is said, a block-long street named Maverick Place, because in the late nineteenth century the elder inhabitants had a vague memory of the first settler who was "a Maverick." The

* The farm extended from the Belleville Road, now Broadway, east to the river, the south boundary being along an extension of the present line of Oriental Place (between Mt. Pleasant and Ogden), and the north boundary running about fifty yards north of the present southern line of Mt. Pleasant Cemetery. The woodlot was across the Belleville Road and extended to "the Long Hill Road" to Bloomfield. This old Bloomfield Road turned to the west from the present junction of Second Avenue and Broadway, bent north through Mt. Prospect Place and along Mt. Prospect Avenue for about a quarter of a mile, and thence veered to the left, along a route no longer existing, to Franklin Street and into Bloomfield.

39

name is gone now, and the street has apparently gone also. It is likely, however, that the location marks one of the three homes which the restless Maverick seems to have had in Newark.

There can be little doubt that Peter's early years in Newark were years of busy progress, whatever his later difficulties may have been. He paid $3125 for his home and some twenty acres of farm land and woodland, and in the next five years he invested nearly as much more in various pieces of land north and west of his first homestead. In acknowledging receipt of a payment for engraving work in 1812 he commented that he was busy purchasing and building far beyond his current income. In 1813 he advertised for rent a two-story residence near Belleville with ten acres of land, garden, orchard, and outbuildings. In the spring of 1813 he advertised for apprentices to the copperplate printing business, though we know that he already had some apprentices in his shop at the time.

Another venture of Peter's illustrates his ambition to make himself a country squire in his estate on the banks of the Passaic. A decade earlier David Humphreys, American minister to Spain, had brought to America the first merino sheep, and had been honored by American agriculturists for this contribution to the national wealth. Humphreys engaged Maverick to engrave a reproduction of one of the medals awarded him. Perhaps Humphreys paid for the engraving in sheep, or perhaps the engraving called Peter's attention to the merino breed, but whatever the stimulus, it appears that Peter boldly plunged into the currently popular business of raising sheep. Perhaps he plunged too far, and was trying to get out of his venture when he advertised for sale, in repeated issues of the *Newark Centinel of*

Freedom during the fall of 1812, five pure-bred merino rams and nine others that were seven-eights or half merino. With fourteen rams to sell, Maverick must have had a large flock, and his acres along the Passaic must have been well grazed.

But, in spite of farming and ventures in real estate, his engraving business continued, and in variety as before. On a few bookplates we find the Newark address accompanying his signature. The bank-note business continued in ever-increasing amounts, and there were commissions for magazine illustrations and for title pages of books, and many orders for book illustrations. He made several important maps, and in his spare time, or that of his apprentices, he launched some little publishing ventures of his own.

One of the contracts which must have kept many workers busy for a long period was that for the American issue of Calmet's *Dictionary of the Bible.* The promoter of an English edition of this work, who had engraved or directed the engraving of many plates for it, followed this promotion by publishing an edition in America. He turned over to Maverick about forty of the original engravings for him to copy, which Maverick did with a fidelity that was not always praiseworthy, for the originals were sometimes crude. Much of the work of this contract, however, was well within the ability of learners, and we know, both by inference and by testimony, that many hands worked on the Calmet plates.

In studying Maverick's work, it must be kept constantly in mind that the apprentices in his shop were not only learning under him, they were also working for him, and that many of the lines on plates signed by him were cut by their hands. Sometimes these subordinates were given credit in the signature, as

41

in the Caracas plate of 1806, where we find the inscription "Water by R. Tanner" (though "the water" is only parallel ruling which filled the space beyond the line of the shore); more often their work is not identified. Nor is there any record of their names. We do know that Asher Brown Durand was one of them, but his subsequent relationship with Peter gave him an importance deserving a fuller consideration a little later in this volume. Dunlap reports that one Robert C. Bruen was an apprentice of Maverick's along with Durand. There were Bruens among the founders of Newark and it seems reasonable to suspect that Robert was a local boy. His premature death ended a life of great early promise.

Another boy, Samuel Dodd of Bloomfield, was also very likely Maverick's apprentice, and since he was only a few months younger than Durand, he probably worked in the shop at the same time. Samuel, and his two sons after him, later carried on engraving work in Newark; there is a slight hint that he might also have done some work with Maverick after his apprenticeship.

Another possible apprentice was Jersey-born William S. Potts, engraver, preacher, and later president of "Marion College." William D. Smith, an engraver in Newark in 1829 and later in New York, may have learned his trade under Maverick, as may also a William S. Griffin (probably Mary's brother). A printer by the name of William was in Maverick's employ for several years, and he may have been one of these three.

In 1818, Maverick and Durand nursed another William, a very seriously ill young man by the name of William James Stone, because Stone's relatives were too far away even to know of his illness. Since, a dozen years later, Stone was established as an engraver in Washington, D.C., it is probable that he was one of Maverick's apprentices at the time of his illness. We also have a rather confused report of an R. M. Gaw as an employee of Maverick; and a decade later a man known as Gaw did work for Samuel Maverick in New York.

These apprentices paid for their training or gave notes for future payment. Normally they lived with their master; along with Maverick's continually increasing family, they provided a use for the field and garden products, and for the milk from "the old dark-brown cow, with long horns, a white streak on the back, white belly and legs, and large udder," which strayed away on June 7, 1816 (according to an advertisement in the *Newark Centinel of Freedom*). Could it have been busy, city-bred, country squire Peter Maverick who milked her? Probably not, although cows were not entirely foreign to people bred in the city; in the year Peter took his bride to live in Beekman Street, a man was reported killed in that street by a cow. Perhaps milking and other farm duties fell to the lot of the girls or the apprentices, but more probably many of these tasks were done by Susan and Pompey, "persons of color and servants of Mr. Maverick," whom the rector of Trinity Church married about 1810; on April 8, 1818, the same rector recorded his reading of Pompey's burial service.

Peter's immediate family continued to grow rapidly. When he purchased the farm in 1809, his surviving children were Emily, Maria Ann, Lavinia, and Cornelia. On October 26, 1809, a few weeks after the purchase, a seventh child, Peter, was born, although it is not clear whether or not the family had actually moved to New Jersey at the time of his birth. On February 7, 1811, came Catharine, named for two of her mother's ancestors, and on May 9 of the next year Elizabeth. The following year, 1813, brought another girl on July 19, and she was named Octavia. On August 3 of the next year Octavia died, but a sister who was born on September 17 was given her name. June 21 in 1816 brought Penelope, and August 12 of the next year Julia Augusta, who lived only to January 7. Angelica was born on December 3, 1818, and Caroline on March 1, 1820. Peter and Mary had been married twenty years when Raphael, the last of their sixteen children, was born on April 21, 1822, after their return to New York.

Peter continued to plan and build for his growing family. He was proud of his progress and his new status as an owner of land, of which he has left us a strange and half-whimsical record. In 1812 he engraved for the New York firm of Prior and Dunning a map of the country thirty miles around the city of New York, a beautiful map on a generous scale. Included in it, of course, were Newark and the towns and roads around it. On this map, at a point just north of the junction of the Road to Belleville and the Long Hill Road to Bloomfield, Peter covered the area of his own holdings with the inscription "P. Maverick." And on the east side of Belleville road, a little north of the place where the Bloomfield road joins, he dotted in the house on his farm.

Three years later he was at work on another map covering "the southern part of New York including Long Island, the Sound, the state of Connecticut, part of the state of New Jersey and islands adjacent," and again Peter remembered that he and his were part of it. He omitted his name this time, but the house is dotted in, and nearby is the label "Cottage." But this house is farther up the Belleville road than is the one in the 1812 map, and on the west side, for by this time Peter had moved to a five-acre piece of land on the "drift road." He had bought the land in December of 1812 for $250, and had built a new "Cottage" there for his family.*

It seems likely that he moved again before returning to New York in 1820. In 1814 he bought a piece of land on the River Road, north of where the Gully Road reached it. It was here that it was later rumored that "a Maverick" had been the first settler. The same reminiscence places one Mathew Banks there from 1820, which coincides with the date of Peter's return to New York. This third home was just a short distance north of where Frank Forester was later to build his home, "The Cedars," and near where Maverick Place was apparently once a street name. The house was on the hill, slightly north and west of the present Riverside Station of the Erie Railway.

Not only did Peter's skill and his diligence in business bring him financial rewards, but they began to attract recognition as well. At the beginning of the century, a group of artists and patrons of the arts in New York had formed an American Academy of Arts (later renamed the American Academy of Fine Arts) to foster and encourage the arts in America, and to recognize ability and accomplishment by electing to its membership those whom its governing body considered worthy to honor. In December of 1816 Peter Maverick was elected. In his reply to the notification by the society's secretary, Alexander Robertson, he asks Robertson "to express to the Gentlemen

---

* This home was near a point west of Lincoln Avenue and north of Chester. Lincoln Avenue, Elwood Place, and Summer Avenue constituted the "drift road" to Belleville, while the River Road left the present Broadway by Herbert Place and the River Road. The present Broadway above the junction with Lincoln was not then cut through. The "drift road" is said to have been so named because the snow drifted over it heavily in winter.

composing the Board of Directors the high sense of the honor conferred [*sic*] by this unlooked for mark of their favor. No one," he continues, "has the welfare of the institution more at heart, and I shall be glad to be informed wherein I can be of service best." The recognition was a significant one, in spite of the fact that the academy was a weak and ultimately futile attempt on the part of benevolent and public-spirited laymen to give recognition in a field where they had small ability to do so. The practicing artists in the group were already chafing under the controls of these sponsors, and a decade later were to form a new academy, but when they did so Maverick was one of the group.

While Peter was enjoying this new association with New York artists, there is strong evidence that Mary was feeling the lack of a kind of association which to the son of the deist Peter Rushton Maverick apparently meant little. There are indications that the reverent among his family considered him not one of them, but there is no evidence as to whether or not he actually opposed the participation of his family in the rituals of religion. Nevertheless, the first dated record of any alliance between the Mavericks and Newark's Trinity Church is found in an entry for October 8, 1814. With the mother as sponsor, eight children were baptized on that date by the Reverend Lewis P. Bayard, the rector: eleven-year-old Emily, nine-year-old Maria Ann, seven-year-old Lavinia, six-year-old Cornelia, five-year-old Peter, three-year-old Catharine, two-year-old Elizabeth, and the baby of three weeks, the second Octavia. During the remainder of the family's residence in Newark, two more children were baptized soon after birth. From this time on, Mary is listed among the communicants of the church, but

46

Peter is not, although he is regularly listed among the contributors to church expenses. Perhaps religious matters were a source of conflict between Mary and Peter which culminated in Mary's revolt and the subsequent baptisms. But the truth may also have been very different. Mary was busy with childbearing, so busy that she might well be excused for long neglect of a duty; we have ample evidence of her strong religious faith, and of the reverence she instilled in her daughters. Whether her delay in active participation in church affairs was due to her husband's opposition or to her own inertia, we can be sure that from that October Saturday she felt a renewed kinship with both God and mankind.

SIX

Maverick and Durand

IN THE autumn of 1812 there appeared at Maverick's shop a
sixteen-year-old-boy, Asher Brown Durand, who had come
in from his farm home on the slope of the Newark Mountains,
in what is now Maplewood, in the hope that he could make a
satisfactory arrangement for apprenticeship. Asher came from
a family well known as skillful watchmakers and general ar-
tisans, and his first engraving was self-taught in his father's
watchmaking shop. A visitor to that shop, Enos Smith, himself
an amateur painter of miniatures, became interested in Asher
and urged him to study engraving. Smith recommended W. S.
Leney as the most prominent engraver in New York, and many
years later Durand told of his trip to interview Leney. Making
the journey on foot from Maplewood to Newark and thence to
Elizabeth Town Point, with his two brothers and Smith he took
a periauger from Elizabeth Town to New York, landing near
the Battery and staying in a nearby hotel over night. The next
day they walked up Broadway, viewed the print shops near City
Hall, and went thence to Leney's home in the upper Bowery.
Leney stated his terms: he wanted a thousand dollars as premium for admission as an apprentice, and stipulated that all

other expenses be assumed by the applicant. Durand could not afford such an arrangement, but Smith refused to let him be discouraged and arranged to have him approach Maverick, "the most prominent writing engraver in the country." * Maverick agreed to take the boy into his household for one hundred dollars a year payable after the end of the apprenticeship five years later, the boy to provide his own clothing and incidental expenses. Durand later recorded somewhat cryptically that the next eighteen months were the happiest of his life.

Asher's first task as an apprentice was to make a pencil copy of a small engraved head — obviously a bit of training in the handling of lines. The lettering of a copperplate for a title page of *Pilgrim's Progress* followed, apparently as further practice work. Then he was put to work on the project then occupying the shop, the Calmet engravings. In the New York Historical Society collection of Durand's engravings is a print, in a partially completed state, of the Calmet engraving of agricultural implements. One wonders whether it was saved through Asher's long lifetime as the first product of his burin. "I soon surpassed my shopmates, and became the chief assistant," said Durand later, and there is surely no reason to doubt him, but his son's later statement, that the business of the firm was almost entirely dependent on Asher's talent, is something of an overstatement.

Asher was not the only member of the Durand family whose interests were linked at this time with those of Peter Maverick; John and Cyrus, his brothers, were busy inventing

* Maverick's skill in lettering was frequently singled out for praise, and several commissions, such as the Declaration of Independence (the document) and Dean's and Jenkins's textbooks in penmanship, gave him a chance to exhibit his skill.

an important engraving device. Aside from the general engraving tasks which had been part of the work of the shop for years, the engraving of bank notes had come to be of increasing importance with the effort to devise various means of making them more difficult to counterfeit. The simple ruled panel used as a border for notes soon was made obsolete by a device for ruling wavy lines—a device which was developed, apparently, by several persons at about the same time. The curves of the lines were not kept parallel; successive lines verged toward their neighbors with a consistency of relationship that gave to the whole pattern of the panel the casual regularity of moire or watered silk. This device may be the machine which Dunlap says that John Durand invented "for bordering bank notes," or it may be Rollinson's, for he is credited with such a machine and worked with Maverick on some bank notes.

But it was Cyrus Durand, with his home background of careful machine work, who went further in developing this control of curved lines and of their relationships. In 1815 he produced the geometrical lathe, which in 1816 and 1818 he improved by the addition of wheels and gears, allowing more intricate geometrical patterns. A further development was made in 1823; the resulting machine was later presented to the New York Historical Society with Cyrus's claim of having invented the "first perfected geometrical lathe." It is not clear whether or not Cyrus's claim was justified or to what extent Maverick was involved in the invention.* All we can be sure of is that Maverick and the two Durands, and possibly also a third, were

* No patent was issued to any Maverick or Durand for this or any related device, and a fire in the United States Patent Office a few years later destroyed records which might show whether any application for a patent was made.

at work during Asher's apprenticeship on an important engraving device.

The geometric lathe was a tight cluster of heavy brass disks and wheels with levers for setting adjustments; the machine was small enough to have been easily contained in a gallon measure. A fine diamond point cut the design. It did not cut the copperplate, however, as a burin would do, but cut through a protective coating of wax or rosin; the metal itself was then bitten with nitric acid. The results of the process can be seen in a few of the bank notes which were done when Maverick and Durand were partners, and in a few of the later Maverick products. The mechanically regular work which the machine produced, though it set the norm for future engraving of bank notes and similar paper certificates, was not, however, in line with Peter's idea of what engraving should be.

Durand's term of apprenticeship ended in the fall of 1817, and the partnership with Maverick probably followed immediately. The partnership seems to have had two phases. The first was characterized by the signature "Maverick and Durand," denoting the simple partnership of the two men who had just previously been master and apprentice. From sometime in 1818, when Cyrus's geometrical lathe got its second elaboration, the signature "Maverick Durand & Co." appears, the *Co.* in the firm name being Cyrus,* who was a pressman with Maverick at that time. It is just possible, too, that John may have shared in the company in some way; at least he shared some of its work.

The partnership was a very loose one, with the partners

* Note that the Durand firm, after 1820, was A. B. and C. Durand.

separated geographically from the beginning. At least as early as October 30, 1817, Durand was established at the corner of Pine Street and Broadway in New York, and throughout the partnership 2 Pine Street continued to be the New York address. Products of the partners were signed with the firm name, with possible exceptions if the plate promised personal fame to the engraver. In a few instances the initials *M* and *D* were used to indicate the individual artists; on many plates both partners worked. Maverick was to have the first choice of any work coming to the company; second choice was to go to Durand. If Durand did not want it, then Maverick was to farm it out as he saw fit for his own benefit. Each man kept his own accounts, though each might act as agent for the other in collections. Printing seems to have been handled in various ways as firm business; the second stage of the partnership was marked, apparently, by an attempt to organize the work of the presses under Cyrus's leadership.

The partnership began auspiciously; orders were abundant and Maverick's pride and hope were high. He signed letters to his former pupil "Yours respectfully" and "Yours with esteem." When a prospective pupil sought him out for instruction, he recommended Asher as the person most capable of teaching him. Although Peter in his late thirties was not the healthy man he had been in his twenties, he was strong in will, and we find him, in letters to his partners, exultant about the future. "I shall," he said in May of 1818, "with the blessing of God make the two coming months produce me a more abundant harvest than ever I before reaped in so short a period."

But the times were not right for reaping abundant commercial harvests, and Peter became convinced that he must return to New York. He advertised his country place for sale or for rent, planning to establish a new home in New York with a new and finer shop. Elaborate farm properties were not in demand, however, and he remained in Jersey, tied by necessity to his farm and kept by that necessity away from the sources of business in his craft.

Perhaps both these necessities rendered him too readily vulnerable to rumors and suspicions. Perhaps, in spite of his many recorded kindnesses and sacrifices, he was a hard man to have as a partner. Or perhaps Peter had just heard rumors of Durand's March 7th contract with John Trumbull to engrave his painting of the signing of the Declaration of Independence. In any case, by 1820 he began to feel that he must manage his New York office himself, and in March of that year he asked Durand to give up the New York quarters and to relinquish his right to the company mail. He asked Durand for a reply "this afternoon."

The Durand files show letters from Durand to Maverick on the 13th and 17th of March, and there may have been others. At this time Durand told Maverick of Trumbull's proposal (which he did not say he had already secretly accepted) that Durand alone should engrave the painting of the signing of the Declaration of Independence. In a letter dated March 17, Maverick protested, claiming his right to the first choice of business offered. "Colonel Trumbull nor no other man," he said, "shall dictate to me how my business must be conducted. I have always been much pleased with your progress and shall rejoice in your acquisition of fame, but it must be done without derogating from mine. I am also ambitious and jealous of my reputation."

Maverick's next letter to Durand was begun on March 25, and it shows the culmination of his suspicions. He had found out by then that Durand had made a first choice of contracts three times in a month, and he emphatically repeated that it was he, Maverick, who was entitled to first choice. He refused to accept Durand's dictation regarding work, and he threw back in Durand's face some plates which the younger partner had sent out to Newark for lettering. He sarcastically thanked Durand for making the Maverick blood circulate more briskly. He did not send the letter that day, and by the next the briskness of his circulation had stimulated him even more. He added further charges, that Durand had sent him no work from the New York office for six months, that Durand had professed friendship but had used every means to injure his partner and undermine his reputation. Further, he reminded Asher, this base and ungrateful conduct had been going on when Asher knew that Maverick was suffering for want of the means of providing for the necessities of his family. As he wrote this last bit, or as he reread the whole letter, Peter, apparently convinced that he had not put the matter strongly enough, made an interlinear addition after the comment about Asher's derogatory remarks: "Lightning blast the wicked that would descend to such business."

He must then have sent the letter promptly, for Durand's answer is dated the next day. He protested first that he had not violated the friendship that he had pledged, nor had he broken his partnership agreement except in the interest of the firm. (In the light of the peculiar nature of the partnership, this claim is somewhat puzzling.) He hinted that Maverick had not stated the real cause of his charges; that it was Maverick's "mortification" at his pupil's improvement which was at the root of the controversy. Then, repudiating all obligations (except a debt which to his shame he could not pay), he ended with, "God willing you shall yet find a friend not unworthy of your confidence in the despised and guilty [*sic*] A. B. Durand."

Peter's reply was somewhat conciliatory. "I suffered my passion not to cool before I wrote," he began, but then went on to list the rumors he had heard that Durand was playing down his senior's reputation, saying that the partnership was of no value to him, but rather an injury, and that Maverick was surprisingly little known as an artist in New York. He denied that he had envied Durand's progress, insisting that all his friends knew the falsity of the charge, but he said he would never "let you or any other engraver excel me," and repeated his ambition to rank high as an artist, "as high as any person on this side the Atlantic."

Thus the Maverick-Durand partnership dissolved. Three years later Maverick made some sort of attempt to return, though still as the senior partner, and was rebuffed. After the death of both principals, the story, as told by Durand's son, strengthens the suspicion that some of Maverick's resentment at his partner's attitude toward him was not without foundation, but it is probably not correct to think that the rift made enemies of the persons concerned. When in 1825 a group was re-forming the pattern of the old American Academy, Maverick and Durand worked side by side in the new movement. Three years later a letter from Maverick to Trumbull mentioned the recent receipt of money, and asked for the remainder of the account because of new and unexpected needs. Trumbull's reply, which he recorded on Maverick's letter, showed no suggestion of a strain in their cordial relations, even though Trumbull had to ask Maverick to wait for payment. Not only do the letters show a friendly relationship, but they also show that Trumbull was still employing Maverick's talents in some way.* And in 1831, when Maverick died without a will, relations between the family and Durand were good enough to make Durand acceptable as an appraiser of the estate. Such evidence does not point to any serious breach of friendship as the result of ending the partnership.

Undoubtedly Trumbull did look with favor on Durand as the engraver of his painting, and he well might. That painting had been going begging, however, for some time. Trumbull wanted a foreign engraver, and tried to get James Heath of London to do the picture; but Heath asked six thousand dollars, and Trumbull refused. A contract was actually made with an Italian, Mauro Gandolfi, whose price was four thousand dollars, but when Gandolfi came to New York to begin work he found living expenses too high and refused to go on. Durand's figure was three thousand, with payments spread over four years.

A wider view of the situation in 1820 shows many reasons for the dissolution of the firm and the move of its principals to New York. The Durands were capable young men with a machine which made them strong candidates for leadership in the fast-growing bank-note business; there were few advantages

* Possibly in printing from the Declaration of Independence or some other plate. As if Peter had not already been humiliated enough by losing to his young partner the choice contract to engrave Trumbull's Signing of the Declaration, he was called upon to do the printing from Durand's plate, Durand probably having no equipment for such a task. Perhaps necessity would not let him refuse the contract. He and his assistant, Mr. Neal, requisitioned in January and February of 1821 a total of 506 sheets of paper for the work, paper which had been made by the Gilpin mill at Brandywine, Pennsylvania, at a price of $75 a ream. Records of later printings continue for several years in Trumbull's account books. The completed prints sold at $20 a copy.

which continued partnership with Maverick could offer. What Maverick had to give he had already given in his training of Asher.

Newark, moreover, which had been an enterprising city ten years before, had suffered greatly from the general business depression which began in 1817 and reached its worst in 1820. Industries had failed or moved away, the population had decreased greatly, land values had disappeared. Though Maverick's business was never dependent upon its immediate surroundings, there was no advantage in staying where such conditions were prevalent. There must have been other reasons also for Peter's return to New York. We know little of the education of Peter's family, but we know, from their later careers, that the girls and the boy were not left uneducated. In 1809 the woods and fields and river bank were a tempting setting for the girls, but now the young ladies and the young lad had other needs, needs which New York could meet better than Newark.

So in 1820, the year that marked the end of his partnership with Durand, Peter Maverick took his wife and eleven children and his furnishings and equipment to New York for a fresh start. To help that start he raised a thousand dollars on a mortgage of all his Newark property, the six plots which he had bought for nearly six thousand dollars during the preceding eleven years. He showed no further interest in the life of a landed proprietor. After his death the holder of the mortgage was apparently the only bidder at the foreclosure sale, bidding enough to cover the debt and an additional sixteen hundred dollars in interest and costs.

SEVEN

Maverick's Last Years

SOME of Maverick's friends were inclined to feel sorry for him as he made his new start in New York. They pitied him for his limited prosperity, and they pitied him for his large family which included no boys to share the economic burden (his son Peter was only eleven). But we have no indication that Maverick himself wasted any energy in self-pity as he plunged into this last decade of his life which was to bring him sorrows and disappointments and strains in his formerly happy family relationships, but which was to bring him also new adventures in the reproductive arts and new successes as a commercial pioneer.

The two eldest girls, Emily and Maria Ann, worked in their father's shop as his pupils and assistants in drawing and engraving, and when about 1824 Peter turned to the new field of lithography, both girls became his active associates, reproducing drawings and doing some original ones. Like other apprentices, they must have done also much of the simpler work on plates and stones signed by their father. They were not, however, the first American women engravers; a dozen years earlier a Mrs. James Akin and an Eloisa R. Payne had made a beginning for women in this field, and about 1816, in Collin's *Quarto Bible*, a print of Ruth and Boaz was done by a Miss H. V. Bracket. In the Maverick family, however, the engravings by Emily and Maria Ann for an edition of Shakespeare marked a family triumph.* Peter must have experienced some of the same pride in his daughters that many years before his father had felt in his son.

There were other apprentices and employees in the shop, but records are not very satisfying. R. M. Gaw may have been still doing some work for Peter, as well as for Samuel, and Dodd seems to have had some continued connection with the shop (see p. 42). One boy, an apprentice of Peter Maverick "at the age of fifteen," seems to belong definitely to this period. He is John W. Casilear (1811–1893) who was to become a National Academician at the age of forty and to win prominence in nineteenth-century bank-note and postage-stamp engraving.

The 1820's were years of keen competition in the New York engraving field, and Peter's re-establishment of his business was marked by the same aggressiveness that he had shown in his many ventures in the past, and by the pride of a workman who feels sure of the quality of his work. Some years earlier, in answering a protest to a charge for repairing a plate, he had confidently said, "Any work I do will command that price." And his opinion had not changed, for in an advertisement in the city directory of 1821, he pointed out the value of having the work of artists engraved and printed by one who was himself an artist; he boasted that his shop had "several" good workmen, that a larger press was soon to be installed, and that the work of

* In the theatre collection of Harvard University the publication date for this volume is listed as 1822, but this date is from H. Heath's original English designs which the girls reproduced. No copies of the American edition appear to be available, but Stauffer's guess of an 1830 date seems reasonable.

the shop was "conducted after the English manner." A few years later, in a letter soliciting business, he proclaimed himself "prepared to engrave plates . . . on copper or steel as successfully as can be done by any engraver in this country."

Along with that boast, however, is a note of humiliation that the business was not seeking him without his stir. "I feel it a duty I owe myself and family," he wrote in a letter, "to conquer the repugnance I have to applying for business." The letter was written to a bank, and since it was not primarily seeking commissions to engrave notes, but instead commissions to print them from already engraved plates, Maverick adds the explanation that the latter work is far more profitable.

The fact seems to be that Maverick, without the aid of the recently elaborated engraving lathes possessed by the Durands, was finding competition hard. Skilled handwork could scarcely meet the lower prices which were possible when much of the work was done by machine, and the value of the involved mechanical scrollery as a deterrent to counterfeiting was hard to deny. Furthermore, there is little reason to think that the bank officials were aware of the bad taste which characterized many of the designs done by the rotary lathe as it came into more and more frequent use; the quiet vignettes and panels of the Maverick designs could have seemed old-fashioned to the customers. In spite of these difficulties, however, Peter Maverick did make a good many notes in this period, as the check list shows.

But his chief interests were not in this kind of work. Throughout the decade he developed and expanded his shop. When engraving on steel was initiated, he promptly began to offer the durable steel plate for engravings needing long use of plates. He even did some multiple-plate color work in intaglio.

60

Six years after the first lithography was done in America, and two years after the first commercial work in New York, he was taking regular commissions in lithography. Near the end of the decade he was advertising his varied business along with "a new method combining the beauty of copperplate with the cheapness of type."

Earlier in the decade, however, he had regarded letterpress printing not as an ally but as a competitor. A manuscript of printer's reminiscences preserves for us a minor triumph of Peter Maverick, the engraver, over the letterpress printers. There had been developed by Messrs. Edwin and Charles Starr and Mr. Elihu White a method of printing bank notes from type which the self-confident printers maintained was proof against counterfeiting. To back their boast they deposited with Mr. Fleming, cashier of the Mechanics' Bank, a five-hundred-dollar forfeit to be awarded to anyone who, in the opinion of Mr. Fleming, should engrave a successful counterfeit. Maverick accepted the challenge and won the award, though others criticized the decision on the ground that the backs of the notes done by Maverick could be distinguished by their lack of the raised impression which is peculiar to letterpress. Maverick, however, had met the requirements of the challenger, and thus had defended his craft against one threat of competition.

The varied kinds of work carried on in his shop required extensive equipment, and from the inventory of his estate at his death we know that Peter's shop was well equipped. In addition to one copperplate press, there were four items identified only as presses, two items which were listed as iron-screw presses, three called lithographic presses, and one called an iron lithographic press. In the sale which followed his death these eleven presses ranged in price from twenty to seventy-six dollars. We find listed also three ruling machines, as well as an item called merely "a machine" which was sold to Durand. Of materials, about two thousand square inches of copperplate sold at from two to three cents an inch, though some twenty-four dollars' worth of copperplates were sold without measurement. Paper of various kinds, sometimes with the quantity specified but sometimes merely " a lot of paper in the corner," brought nearly three hundred dollars. The largest, and heaviest, asset in Peter Maverick's estate was lithographic stone. The various lots of this, which sold almost always for ten cents a pound, total more than two and a half tons. Other materials of the trade were in proportion.

In the 1820's Maverick also turned more and more to independent business ventures in which he functioned both as engraver and as publisher. He had already produced a small school atlas and was beginning to be interested in portraits. He engraved portraits of Henry Clay, Edward Mitchell, and Richard Channing Moore; several others not so well dated may have been done also at this time. He was interested, too, in producing books of art instruction, such as *Rudiments of Drawing*, a textbook which he designed to illustrate the drawing of the head or full figure through the various stages from simple geometrical designs to finished drawings.

There seems to be no record which reveals Peter Maverick's political attitudes, but it seems safe to assume that he was thrilled, in the summer of 1822, to find himself working with Thomas Jefferson, even though he had only a small part in the company of those surrounding the former President in the culminating act of his life, the launching of the University of

Virginia. Although the institution was not to open its doors until three years later, in 1822 Jefferson and his associates were pressing the matter vigorously against much public inertia and many political cross purposes. The plan of the buildings and grounds of the academic community had taken form, and as an aid to publicity the committee proposed reproducing the design. The details of the transaction, which can be traced through various collections and records in Virginia, not only give us a point of contact between Maverick and Jefferson, but they furnish us also with a body of specific data regarding the conduct of Maverick's business not otherwise available.

Sometime before July 10, 1822, Maverick had had correspondence regarding the engraving, had offered to do it in line for $112, and had said that such a plate would give six to eight thousand impressions. On this date Jefferson wrote William J. Coffee asking him to order such a plate with 250 impressions, and to have Maverick keep the plate in his shop in anticipation of further orders "if we find the impressions sell readily." Further negotiations were interrupted by the epidemic which caused Maverick and his family to flee the city, but on November 22 Jefferson wrote acknowledging receipt of the proofs of the engraving, commenting on the paper to be used, and confirming the initial order for 250 copies. On December 7 Maverick wrote Jefferson that he had sent the copies to Colonel Peyton at Richmond and had retained the plate. The itemized bill was $112 for the engraving, $25 for printing 250 copies, $12 for the paper used, and $1 for boxing and cartage. A check for payment went promptly from the proctor of the university to Peyton, and on December 23 Peter again wrote to Jefferson acknowledging the receipt of the payment. Before the university was ready for students, however, there were changes in the building plan which necessitated changes in the engraving. With the charges for a second printing of 250 copies in 1825 was included a $13 charge for alterations. The bill was paid on March 3, 1825, four days before classes began in the new institution.

Engraving was not a cheap method of reproduction, even if enough copies were printed to make the cost of the original plate relatively small, as bills of Maverick and his contemporaries testify.* For each operation of inking this plate, wiping it clean, and running the plate and paper through the press, Maverick charged ten cents, and for the sheet of paper for this engraving of approximately sixteen by eighteen inches he charged about five cents. If only five hundred copies were made from this plate, the cost of cutting the plate added twenty-five cents for each copy. To these costs must also be added the shipping charges from New York to Richmond. In the light of such costs, it is no wonder that the cheap and easy process of lithography—though it resulted in a muddy surface and a ragged line which must have set many a good engraver's teeth on edge —pushed very rapidly to the fore.

During this period Maverick also included commissions for the South American trade. He did work for a Spanish gift book intended for South America, and his portrait of Clay was printed in a Spanish edition. The inventory of his estate refers

* The Durand-Perkins firm, in 1828, for instance, charged $250 for engraving a copperplate of four bank notes, and half that amount for retouching it after the guaranteed six thousand impressions, to make it good for six thousand more. Steel engraving was then just becoming possible, and the same work on steel cost twice as much, though the guaranteed product was thirty thousand impressions before retouching, and twenty thousand more afterwards. The charge for printing these plates, however, was given as two dollars a hundred, with no mention of an extra charge for the paper stock.

vaguely to engravings for a Spanish prayer book, and elsewhere to a plate for a portrait of Bolivar. When Simon Bolivar
was constructing the financial pattern of the Republic of Colombia, Peter Maverick tastefully designed and engraved with
skillful care a sheet of notes for him. It is possible that an extensive search of South American libraries and museums might
produce evidence of much more of Peter's work in that part of
the world.

Perhaps the most important bit of professional adventuring in Maverick's shop at this time was his work with the entirely new process of lithography. We have seen him at work
first with a relief block, in which his task was to carve away all
but the lines and surfaces to be printed, and then to press these
inked lines and surfaces on paper to make the impression. We
have seen him at work in a long career with the intaglio process
in which the printing is accomplished by pressing paper into
channels and tiny pits filled with ink. Now he turned to a plano-
graphic process, with no raised surfaces to take the ink from the
roller, nor any channels to hold the ink against the cleaning action of the wiper.

The process of lithography was invented and developed in
Austria just before the turn of the century, but its first recorded
use in America was by Bass Otis, in a portrait frontispiece for a
book published in 1818. The basic process was simple, though
it was capable of an infinite refinement, the extent of which was
never even dreamed of in Maverick's time. Upon the smoothed
surface of a kind of stone found in the region of lithography's
origin, the drawing was made with a greasy crayon. When water
was applied to the stone, the crayon lines, being greasy, repelled
the water, and when oily ink was rolled over the surface it ad-

hered only to the lines from which the water had been repelled, so that the paper laid upon the stone took the impression of these inked lines of the original drawing. This brief exposition is far too simple for even the work done by the Mavericks, and is quite inadequate for later developments, but it serves to distinguish the process from Maverick's previous work.

One of the contracts in the Maverick shop at this time was for plates for the *Annals of the Lyceum of Natural History of New York* for 1824 and 1825. Out of a group of more than thirty plates, several were done in lithography and the remainder in stipple and line engravings. Emily and Maria Ann did many of these plates. Octavia and Catharine were already hard at work learning the process, and after Emily's marriage and departure in 1830, and their father's and Maria Ann's deaths in 1831 and 1832, respectively, they joined their brother in carrying on the family business of lithography.

Because lithography was a cheap and rapid process compared with engraving, it offered strong competition to the older art, and lithographic items were turned out in great abundance for the popular trade which Currier and Ives were soon to serve. Maverick used stone for reproducing at least one popular song, for Lambdin's portrait of Robert Owen and for Lawrence's *Daughters of Charles B. Calmady*, for Herring's drawings of snipes and woodcocks, for a dog and a girl with a title *Le Fidèle Ami*, and undoubtedly for many more pictures. His final inventory abounds in items which might be either engravings or lithographs, but the titles suggest the popular taste which lithography was soon to cater to. We find, with the number of copies and the price (of a cent or two a copy), such titles as *Maid and Milk Pail; Distress; Gentle Tooth Drawer; Grandfather's*

Wig; Rabbits; Perfect Felicity; and other similar items for which the inventory shows no identified plates to prove them engravings. We find also one item "1 Stone and Drawing, Puppies" which sold for five dollars; the price can hardly mean anything else but that the surface of the stone was still good for printing before the impression should be cleared off and the stone used again.

The American Academy of Fine Arts, which had elected Maverick to membership in 1816, was now having difficulties with an active group of practicing artists among its members who felt that the "gentlemen of taste and fortune" who were in authority over their body ignored proper business methods, lacked administrative abilities, and tended to rebuff rather than attract young artists. Accordingly there developed a group called the Drawing Association, whose members made use of certain facilities of the Academy in their own way, and threatened complete separation when the governing board exercised a control which they felt not warranted. Leaders in this movement were Samuel F. B. Morse, Durand, Inman, and Wall. In the winter of 1825–1826 the efforts of this group to get satisfactory representation on the governing board came to an impasse. The discontented group withdrew to form the National Academy of Design. Maverick appears to have played no great part in the politics which stirred the younger men to high emotion, but he identified himself with the new movement and was one of the founders. He was also one of the committee that prepared its first exhibition in 1826. The American Academy made several futile attempts at conciliation, but before long the National Academy had the field to itself.

In the late spring of 1826 Maverick was host for a period

to the portrait painter, John Neagle,* and his wife of Philadelphia. Neagle appears to have used the days of his visit to good
purpose, for he records that he did portraits of half a dozen important theatrical folk of the time, a minister, and several others.
In recognition of the hospitality which he and his wife had received, Neagle also began a portrait of his host, which he
finished in Philadelphia later with Mr. Townsend (perhaps
one of Maverick's future sons-in-law) "sitting for the coat."

This portrait, which Neagle presented to the Maverick
family (reproduced as the frontispiece to this volume), gives us
our only knowledge of the physical appearance of Peter Maverick. It was exhibited in the National Academy show of 1827
and drew from John Neal, in his review of that exhibit ** the
judgment that it was "a very bold, straightforward, generous
picture." A process reproduction of it was made in the late
nineteenth century, but the original was lost to public record until (in connection with the present study) it was discovered in
the possession of Mr. Charles E. Townsend, Maverick's great-
great-grandson; in an exhibit at the Newark Museum in December, 1947, it was shown in a collection of early American
portraits.

Maverick's personal affairs during this last decade of his
life were less happy than his professional activity. First death
claimed two of his children: on September 13, 1822, five
months after birth, he lost his son, Raphael, and on July 8,
1823, three-year-old Caroline died. In the summer of 1825 his
wife, Mary, who had been subject to consumption, suffered a

* Neagle is often mentioned as an
engraving apprentice of Maverick. The
statement is completely plausible, but I
have found no contemporary evidence.
** (*The Yankee*, New Series, No. 1,
1829, p. 51.)

serious decline. On August 10 her suffering became intense and by seven o'clock the next morning she, too, was claimed by death. Consumption was a disease that was destined to be the cause of much sorrow in the family; already the cause of death of one child, Julia Augusta, it was later to claim also the lives of several other of his children.

In the following spring came the death of Peter's brother Andrew at the age of forty-three. Although the evidence is slight, it suggests a cordiality in many personal and business relations between the two. Peter engraved business cards for Andrew, and Andrew's home was Peter's New York address during part of his residence in Newark. Andrew may have worked with Peter in his Newark establishment (the records hint at such a relationship).

About this time an important rift occurred between the Peter Mavericks and Peter's brother-in-law Patrick Munn, for whom Peter and Mary had named their first son. In 1819 Munn had made a will which provided for the division of his estate, after his widow's death, among his and his wife's relatives, the Munns themselves having no children. This meant that half of Munn's estate was to be divided among the grandchildren of Peter Rushton Maverick. Peter Maverick was nominated as one of the executors. In 1827, however, Munn added a codicil removing the nomination of Peter as executor, and removing all Peter's children from any share in the estate. The shares of his other nephews and nieces were left undisturbed. An explanation of Munn's action can only be a matter of speculation. The religious issue suggests itself, for Ann Munn, Peter's sister, was, contrary to Peter, a devout person; but so were many of Peter's daughters. Whatever the cause, we may be sure that, unless Peter was well fortified by a conviction that he was not at fault, this incident must have added further strain.

A year later the family tensions reached a climax. Since their mother's death the older daughters had continued to maintain the family unity and to carry on the household for their younger sisters and their father and brother. When it was learned that their father planned to bring into the household a new mother, and one only seven years older than his eldest daughter, their resentment was strong. Perhaps Peter did not lessen the resentment when he, or his intended wife Matilda Brown, chose May 15, the twenty-sixth anniversary of his marriage to Mary, as the date of his second marriage; Matilda never felt herself received into the family of her husband. On September 25 two daughters left the household after Maria Ann, the engraver and lithographer, married John Franklin Townsend, and Cornelia married William Henry Townsend, his brother. A little over a year later, on January 4, 1830, Emily married Tobias Abraham Stoutenburgh of Johnstown, N.Y. The younger members of the family presumably stayed at home during the life of their father. To this father and his new wife was born an unnamed daughter who lived only a short time. On August 23, 1830, a second child, who was destined to achieve some eminence, was born and named Augustus.

In the fall of 1830 Peter completed his fiftieth year. He had worked hard, and apparently was still working hard, for there are none of the indications of the slow relinquishment of activity that his father's last years showed. His advertisements emphasize the new techniques available at his shop, or call for additional helpers. But the work, the worries which commercial planning and adventuring must have entailed, the worries of births and deaths and family rifts must have taken their toll. On the 7th of June in 1831 he died of what the signer of the death certificate called "decay of the heart." The funeral was held two days later from his last home, 61 Grand Street, and burial was in St. John's Burying Ground, beside Mary and their child Caroline.

On January 12 of the following year Maria Ann died, and her death was recorded in her mother's family Bible, on the inside cover of which were recorded all the births and deaths of Mary's family and of her mother's family. Whoever recorded Maria's death (perhaps kindly Cornelia) also recorded, in the sequence given, the following notes, which tell as much by their reticences as by their utterances:

Maria Ann. *Departed this life on the 12th of Jan. 1832 at 5 o'clock* A.M.; *in the joyful hope of a happy immortality through the merits of her crucified Redeemer. Her complaint Consumption. Her age 26 y. 7m. 28d.*

The mother of the preceding, August the 11th 1825, at 7 o'clock A.M. *of a pulmonary complaint terminated by extreme agony of 18 hours continuance during the whole of which trial, the mind remained calm; not a murmur of impatience could proceed from a heart so fortified by the Christian's hope of a happy immortality. Her short time of existence, 43 years—her walk through life exemplary; her exit happy.*

Peter, *the Husband and Father of the foregoing—of a disease of the heart which terminated his existence on the 7th of June 1831 at 1 o'clock* P.M. *aged 50 y. and 7 mon.*

In St. John's Burying Ground a stone was set with the simple inscription "Sacred to the memory of Peter Maverick who departed this life June 7th 1831 aged 50 years & 8 months." Near the end of the century the burying ground was taken by the city for a public park. After a careless record of the inscriptions had been made, the stones were buried. The park has now become the commercial parking area which motorists emerging from the Holland Tunnel see at their right.

EIGHT

The Maverick Name and Engraving

ALTHOUGH Peter was the most important Maverick in the field of graphic arts, the name continued to be closely associated with engraving and lithography long after his death. Among his descendants and those of his brother Andrew and his half-brother Samuel, skill in engraving and lithography continued until the craft itself gave way to quicker and cheaper methods of reproduction.

Six years after the death of Andrew, the copperplate printer, his twenty-three-year-old son Andrew R. married Ann Anderson, the daughter of the wood engraver, Alexander Anderson, who in 1788 had marched in the federal procession with old Peter Rushton Maverick. A few years later Ann was left a widow with two children: a daughter who was destined to die in childbirth while still very young, and a son, William, who after apprenticeship to a bookbinder was employed in the early 1850's as a journeyman. When he married a fellow shopworker in 1854, William moved his business and home to Brooklyn, where he lived till his death at the end of the century, being survived by his wife (who died in 1903) and three daughters.

But in Andrew's immediate family it was Ann's career that kept the name of Maverick connected with the graphic arts, for her signature appears on many prints. From her father, Ann had learned intaglio engraving and the art of engraving wood or type-metal blocks for relief printing; and when left a widow, she turned to engraving for a livelihood, and was soon regularly employed. A half dozen years later she was courted by a Joseph Riley, a former Bostonian who represented himself as a widower. After some hesitation Ann married him in 1842, and for a year or two, his business prospering, he made a home for Ann and her two children, and also presumably for two children of his own. Then he deserted the family, and upon investigation Ann learned that his former wife was still living and still undivorced. Ann resumed the name of Maverick and returned to engraving, putting her children out to board, as she had done before marrying Riley. She was soon regularly employed again, in her later years by an Episcopalian publishing house, doing work for their Sunday school and church books and periodicals. Her work, in the relief block which could be printed with type, has a neat correctness which suggests sometimes the products of those mechanical processes that soon were to replace handwork in all commercial engraving, but it is skillful work of its kind, and it drew the praise of the old master, Ann's father. She continued this employment until the onset of her final illness; after months of suffering she died in late September or October of 1863. For nearly thirty years she had practiced the trade of engraving in New York City under the name that Peter Rushton Maverick had begun to make famous ninety years before.

Throughout the nineteenth century, Samuel Maverick and then his son, Brewster, kept the name of Maverick closely connected with lithography. Mary Howell, Samuel's first wife, apparently was influential in his decision to become an engraver instead of a mariner. After her death he married Clara Reynolds, the granddaughter of his mother's half-brother. Both his mother and Clara survived him when he died on December 4, 1845,* but his engraving business did not continue very long after Clara's death three years later.

Although scarcely fifteen years old at the time of his father's death, Samuel's eldest son Brewster early became interested in lithographic work. In 1866, after some ten years of work in lithography, Brewster shared in the establishment of a lithographic firm in partnership with Louis Stephan, and twelve years later with J. G. Wissinger. His wife, the former Ellen Maria Boleyn of London, survived his death in 1898 by ten years. Although Brewster had no children, his lithographic business continued and is still (1949) in operation in New York under the firm name of Maverick and Wissinger.

In spite of the fact that the majority of Peter's children were girls, it is in this branch of the family that the association of the name of Maverick with the arts was most strongly con-

* His mother, Peter Rushton Maverick's second wife, died in 1852, and his wife, Clara, in 1848. Two lines of descent from Samuel have been traced in recent genealogical studies of the Maverick family. Both are through Samuel's daughter Harriet Matilda, who married Smith A. Parkes. Her son Woodworth's daughters, Harriet M. and Grace E. Parkes, still live in Iowa, where their father was taken after the death of his mother in 1859, and they have been of great help in tracing many of the relationships outlined in this book. Woodworth had a sister Mary Louise, and her great grandson, Raymond Maverick Hunter, Jr., born March 26, 1925, is the eleventh generation from the Rev. John Maverick who brought the name to America.

tinued. The work of Emily and Maria Ann in their father's shop has been noted in earlier pages (pp. 58–59). While their father was still living, both girls became associates of the National Academy of Design. It is not certain whether or not Emily continued her interest in lithography from her move in 1830 to upstate New York until her death in 1850. From her marriage in 1828, Maria Ann probably did very little work in the graphic arts; she was not in good health and lived only to 1832.

On January 31, 1834, when the aging William Dunlap was completing his *Rise and Progress of the Arts of Design in the United States,* he was visited by "two Misses Maverick" who brought with them samples of lithographic work. These girls may well have been Octavia and Catharine, the only other daughters of Peter whose signed works testify to their abilities in the graphic arts.* Since there is record of a letter written by Dunlap to their brother Peter Jr. (then the head of his father's business) only a few days before their visit, it is conceivable that they had come at Dunlap's request. Later in their lives these two sisters turned to teaching. Octavia married a teacher, Edwin Spafard, in 1846, and from 1855 to 1863 she herself taught drawing and painting in the Packer Institute in Brooklyn. Catharine began her teaching career in 1847 in the Troy Female Seminary (now Emma Willard School) where she taught drawing, water-color painting, and later pastel until 1862. Octavia died on June 23, 1882, and five years later, on January 11, 1887, Catharine died.

There is little reason to believe that at the death of Peter

---

* What appears to be their only publicly available signed work may be found in the scrapbooks acquired by the Newark Public Library in 1947.

Courtesy of the New England Historical
Genealogical Society

Reproduction of the Jarvis Portrait
Courtesy of Harriet M. and Grace E. Parkes

SAMUEL MAVERICK

B. Walker.

P. Maverick n Newark.

BOOKPLATE
[208]

LIBERTAS ET PATRIA MEA

James Giles

BOOKPLATE
[130]

Sam.ₗ Maverick

COPPER-PLATE-PRINTER

N.º 73

Liberty Street.

NEW YORK.

TRADE CARD
[1024]

THEATRE TICKET
[721]

TRADE CARD
[1017]

LITHOGRAPH BY
EMILY MAVERICK

[1802]

VIRGIL'S ÆNEIS.
TRANSLATED
by
John Dryden.

The serpents strangled with his infant honde.
Æneis Book VIII

Nvins del.   P. Maverick

PHILADELPHIA.

[764]

TYPICAL TITLE PAGE

Gonzales pinx.   P. Maverick sculp. Newark. N.J.

CHRIST AND DISCIPLES
[450]

LITHOGRAPH BY CATHARINE MAVERICK
[2001]

[1905]

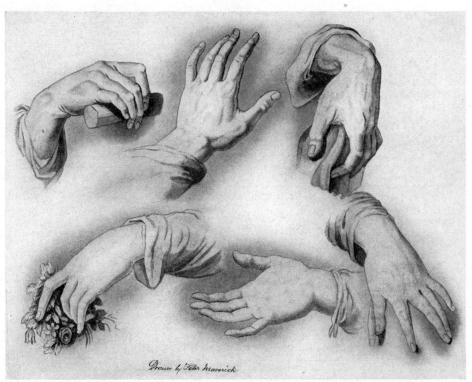

ORIGINAL DRAWING
[663]

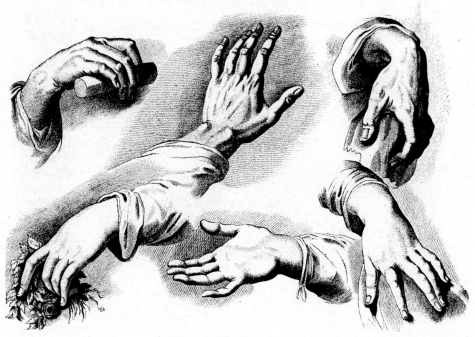

DRAWING-BOOK ENGRAVING
[500]

[1563

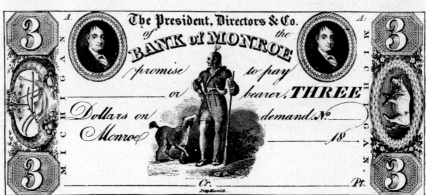

[1223

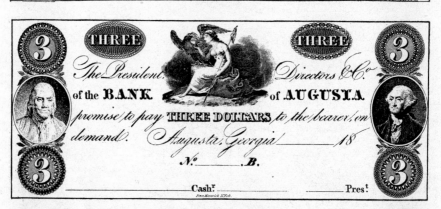

[1213

[1405

Courtesy of Newark Public Library

Reproduced with special permission
of the U.S. Secretary of the Treasury

MAJ. GEN. ANDREW JACKSON.

[575]

PRINCE KOUTOUSOFF.

[598]

LITHOGRAPH BY OCTAVIA MAVERICK

[2103]

WOODCOCKS

Drawn by J.Hering.

Printed by P.Mavoroft

Published by M.Bancroft, 403 Broadway.

[779]

W.G.Wall pinx.^t   Peter Maverick sc.^t

TICONDEROGA.

[761]

W.G.Wall pinx.^t   Peter Maverick sc.^t

NEW-YORK.

[657]

MASONIC JEWEL-MARK

[70]

in 1831 the family rift occasioned by his second marriage to Matilda in 1828 had been mended. Matilda with her baby Augustus continued for some time to make her home at 61 Grand Street. Augustus, who early began his career as Horace Greeley's office boy, became prominent in New York and Boston journalism as editor and author. After fifty-seven years of widowhood Matilda died only a month earlier than her son.* Since the children of Peter and his first wife Mary left the home on Grand Street soon after their father's death, it is scarcely strange, in view of the family separation, that the officiating clergyman at the funeral of Augustus spoke of him as an only child, in spite of the fact that a few weeks earlier his half-sister Angelica had died but a few blocks away, and another — Catharine — only the year before.

The center for Peter and Mary's children after they left Grand Street appears to have been Cornelia's home. This is not difficult to understand, for from the meager records available she emerges as an interesting and kindly personality. In the record of her testimony for an acrimonious lawsuit, for instance, her quiet kindly effort to be fair to all concerned is evident in every sentence. Except for her residence in Staten Island ** from the spring of 1840 until her husband's death six years later, Cornelia made her home in Manhattan. Church records show that, when Cornelia and her husband transferred their membership from St. Luke's Protestant Episcopal Church in New York to St. Paul's in Staten Island, Penelope, Lavinia, Catharine, and

* Augustus had two children, Grace and Manton. Of the many descendants of Rev. John Maverick of New England, Manton appears to have been the last to bear the name of Maverick; at his death on Sept. 23, 1943, he left no children.

** The Townsends lived at what is now 104 Townsend Avenue. Called a stationer, he and his brothers were also large land-owners in the vicinity.

in the following year Angelica * also transferred their member-
ships. Nor were her sisters the only ones to enjoy Cornelia's
home. When the wife of her half-brother Augustus died in
1870, Cornelia took the two children, Grace and Manton, to
live with her for a time; and after Cornelia's return to New
York from Staten Island Grandmother Rebecca also lived with
her.

Cornelia's husband, William Henry Townsend, may have
been one of Peter Maverick's apprentices. After Peter's death,
his business was carried on by a kind of partnership of Townsend and Peter's twenty-one-year-old son Peter; the older Peter
died without a will and in the 1831 sale of his goods, Townsend
and the younger Peter shared in some of the purchases of shop
equipment.

Young Peter's contemporaries seemed to regard him as an
unworthy son of a worthy father, but the records do not indicate
whether this opinion was based on a comparison of their business
efficiency, their social behavior, or their technical skill. At any
rate, he continued to work in lithography up to his death on
September 6, 1845.** At a recent sale, because of its rarity, his
lithographic view of Wall Street, New York, sold for nearly
four thousand dollars. This print was long assumed to be the

* Lavinia married the blind Warren
Waterbury in 1850 and lived until April
19, 1874. Of Penelope, little is known
beyond the fact that she died in 1864.
Another sister, Elizabeth, who married her
cousin James Woodham, Jr. (son of James
Woodham by his second wife, Maria Maverick) died in 1865. From 1850 to 1855
Angelica was a colleague of her sister
Catharine at the Troy Female Seminary
where she taught language and literature;
she may earlier have been a teacher in
Virginia. Her death is recorded for
March 27, 1888. For Catharine, see
pages 76 and 79.

** An unexplained New York Trinity
Parish burial record, "Mary, wife of Peter
Maverick, died March 1833," might indicate that young Peter married a Mary
and early became a widower, but it is
more probably another example of the
careless copying to be found in this record
of the tombstones in St. John's Burying
Ground made at the time the burial
ground was turned into a park.

work of his father, and it is possible that other lithographs attributed to his father are instead the work of the son.

Charles (1836–1894), one of the children of Cornelia and William Townsend, showed some of the Maverick interest in the arts. Although an accountant by vocation, he was a painter by serious avocation, and exhibited his pictures in the shows of the National Academy which his grandfather had helped to found.

Although most of the Mavericks lived and worked in New York City the greater part of their lives, the location of the family burial plot in Newark reminds us again of the family's interim residence in that city. Presumably the family lot * was purchased for the burial of the first Octavia in 1814. Although only the burials of Octavia and Raphael are listed during their parents' lifetime, it is a fair assumption that Julia Augusta was also buried in this plot during this period. According to a manuscript copy of the tombstone inscriptions made in 1904, Lavinia, the second Octavia, Angelica, Catharine, and two of Cornelia's children, William Henry Townsend (1834–1864) and Mary Townsend Walsh (1838–1863), are also buried here. A mysterious Hebert Maverick, who died in 1864 at the age of 48, is also listed. Since Penelope died in 1864 at the age of 48, this may be an error in deciphering or copying the tombstone inscription; if on the other hand there was a Maverick who gave his son the name of the French revolutionary martyr to reason's cause, there is apparently no other record of his life. And as errors go, this is surely more interesting than most blunders of copyists.

* No. 2 in Trinity Yard now included within the walls of the Cathedral House.

This, then, is the family of Peter Maverick, from his father, who founded the business with the help of his grandfather's estate, on through the span of a century to the sons and daughters of Peter who reflected in their vocations their training in the shops of Newark and of New York. There must be still further influences and results of his life and work. There must be influences in interests and skills transmitted from parent to child in the various families founded by the daughters and granddaughters under various names. There must be influences among pupils who studied under the teachers of art who had learned their first principles in Peter's shop. We cannot trace them all, but, traceable or not, they are the results of the Maverick skill and industry, for these are the ways in which a culture lives and grows and develops. As a master craftsman in the engraving of his time, and as a pioneer in lithography, Peter was an important worker in movements which, for better and for worse, have strongly affected America's artistic culture.

[2]

MAVERICK ENGRAVINGS

AND

LITHOGRAPHS

1. Explanation of Check List

THE CATALOGUE which follows is the result of a ten-year search for information about the Maverick family and their works. It is intended to list all the Maverick engravings and lithographs about which data are available. However, in spite of careful search, there must be errors and omissions, and the author hopes that any additional items or corrections will be brought to his attention. The inventory of the 1831 auction of Peter Maverick's possessions gives information about many Maverick prints, and this information is also included in the listing, even when no other data for any one item are available. Such an entry as "1831 sale, 213 for $4.15. Plate for 75¢" means "In the 1831 auction of Peter Maverick's goods, 213 copies of a print (in one lot or several) were sold for a total of $4.15, and the copperplate from which the print was made sold for 75 cents." When there is any doubt as to the identity of an invoiced item, the exact notation on the invoice is quoted.

For each item I have tried to include the following: (1) the exact title, or, if untitled, a descriptive phrase of identification; (2) the type of engraving, i.e., vignette, circle, rectangle, and whether executed in line or stipple, etc; (3) height and width, i.e., 4.6 x 2.14 indicates a height of $4\frac{6}{16}$ inches and a width of $2\frac{14}{16}$ inches (*Note:* figures following decimal points indicate sixteenths, not hundredths); (4) a description of salient features; (5) the entire inscription if the inscription seemed important enough to include; and (6) regularly the complete signatures reproduced exactly with one exception: the superscript letters in abbreviations are brought down to the line. In addition, wherever possible, information is given concerning uses of the plate, books and magazines in which engravings appeared, and modern reproduction of prints. I had hoped that at least one public location of each print could be indicated, and where it was possible, this information has been included. Many unique and rare items, however, are at this time only in the possession of private collectors.

2. Maverick Signatures

ALTHOUGH in his early years Peter Rushton Maverick often used the signature "Peter Maverick" in his business and social affairs, no engravings with this signature in the list which follows appear to be his work. Up until the time when he recognized the necessity of distinguishing his signature from that of his son, he most commonly signed his engravings simply "Maverick"; only occasionally did he use instead the "P. R." or "Peter R." that later became his characteristic signature. Occasionally, in this later period, he also used "Maverick Senr."

The elder Maverick signed his work in script. His capital letter M was usually pointed at the tops and preceded by the loop (similar in appearance to a large, lower-case, script "e"). In the 1790's this loop decreased in size, until finally there was only a fatness of line at the beginning of the letter M. When his son Peter began to sign his work, he used the signature "Peter Maverick," and in his early work his script signature bears close resemblance to his father's later style. It seems probable too that this signature was used on many plates on which both father and son worked.

When Peter began his independent career, he stopped using script and used, instead, neat printed letters. At first the angularity of the letters suggests the use of a square, but the neatly curved lettering by which his later engravings are usually identified soon developed. His occasional substitution of the initial for his first name, his use of a variety of abbreviations for *sculpsit*, and his use of other abbreviations give no guide in dating, except that there is a tendency to simplify his signature through the years of his career. He commonly added his post-office address to his signature while he was living in Newark; while he was living in New York he sometimes, though not frequently, used a street address.

During the period from 1817 to 1820, when Peter was in partnership with Asher Durand, two signatures were used. The first signature of the partnership was "P. Maverick and Durand," but soon (probably in 1818) it became "P. Maverick, Durand, & Co." Sometimes to this signature was added an M or D to indicate that the plate was the sole work of either Maverick or Durand. With somewhat the same purpose of identification, he later added "dir" or "direx" to his signature for those plates which his daughters had worked on under his direction and which sometimes also bore the daughters' signatures.

3. Location and Typical Examples of Maverick Work

THE READER who wishes to examine Maverick prints will find many available at NPL, NYHS, NYPL, AAS, and WMFA. Almost any library or museum with a few early American prints or books will contain Maverick material, but seldom is it catalogued under the engraver's name as it is in the above institutions.

Peter Rushton Maverick—General Works. The general work of P.R.M. was often quite crude and primitive, but in the stipple portrait frontispiece for Elizabeth Rowe's *Devout Exercises of the Heart,* he achieved a delightful result; and in his New York City map of 1799 he was clear and firm of line. Many of his certificates and allegorical designs are somewhat fearful to behold, but in his diploma for Columbia College he cut the plate with assurance and a firm hand, and Columbia found the result good enough to use for a century.

Peter Rushton Maverick and Peter Maverick—Bookplates. Of the hundred or so bookplates of Peter Rushton Maverick, some may be the work of his son Peter while he was still in his father's shop. The young Peter's bookplates were superior to those of his father both in design and execution, and the best work of the father is often suspected as being that of the son. Typical examples of the work of the father are the bookplates for DeWitt Clinton, for Benjamin S. Judah, for Rufus King, for Edward Livingston, and for William Smith Livingston. Of special interest are his plates for John Pintard, for Bishop Provoost, and for P. J. Van Berckell, as are also two plates for the New York Society Library.

Any unsigned item which has been attributed to Maverick is included with comment concerning authenticity. For example, some of the items in the Frederick DePeyster contribution to the New York Historical Society (*A Collection of Book Plates of Several Old Citizens of New York,* bound sheets with impressions made from the original coppers) are not only unsigned but are quite different in style from Maverick's work. Yet Allen assigns all the items in the list to Maverick (in one case he later changed his mind).

The list of bookplates is based chiefly on the half-century-old lists of Allen and of Fincham (see Bibliography); items from the Allen list are indicated by the letter *A* plus the number of his listing; items from the Fincham list are indicated by the abbreviation *Fm* (Fincham's listing is unnumbered). Similarly, *St.* and *F.* with numbers indicate, respectively, Stauffer's *Dictionary of American Engravers* and Fielding's supplement to it. Items from the bookplate collection of Mrs. Bella C. Landauer, which is housed in the New York Historical Society, are indicated by the addition of her name to the abbreviation NYHS.

Other sources for the listing are the notes and collections now in the possession of the American Antiquarian Society, the Metropolitan Museum of Art in New York, and the New York Historical Society; other scattered sources were used, when the indexing and notes made it possible to find pertinent information.

Dates in the listing are the author's approximation and have been based on the style of the work or on the form or content of the signature.

Peter Maverick—General Works, Trade Cards, and Maps. Many of the items in this listing of some five hundred general works of Peter Maverick are book and magazine illustrations which he copied from the illustrations in English books to be published in the United States. Of the other items, some are the result of his independent print–publishing ventures in which he engraved for an entrepreneur as, for example, the large reproduction, with facsimile signatures, of the Declaration of Independence. Others were the results either of a venture entirely on his own or in partnership with the artist; examples of the latter are Charles Ingham's picture, "Christ Blessing Little Children," or William Dunlap's portrait of Bishop Richard Channing Moore. As to lithographs, the chief items available for public inspection are in NPL, AAS, and NYPL print room.

Peter also did many certificates for various societies of which NYHS, NYPL, and MCNY have typical examples. A diploma which he made for Rutgers College was used by Rutgers for over a century.

The principal collections of his trade cards and business forms may be found in NYHS (particularly NYHS Landauer). Some twenty of his maps may be found in the collections of LC, NYPL, NYHS, AAS, AGS, and NJHS.

Bank notes—Peter Maverick. Bank notes were made by Maverick in one or more sheets, normally of four notes each, for at least thirty-five banks. Since the lowest denomination was usually one dollar and the highest either a hundred dollars or a blank post note, numbers with a span of ten for each bank have been allotted to enable cataloguers who discover additional items to locate them near or at their proper positions. Bank-note items, not catalogued under Maverick's name, may be found in AAS, ANS, CNB, and especially in the private collection of Mr. J. N. Spiro of Maplewood, New Jersey.

Samuel Maverick. Samuel Maverick's work is to be found in most of the collections mentioned. I have found some eighty prints signed with his name and varying greatly in quality. Almost surely his signature means often that he contracted for the engraving and farmed out the work. Asher Durand did some work for him in his early years; Peter did also, but later refused to do further work until Samuel should stop advertising himself as an engraver.

Peter Maverick's children. Samples of the signed work of Peter's daughters may be found in NPL. See Item 2201 for the only important work of his son, Peter Jr.

4. List of Abbreviations

AAS: American Antiquarian Society, Worcester, Mass.

AGS: American Geographic Society, New York, N.Y.

AMNNJ: Academy of Medicine of Northern New Jersey, Newark, N.J.

ANS: American Numismatic Society, New York, N.Y.

BA: Boston Athenaeum.

BMFA: Boston Museum of Fine Arts.

BPL: Boston Public Library.

CNB: Chase National Bank, Collection of Moneys of the World, New York, N.Y.

CU: Columbia University Library, with references to Plimpton and Columbiana collections added.

DC: Dartmouth College Library, Hanover, N.H.

EI: Essex Institute, Salem, Mass.

GC: Grolier Club, New York, N.Y.

HU: Harvard University Library, with added references

for the Fogg Museum.

LC: Library of Congress.

MEHS: Maine Historical Society, Portland, Maine.

MCNY: Museum of the City of New York.

MHS: Massachusetts Historical Society, Boston, Mass.

ML: Library Masonic Grand Lodge of New York, N.Y.

MMNY: Metropolitan Museum, New York, N.Y.

NEHG: New England Historical Genealogical Society, Boston, Mass.

NJHS: New Jersey Historical Society, Newark, N.J.

NPL: Newark Public Library, Newark, N.J.

NYHS: New York Historical Society, New York, N.Y., with added references to the Landauer collection and the Print Room.

NYPL: New York Public Library, New York, N.Y.

NYSL: New York Society Library, New York, N.Y.

NYSMT: New York Society of Mechanics & Tradesmen, New York, N.Y.

PAFA: Pennsylvania Academy of Fine Arts, Philadelphia, Pa.

RU: Rutgers University Library, New Brunswick, N.J.

UM: University of Michigan Library.

UV: University of Virginia Library.

WMFA: Worcester Museum of Fine Arts, Worcester, Mass.

NOTE: To the institutions listed above, and to the following institutions, I want to express my grateful appreciation for their help and co-operation at all times: National Museum, Washington; United States Patent Office; United States Bureau of Engraving and Printing; Philadelphia Museum, Pennsylvania Historical Society; Trinity Church, Newark; Trinity Church, New York; the records divisions of Essex and Hudson Counties in New Jersey and of Richmond, New York, and Kings Counties in New York State; and the city records of New York City; Long Island Historical Society; Staten Island Historical Society, Morgan Library, Frick Art Reference Library; Packer Collegiate School, Brooklyn; Emma Willard School, Troy, N.Y.; Chicago Art Institute; Chicago Public Library; Milwaukee Public Library; University of Minnesota Library; Detroit Museum.

5. List of Maverick Engravings and Lithographs

A. Peter Rushton Maverick

GENERAL WORKS

AGRICULTURE. *Transactions of the Society for the Promotion of Agriculture, Art and Manufactures,* Part I. N.Y.: The Society, 1792. AAS, NYHS. (Items 1 and 2.)

1. Agric. implement. Facing p. 77, line rect., 4 x 6.3. Implement for collecting red clover seed. Sig.: "Maverick Sct."
2. Meterological chart. Facing p. 109, line rect., 6.6 x 10.8. Plan for chart. Sig.: "Maverick Sct."
3. ANATOMICAL ENGRAVING. Line rect., 4.6 x 2.14. Man flayed to show muscles, landscape background. Ins.: "New York, Novr. ——. Anatomy. No. —— Maverick Sct." Ticket for lecture, made about 1790–1795, WMFA copy used 1808. WMFA, NYHS.
4. AYERIGG. Bus. card of Benjn. Ayerigg, painter & glazier, 97 Cherry St. 1794–1802. NYHS.
5. BICKER. Bus. card of Walter Bicker, hatter. 111 Pearl St. 1794–1802. NYHS.
6. CALEDONIAN SOCIETY OF THE CITY OF NEW YORK. Membership certificate. Line rect., 8.2 x 10.4. Indian, Liberty, and kilted Scot, surrounded by eagle with shield of the United States, festoons of plaid, and thistles. Sig.: "Designed & Engraved by P. R. Maverick, No. 65 Liberty Street." 1794–1798. NYHS.
7. CALEDONIAN SOCIETY. Ball ticket. Reported.
8. CARONDELET, EL BARON DE. (As reported.) Line eng., 5.2 x 6.3 on type-printed certificate 11.2 x 17.8. Officer presenting medal to Indian. Landscape background, two alligators at bottom. Flags and military emblems engraved by A. Allardice. View signed "Maverick sculp. N. York."
9. COLUMBIA COLLEGE DIPLOMA. Line, 13.2 x 21, All script and decorative lettering, no pictorial design. Sig.: "Gulielmus Milns Scripsit. Engrd. by P. R. Maverick, 65 Liberty Street." This address was probably added or changed after 1794, the diploma itself apparently dating from the engraver's Crown Street period. On September 8, 1791, Maverick received four pounds, one shilling, and sixpence

($10.19) "for diplomas furnished Columbia College." This diploma was used by Columbia for about a century. CU.

10. COLUMBIA COLLEGE SEAL. Circ. seal, diam. 2.8. The original seal, probably cut in England about 1750, contained the Latin abbreviations for "King's College." In 1788 P. R. Maverick cut these words from the seal and inlaid a section with the new name, "Columbia." The receipt for one pound and five shillings for this work is dated April 12. CU.

COLUMBIAN SONGSTER. *The Columbian Songster, or Jovial Companion* etc. Anon. N.Y.: Greenleaf's Press, 1797. Evans 31961. NYHS, BPL. (Items 11 and 12.)

11. Front. Line rect., 4 x 2.4. Orn. panel with circ. view of Pegasus, landscape, etc. Below, musical instrument resting on panel with four-line ins. Sig.: "Engraved by P. R. Maverick, 65 Liberty Street."

12. Facing p. 97. Line, orn, rect. panel, 5.8 x 3.1 overall. Eagle above with U.S. shield on breast. Liberty. a young woman, treading underfoot crowns, chains, and daggers. Three-line ins. in panel. Sig. like preceding.

13. DE LA CROIX. Bus. card for Joseph De La Croix's icehouse garden, 112 Broadway. See NYHS *Quarterly Bull.*, 20: 110–112. About 1798–1799. NYHS.

14. a. DOCK-CLEANING MACHINE. St2263. Line vign., 3.8 x 4.13. Ins.: "American Magazine Jan. 1788 / A New Machine for Cleaning Docks, &c. &c. / Maverick Sct." AAS.

  b. Same without date.

ENCYCLOPEDIA. *The New Encyclopedia.* N.Y.: J. Low, 1805–1811. Line rect. plates with many drawings in each. Sig. uniformly "P. R. M. Sct." Subjects as follow below. AAS, NYHS. (Items 15 through 23.)

15. Pl XXXV. Botany. 7.14 x 5. Misc. flower pictures.
16. Pl XXXVIII. Bee. 7.14 x 5. Bees, combs, etc.
17. Pl. LII. Canis. 8 x 5. Ten dogs.
18. Pl. LIX. Catoptrics.
19. Pl. LIX alt. Diving Bells. No. sig.
20. Pl. LXXIV. Dialling.
21. Pl. LXXIV alt. Didelphis.
22. Pl. (?) Rodents.
23. Pl. (?) Dioptrics.
24. FIRE SCENE. St2265. Line rect., 3.14 x 5.5. Burning house with fire-

men at work. On Deed of Settlement, Mutual Assurance Co. MCNY copy dated in handwriting, 1787. MCNY, NYPL.

25. FIRE SCENE. Line rect., size *ca.* 4 x 5.5. Same view as the preceding, but different plate. On policy of the same company. Sig.: "Engd. by P. R. Maverick." 65 Liberty Street. 1794–1802. MCNY.

26. FRANCIS. Line and stip. Ticket, Mr. Francis's Ball. About 1800, perhaps the work of Peter Maverick. NYHS.

FRANKLIN. *The Works of the late Dr. Benjamin Franklin,* etc. N.Y.: Printed by Tiebout and Obrian for H. Gain et al., n. d. [1794] NYPL, HU. Port. used also in Johnson & Manchester's 1797 ed., and in Tiebout's ed. of 1799. See Evans 32150 and 35498. (Items 27 and 28.)

27. . . . Title page with bibliog. data as given. Sig.: "Engraved by P. R. Maverick, 65 Liberty Street." WMFA.

28. Portrait. St2259. Line and stip. orn. oval, 3.15 x 2.15. Bust, nearly profile left, fur hat. Sig. like preceding. AAS, WMFA.

29. FRAUNCES. Bus. card, Andrew G. Fraunces, notary and real estate. Sig.: "P. R. Maverick Sct." See also Fraunces bookplate. NYHS.

30. GRENADIERS. F1048. Line rect., 12.14 x 11.4. Cert. of membership in First Company, New York Grenadiers. Sig.: "Archd. Robertson invt. and delent. Maverick Sculpt., Liberty Street No. 65." MCNY.

31. GRIFFITHS. Ticket, Griffiths' Ball. 1794–1802. NYHS.

HOMER. *The Adventures of Telemachus,* etc. trans. by John Hawkesworth from the French of Fenelon. 2 vols., N.Y.: David Longworth, 1796–1797. Evans 30414 and 32126. AAS, MHS. (Item 32.)

32. . . . Front., vol. II. Orn. lettering, 3 x 3.5. Sig.: "Shepherd Script. Maverick Sculpt." Pictorial half of plate engraved by Thos. Clarke.

33. a. INDIAN PRESENTS. St2264. Line vign., 3.10 x 6.12. Four Indian pipes, lettered. Ins.: "American Magazine, March 1788. / Indian Presents to Congress. / Maverick Sculpt."
   b. Same, without date. AAS.

34. KING'S PORTER HOUSE. 9 Wall St. Central design a thistle. Sig.: "Engr. by P. R. Maverick, 65 Liberty St." MMNY.

35. LIDDELL. Bus. card, James Liddell, teacher. NYHS.

36. MANHATTAN COMPANY. Stock cert., script lettering, 1800. Sig.: "Maverick Sculpt. No. 65 Liberty Street."

37. MANHEIM. St2262. Line rect., 7.4 x 4.7. Sig.: "S. Folwell Del. P. R. Maverick Sct. N.Y." Front. to *Affecting History of the Dreadful Distresses of Frederick Manheim's Family* etc. Phila.: Matthew

Carey, printed by D. Humphreys, 1794. Evans 26540. AAS, NYPL, LC, MHS.

MARTEL, MICHAEL. *Elements.* N.Y.: C. C. Van Alen & Co, 1796. Evans 30740. AAS, NYPL. (Item 38.)

38. Allegorical front., 6.5 x 3.11. Man at fire, books about. Ins.: "Legite austeri. Crimen amoris abest. P. R. Maverick, 65 Liberty Street."

39. MASONIC CERTIFICATE. Line rect., 10.13 x 8.11. St. Simon and St. Jude's Lodge No. 12, Fishkill, New York. Sig.: "Engraved by Brother P. R. Maverick, 65 Liberty St., New York." Cert. and copperplate, Library of the Grand Lodge of New York, 71 W. 23 St., New York City.

40. a. MASONIC CERTIFICATE. F1043. Line rect., 11 x 11.9. Above, vign. of herald angel. At left, column supporting woman with Bible, at right woman with anchor. Woman with children at base of center column. Statement in English and Latin. Alexandria Lodge No. 22. Sig.: "A. Chevalier delt. Philadelphia. Brother Maverick sculpt. New-York." Alexandria-Washington Lodge, Alexandria, Va.

b. Change reported made in 1805 to "Alexandria-Washington Lodge." Cert. and copperplate in that lodge's archives.

41. MASONIC CERTIFICATE. Line rect., 10 X 8.4, lettering and Masonic symbols. Harmony Lodge No. 31 of Catskill, N.Y. Sig.: "Brother P. R. Maverick, 65 Liberty Street." Used 1795. Greene County Historical Society, Coxsackie, N.Y.

42. M'CULLUM. Bus. card, Archbald M'Cullum, saddler, 102 Broadway. Advertising inscription in French. Sig.: "Maverick Sct." About 1790. NYHS.

43. MICHEAU. Line vign., 6 x 6.4. Body and thighs, with hernia support in place. Sig.: "Maverick Sculpt." Front. to *A Dissertation on Hernia Humoralis,* by Paul Micheau. N.Y.: Printed for Samuel Campbell, 1788. Evans 21255. AAS.

44. MIDDLE STATES. Line rect., 14.10 x 15.8. Ins.: "Map of / of the / Middle States of North America / Shewing the Position of the Genesee / Country Comprehending the Counties of / Ontario and Steuben as laid off in Town- / ships of Six Miles square each. / Maverick Sculpt. 65 Liberty Street. N.Y." NYHS, NPL. Without sig., NYHS. Found in Charles Williamson's *Description of the Settlement of the Genesee Country* etc. N.Y. T. & J. Swords, 1799. AAS, NYPL. Aso in Williamson's *Observations on a Proposed State Road,* etc. N.Y. 1800. NYPL.

45. NEW JERSEY SEAL. Line vign., 3 x 3. Sig.: "Maverick Sc." Front. to Andrew Beers's *Washington Almanac, 1805.* Monmouth Co., N.J.: Robert Stewart.

46. NEW JERSEY SEAL. Relief block, 3 x 3.2. Sig.: "Maverick sc." On title page, *Laws of New Jersey, 1800.* An unsigned cut, slightly larger, is found in the following years.

47. NEW YORK CITY. New York in 1789, reportedly engraved by P. R. Maverick, reproduced in King's *Handbook of New York City,* Boston, 1892. NYPL, NYHS, LC.

48. a. NEW YORK CITY. F1047. Line rect., 15 x 21. Sig.: "J. A. Del. Engrd. by P. R. Maverick, 65 Liberty Street. Drawn and Engrav'd for D. Longworth Map and Print Seller. No. 66 Nassau Street." This is apparently the "New Map of the City" authorized by the City Council to be engraved "by Mr. Maverick or other competent person" on July 15, 1799. On May 9, 1803, he was paid a balance of $480 for engraving the map, and on the following Dec. 6 he was paid $69 for additional copies. Reprod. in Emily J. DeForest's *A Walloon Family in America.* Boston & N.Y., 1914. NYPL, AGS, NYHS, LC.

  b. Later issue, dated 1804. LC.

  c. Later issue, dated 1808. NYPL.

49. NEW YORK MEDICAL SOCIETY. Line rect., 9.1 x 11.13. Latin diploma, with "Maverick sculpt." in the inscription, and "Maverick sct." on the attached seal. Society founded in 1789; this engraving gives evidence of being done near that date. MCNY.

50. PALMER, ELIHU. Stip. oval, 4 x 3, with lettering below. Three-quarter seated figure, almost profile right. Hands on cane, tricorn hat. Name and four-line insc. below. Sig.: "Engrd. by P. R. Maverick, 65 Liberty St. N. York." 1794–1802. This blind Deist orator was a friend of the elder Maverick. NPL.

51. PROVIDENT SOCIETY OF NEW YORK. Memb. cert., line rect., 7.7 x 9.6 plate size. Grape arbor design, eagle above, three figures and beehive below. NYHS copy has wax seal, dove with olive branch, probably also Maverick's work. Sig.: "Maverick Sculpt." About 1790. NYHS.

52. QUICK AND DEGROVE. Bus. card, grain brokers, 124 Cherry St. NYHS.

53. REMINGTON. Bus. card, Wm. Remington. NYHS.

54. REPUBLICAN SOCIETY. Library card, Republican Society Library, with

motto, "Mutual Improvement." Sig.: "P. R. Maverick Sc. No. 3 Crown Street, N.Y." NYHS.

Rowe, Mrs. Elizabeth. *Devout Exercises of the Heart*. N. Y.: Tiebout & OBrien for E. Mitchell, [1795]. NYPL. (Items 55 and 56.)

55. . . . Title page. Lettering, 2.15 x 1.12, no vign.

56. . . . Front. Line and stip. oval port., 2.1 x 1.9 in orn. panel 3.2 x 1.13. Ins.: "Mrs. Rowe. / Engrd. by P. R. Maverick, 65 Liberty Street."

57. Ruth. St2266. Line rect., 10.6 x 7.2. Draped base, festoon of flowers above. Ruth, Boaz, and others in field. Sig.: "Maverick Sculpt." In Rev. John Brown's *Self-Interpreting Bible*, first American edition. N.Y.: Printed for T. Allen, 1792. Engraving a copy of picture in Eng. ed. 1780, pub. by Fielding & Walker. Used also in Maynard's *Works of Josephus*, Phila.: Archibald Woodruff & John Turner, 1795. RU, AAS, NYPL.

58. Speller. Hugh Gaine's receipt book, NYPL, shows on Dec. 19, 1787, a payment to P. R. Maverick of eleven pounds ($27.50) for "the cuts of the Universal Spelling Book and all accounts."

59. St. Andrew, Society of, Alexandria, Va. Memb. cert., line, 7 x 8.10. Festooned and foliaged border, vase at bottom, St. Andrew at top. Sig.: "Maverick Sct. New York." About 1785–1790. NYHS.

60. St. Andrew, Society of. Memb. cert. Line, 5.7 x 8.14. St. Andrew at top, with his cross. Wax seal at bottom, bearing thistle surmounted by crown and inscribed *"Nemo me impune lacessit."* (Seal probably also Maverick's work.) Sig.: "Maverick Sculpt. Crown Street N. York." Before 1792. NYHS.

61. Schieffelin, Jacb. Billhead. At left, vign., 2 x 3.10, of mortar, pestle, vessels, funnel, and scales. At right, bill form. Vign. prob. also used as trade card. Ins.: "Jacb. Schieffelin, late Lawrence and Schieffelin, drugs and medicines, 125 Pearl St., facing the Fly Market. Engd. by P. R. Maverick 65 Liberty Street." On ribbon above, "Inspected store" etc. This is F1036, the "& Son" of Fielding's description being a ms. addition in copy used 1811; orig. made 1794–1802. MCNY.

Tyler, Royall. *The Contrast, a Comedy in Five Acts*. Phila.: Thomas Wignell, printed by Prichard & Hall, 1790. (Item 62.)

62. . . . Front. Line rect., orn., 6.11 x 4.2. Scene from Act V, final scene. At bottom, "Jon. Do you want to kill the Colonel?/ I feel chock full of fight./ W. Dunlap inv. & del. Maverick Sct." NYPL, UM. Included in the facsimile edition of the play published as Publication

No. 1 of the Dunlap Society, N.Y. 1887. NYHS. Also reproduced in J. G. Wilson's *Memorial History of New York*, 1893.

63. URANIAN SOCIETY. Line script, cert. of memb., 5 x 9, no vign. Sig.: "Maverick Sct." 1787–1790. Note on reverse of copy seen "Copper & Engraving 2–16–0" [$7]. NYHS.

64. VAN BEUREN. Bus. card of Wm. Van Beuren, gold and silver smith, 22 Maiden Lane. 1794–1802. NYHS.

65. VOLNEY. St2260. Stip. oval, 3.10 x 2.14. Ins.: "Engrd. by P. R. Maverick, 65 Liberty Street./ C-F. Volney." Stauffer, because of the excellence of the work, says this may be the work of Peter rather than of Peter R. NYPL.

66. VOLTAIRE. St2261. Line oval port., 2.5 x 1.15, in orn. design 5.6 x 2.11. Bust, face ¾ left. Sig.: "Engrd. by P. R. Maverick 65 Liberty Street N.Y." In Voltaire's *Philosophical Dictionary*, trans. from the French and corrected by the author. Catskill [N.Y.]: Printed by T. & M. Croswel for selves and J. Fellows & E. Duyckinck of New York, 1796. AAS, NYPL, WMFA, NPL.

METAL AND SEAL WORK (see also 49, 51, and 60)

67. IN MARGHERITA ARLINA HAMM's *Famous Families of New York* (N.Y.: Putnam's Sons, 1901. 2 v.) Volume I has on page 190 a picture of a gold "freedom" box presented with the scroll granting the freedom of the City of New York to John Jay. It is still owned by the Jay family. It bears a seal of the city, with ribbons and posies in the fashion typical of the elder Maverick, and is signed "Maverick sculpt." According to C. Louise Avery, who gives another view of this box in her *Early American Silver* (N.Y.: Century, 1930), the box was made by Samuel Johnson and bears his initials, Maverick's signature referring only to the engraving. See also J. M. Phillips, *American Silver*, N.Y.: Chanticleer, 1949, p. 120. Authorized by the Common Council, Sept. 11, 1784.

68. STEUBEN, BARON. Avery notes also another box similarly authorized and engraved, now in the Francis P. Garvan collection at Yale University. Boxes were authorized also for Governor George Clinton, Washington, and Lafayette, but their whereabouts I do not know. These are earliest known dated "bright-cut" engraving.

69. THE NEW YORK SOCIETY LIBRARY records show payment to Peter R. Maverick on January 23, 1790, of five pounds fourteen shillings

(one pound equaled $2.50) for a seal and a box to hold it. This is presumably the seal used for some time subsequent to this date.

70. MASONIC JEWEL-MARK OR COIN. Royal Arch Mason's mark, diam. 1.10. Obverse shows grapes and rose with leaves, a ribbon inscribed "William Wright," and sig. "Br. Maverick Sct." Reverse shows man-faced sun, lamb, and tree, with border of letters "H T W S S - T K S." If this is Sen. William Wright (1794–1866. See D A B.), whose family once owned it, the work is probably Samuel Maverick's, *ca.*1830. If it was Wright's father, William Wright, M.D. (Yale 1774, died 1808), the work is, as for various reasons I should judge it to be, that of Peter R. Maverick, *ca.*1790. In author's collection.

B. Peter Rushton and Peter Maverick

BOOKPLATES

101. JAMES AGNEW. A9. Armorial. Shield with two rosettes, crest a helmet surmounted by a bird. Unsigned but attrib. to P. R. Maverick; it may be his, but is not the typical landscape design. MMNY, AAS.

102. ANONYMOUS. A1, illus. p. 161. Fm. French arms, mil. orn., and crown. Sig.: "Maingot delt. Maverick Sct." About 1790. MMNY, NYHS.

103. ANONYMOUS (stock plate). A110, illus. p. 141. Fm. Library interior, youth lounging in chair. Above, on ribbon, "The property of _____"; below, four-line motto. Sig.: "Engrd by P. R. Maverick 65 Liberty Street." 1794–1802. Photo, NYHS Landauer. See Jacob Brown, *infra.*

104. FLAMEN BALL. A48. Fm. Festooned armorial. Sig.: "P. R. Maverick Sct." About 1795. MMNY, AAS, NYHS Landauer, DC, RU.

105. ABRAHAM BANCKER. A51, illus. p. 143. Fm. Eagle holding framed figure 4. Below, sea, trees, and chain of mountains. Sig.: "Maverick Sculpt." About 1790. MMNY; NYHS.

106. ABSALOM BLACHLY. A81, illus. p. 173. Fm. Shield with girdled tree and dog. Quill above and below name. Sig.: "Maverick Scp." About 1790. AAS, MMNY, NYHS.

107. JOSEPH W. BLACHLY. Same as 106, with quills and "Absalom" erased. MMNY.

108. ELIAS BOUDINOT. A96. Illus. in *Curio,* p. 111. Shield, flaming heart, and stars. Crest a wreath. Festoons at side. Allen says it "is the

96

work of Maverick"; it may well be the elder Maverick's work, of about 1800 or a little earlier, but it is not signed. The plate exists with only the surname, and in two different coppers. DC, MMNY, AAS, NYHS, Photo RU.

109. HENRY BRASHER. Landscape with ships, houses, church, trees. Winged figure, above, holds suspended an iron gate with armorial device. Sig.: "Maverick Sct." About 1785–1790. AAS.

110. PHILIP BRASHER. A102. Similar to Henry Brasher's, but without houses and church. MMNY, NYHS.

111. CHARLES BRIDGEN. A105. Festooned armorial. Shield with battlemented wall and three lion-headed fish. Crest a man with globe in hand, anchor at side. No sig., but very like P. R. Maverick's work, about 1790. NYHS, MMNY, AAS.

112. JACOB BROWN. The anonymous stock plate listed above, with name, in ink, on an inlaid slip of paper. MMNY. Same plate, cut for an inlay, at AAS. With this method of adaptation, this plate may well have been used by many persons. Listed as Jacob Brown's plate in BMFA show, 1904.

113. EPAPHRODITUS CHAMPION, JR. A984. Fm. Plain armorial, spread eagle and crosses in shield. Crest an upraised arm with wreath. Sig.: "P. Maverick Sc." Good late work of Peter Maverick, perhaps 1820–1830. AAS, MMNY.

114. CHARLES A. CLINTON. Plate later state of DeWitt Clinton's, below, signed "P. R. Maverick." About 1795. AAS, DC, MMNY.

115. DeWITT CLINTON. A171, illus. p. 55. Fm. Also illus. in *Art Amateur*, Feb. 1894. Shield with two stars and six crosses surmounted by plumed crown. Flowers at side. Sig.: "P. R. Maverick Sculpt." About 1795. AAS, DC, MMNY, NYHS, BA, NYHS Landauer, RU. See also A766 and A992. St.M. 469.

116. WILLIAM COCK. A172. Fm. Illus. *Art Amateur*, Mar. 1894. Festooned shield. Crest a cock, crown around neck, key in bill. Colors indicated by words *gules* and *or* connected by dotted lines to parts of design. Last word of motto is "feceris", not "fueris" as in A. About 1790–1795. AAS, DC, MMNY, NYHS.

117. JAMES S. CUTTING. A197. Fm. Festooned shield, three black birds, three diamonds. Sig.: "Maverick Sct." About 1790–1795. AAS, MMNY.

118. WILLIAM CUTTING. A198. Fm. Copy of James Cutting's plate, but not same copper. Later and better work, possibly done in part by

Peter Maverick. About 1795–1800. Sig.: "P. R. Maverick Sct."
AAS, DC, MMNY.

119. JOHN CUYLER. A199. Fm. Festooned armorial. Shield with lion,
stars, crosses. Crest an arm with dagger. Sig.: "Maverick Sculpt."
About 1785–1790. NYHS.

120. GAIUS DEAN. Fm. Oval scene, tree, coiled serpent beneath, doves in
branches. Sea and hills. Sig.: "P. Maverick Sct. N.Y." Shows influence of P. R. Maverick's designs. Probably early work of Peter,
about 1800–1805. AAS, MMNY.

121. FREDERICK DE PEYSTER. A216. Fm. See *Art Amateur*, Feb. 1894.
Heart-shaped shield supported by two eagles on palm branches.
Sig.: "P. R. Maverick Sct." but Peter may well have had a part in
this. About 1800. AAS, MMNY, NYHS Landauer, NYPL.

122. HENRY CASIMIR DE RHAM. Armorial. Sig.: "P. Maverick, s." AAS,
MMNY, NYHS print room.

123. WILLM. DUER. A253, illus. p. 322. Festooned armorial. Motto: "Esse
et videri." Not signed, but attributed to Maverick. If so, it is the
work surely of Peter, being scarcely within the ability of the father.
AAS, MMNY.

124. H. I. ECKFORD. Cherub each side, one with lyre, one with horn;
books, etc. Sig.: "Inman del. P. Maverick sc." NYPL.

125. BARNARD ELLIOTT. A235. Fm. Armorial. Motto: "Virtute spernit
victa." Sig.: "Engrd. by P. R. Maverick." About 1795. AAS, DC,
NYHS Landauer, NYPL.

126. ERASMUS HALL LIBRARY. A257. Fm. Pictorial, Diana showing youth
temples of Fame and Virtue. Below, wreath enclosing name. Sig.:
"Maverick Sculp. New York." Illus. *Brooklyn Daily Eagle*, Dec.
17, 1899. AAS, DC, MMNY, NYHS Landauer.

127. EBENEZER FOOT. A276. Fm. Festooned armorial. Sig.: "Maverick
Sct." Shamrock in shield, crest a tree. MMNY, NYHS.

128. ANDREW G. FRAUNCES. A289, illus. p. 205. Fm. Shield, crest a sheaf
of wheat, all against draped mantle. Sig.: "Maverick Sct." About
1790–1795. NYHS.

129. JAMES GIBS. A306. A. says, "Armorial. Signed by Maverick." Is this
entry based merely on a mistaken reading of a note on the James
Giles plate?

130. JAMES GILES. A308. Fm. Lion rampant on shield, military emblems
above. Sig.: "Maverick Sculp." About 1788. AAS, NYHS, DC,
MMNY, BA. See *Bookbuyer*, N.Y., May 1895. St.M. 190.

131. JOHN D. GILES. In Baillie collection, MMNY, with Baillie's notation that the name, in pen work, was "inserted by some Londoner who knew it all." The preceding plate mutilated.

132. JOHN GOELET. A313. Armorial Jacobean. Swan on shield, crest a helmet surmounted by swan. Unsigned, but A. says "probably" by Maverick. It may be, but the design is not typical. NYHS.

133. PETER GOELET. Same as 132. AAS, MMNY.

134. PETER P. GOELET. Same copper as 133. MMNY.

135. ROBERT R. GOELET. Same copper as 133. AAS.

136. THOMAS B. GOELET. Same general pattern, except instead of the Jacobean decoration there is a P. R. Maverick type of festoon, with roses, and a ribbon bearing the name. May well be Maverick's, about 1790–1795. AAS photo.

137. SAMUEL HAY. Shield with three inserted shields, orn. of oak leaves, ribbon below with "Laboranti Palma." Sig.: "P. R. Maverick Sculpt." About 1795–1800, perhaps with Peter's help, especially in lettering. AAS, MMNY.

138. —— HERBERT. A374. Armorial Chippendale. A. says "probably" by Maverick; I have serious doubts. I have been able to find only the one form of this, with surname only, in the De Peyster book (see page 85). NYHS.

139. ELIAS HICKS. A376. Fm. See *Ex Libris Journal,* vol. I, p. 45. Oval shield, three fleur-de-lis. Crest a lion's head crowned. Sig.: "P. Maverick s." Good example of Peter's work, possibly about 1820. NYHS, NYHS Landauer, DC, MMNY, AAS.

140. PHILLIP L. HOFFMAN. A382. Fm. Shield, landscape beneath, with water, trees, books, etc. Sig.: "Maverick Sculpt. N. York." About 1790. NYHS Landauer, NYHS, MMNY photo.

141. HORANIAN SOCIETY LIBRARY. A392. Fm. Allegorical figures on shield. Crest an owl perched on books. Festoon and mantle. Sig.: "P. R. Maverick Sct. No. 3 Crown Street N.Y." About 1792–1793. MMNY.

142. WILLIAM J. HUNTER. A400. Fm. Armorial festooned. Sig.: "Engrd. by P. R. Maverick, 65 Liberty St. N.Y." 1794–1802. MMNY.

143. JOHN I. JOHNSON. A431. Fm. Cherub holding drape with name. Oval frame, bordered by brick wall. Sig.: "Maverick St." [*sic*] Early work, about 1785. MMNY, AAS.

144. JOHN JOHNSTON. A437. Fm. Festooned armorial. Sig.: "Maverick

Sculpt." Same design, not same copper, as Thomas Johnston. MMNY, NYHS.

145. THOMAS JOHNSTON, A439, illus. p. 231. Fm. Festooned armorial, crest a winged spur. Sig.: "Maverick Sculpt. N.Y." About 1790. NYHS.

146. WILLIAM JOYNER. Fm. Armorial. Eagle on shield, crest an arm holding battle ax. Sig.: "Maverick Senr. Sct. 73 Liberty St." After 1802, when P. R. Maverick moved to this address.

147. BENJAMIN S. JUDAH. A444. Fm. Festooned armorial. Shield has scales of justice and man-headed lion. Crest a spouting whale. Sig.: "Maverick Sculpt." About 1795. AAS, DC, MMNY, NYHS.

148. JOHN KEESE. A446. Fm. Small Chippendale label, 1.6 x 2.3, books at end, one labeled "Law," center lozenge for name. Sig.: "Maverk Sct." (the "k" is raised.) About 1785. AAS, DC, MMNY.

149. JOHN KEESE. A447. Fm. Shield with rampant lion and griffin, crest a vase in wreath. Flowers and mottoed ribbon. Sig.: "Maverick sculpt. About 1790. AAS, DC, MMNY, NYHS.

150. RUFUS KING. A456. Fm. Festooned armorial. Sig.: "Maverick Sculpt." About 1790. NYHS, AAS.

151. ISAAC L. KIP. A461. Fm. Pictorial armorial. Cherub holds scroll bearing name. Lawbook, ink, etc. Sig.: "Maverick sculpt." NYHS, Reprod. RU.

152. LEONARD KIP, JR. Armorial. No shield, but crest-like design of a crowing cock on wreath. Motto: "Victoria aut Mors." Sig.: "Maverick Senr. Sct." About 1800. MMNY, AAS.

153. HENRY LAIGHT. Armorial. Shield with three swans, crest a swan surmounted by three plumes. Motto: "Suaviter at fortiter." Sig.: P. Maverick sc. Newark, N.J." Copy, with name partly erased, in AGS copy of *Travels on an Inland Voyage* by Christian Schultz, Jr.

154. MORGAN LEWIS, ESQR. A486. Shield with rampant lion, crest the bust of a bearded and garlanded man. Ribbon and flowers. A. says "undoubtedly" by Maverick; it may well be the elder Maverick's work of about 1790 or earlier. AAS, DC, MMNY.

155. ALFRED S. LIVINGSTON. Like the following, with name in autograph below. AAS.

156. EDWARD LIVINGSTON. A493. Fm. Landscape. Shield leaning against broken tree. Crest a ship in distress. Pointer barks at squirrel on bough of tree. Sig.: "Maverick sculpt." AAS, DC, MMNY, NYPL, NYHS.

157. HENRY W. LIVINGSTON. Second state of Walter Livingston plate. MMNY. St.M. 433 (?).

158. MATURIN LIVINGSTON. A495. Fm. Second state of William Smith Livingston plate. AAS, DC, MMNY, BA, Copperplate in NYHS.

159. ROBERT R. LIVINGSTON. Fm. Third state of Walter Livingston plate. Sig.: "Maverick sct." but sig was apparently later removed, for both forms are found. AAS, MMNY. St.M. 104.

160. ROBERT R. LIVINGSTON OF CLAREMOUNT. Similar shield and festoon. Sig.: "Maverick Sct." NYHS Landauer.

161. ROBERT R. LIVINGSTON. Shield against broken pillar, palms in background, books, globe, caduceus. Very much more detailed line work than in other Livingston plates. No sig. Might be the work of Peter Maverick. AAS.

162. WALTER LIVINGSTON. Shield and decoration in usual Livingston pattern. No sig., but attributed to P. R. Maverick, and it may well be his. AAS.

163. WILLIAM SMITH LIVINGSTON. A503. Fm. Illus. *Ex Libris Journal,* Vol. I, p. 83 and *Curio,* p. 63. Festooned shield, ship as crest, motto on ribbon above. Sig.: "Maverick Sculpt." AAS, DC, MMNY.

164. PETER MASTERTON. A565. Fm. Festooned armorial. Unicorn in shield, and another above the crest, which is a helmet. Thistles in decoration. Sig.: "Maverick Sculpt." About 1795. AAS, MMNY NYHS.

165. PETER R. MAVERICK. Maverick used the design of his stock plate, the third on this list. Photo, NYHS Landauer, MMNY.

166. —— MAXWELL. A570. Fm. Festooned armorial, shield in oval frame. Sig.: "Maverick sculpt." Crest a stag. AAS, DC, MMNY, NYHS (offset on fly-leaf) Landauer, NYHS without name, RU with pen-written "W. H. Maxwell."

167. HUGH McLEAN. A541. Fm. Festooned armorial, oak leaves and branches. Sig.: "Maverick Sct." This appears to be early work of Peter, while yet in his father's shop, perhaps 1800. AAS, MMNY, NYHS. Illus. BMFA *Catalogue of Exhib. of Bookplates,* 1904.

168. JONATHAN MEREDITH, JUNR. A573. Festooned armorial. Unsigned, but A. says "apparently" Maverick's; it may well be the work of the father, though I have doubts. AAS, DC, MMNY, RU.

169. JOHN MINSHULL. Shield with flaming star, crest a helmet surmounted by lion's paws poising crescent moon. Sig.: "Engrd. by P. R. Maverick, 65 Liberty Street." MMNY, AAS.

170. NATHL. F. MOORE. A586. Fm. Armorial. Three stars on shield, crest a Moor rising from a crown. Sig.: "P. Maverick sc." Work of young Maverick, perhaps about 1805. AAS, NYHS Landauer, DC, MMNY.

171. RICHD. CHANNING MOORE, M. A. Armorial, wreathed. No sig. but attributed to Maverick; if so, probably with Peter's help, *ca.*1800. AAS, DC, MMNY.

172. JOSEPH MURRAY. A601. Chippendale armorial. Unsigned, but A. says "evidently" by Maverick. I have serious doubts.

173. NEWARK FEMALE BIBLE AND COMMON-PRAYER-BOOK SOCIETY. A presentation bookplate. Line vign., globe in clouds, dove overhead. Sig.: "P. Maverick s." MMNY.

174. a. NEW YORK SOCIETY LIBRARY. A615, illus. p. 61. Minerva, just descended and trailing clouds, gives book to kneeling Indian. Dated in plate, 1789. Sig.: "Maverick Sct. Crown Street." NYSL records show payments, June 25, 1789, of five pounds for the engraving and six pounds seven shillings for 1400 copies (one pound equaled $2.50). Also on Aug. 25, 1791, sixteen shillings for repairing the plate and seven pounds eleven shillings five pence for 2500 copies. AAS, DC, MMNY, WMFA, NYHS, NYHS Landauer.

b. In the second state, the shading on the Indian's legs is in continuous instead of broken lines.

175. NEW YORK SOCIETY LIBRARY. A614, illus. p. 60. Fm. F1050. Similar to item 174, but an interior scene in an oval panel bordered by brick-like cross-hatching. Sig.: "Engd. by P. R. Maverick, 65 Liberty Street." NYSL records show payments, April 24, 1795, of five pounds for engraving the plate, and one pound eighteen shillings and three pence for 625 copies. A. Robertson received one pound twelve shillings for the design. AAS, DC, MMNY, NYHS Landauer, WMFA, NYPL.

176. LEWIS MORRIS OGDEN. A620. Festooned armorial. Sig., which includes date: "P. Maverick Sc. 1801." A good example of Peter's early independent work. MMNY.

177. PETER OGILVIE. Lion on shield, eagle as crest, festoon of leaves. Motto: "Non sibi sed patriae." Sig.: "P. R. Maverick." AAS.

178. FRANS. PANTON. A636. A. says "undoubtedly" by Maverick. I am far less certain. AAS.

179. FRANCIS PANTON, JUNR. A637, illus. p. 259. Fm. Pictorial. Two ducks holding ribbons supporting shield. Below, river with ducks and

boat. Mountains in distance with single trees on tops. Motto: "Spero meliora." Sig.: "Maverick Scp." About 1785–1790. MMNY, NYHS, AAS.

180. WILLIAM PASLEY. A646. Armorial, thistle and rose decoration. A. says "undoubtedly" by Maverick; I should not be so sure, but it may be. AAS, MMNY, NYHS.

181. W. PAULDING. A648. Fm. A. says only, "Armorial. Signed by Maverick."

182. N. PEABODY. Festooned armorial. Shield a standing sheaf of wheat with two suns, with faces, above. Sig.: "Engrd. by P. R. Maverick, 65 Liberty Street, N. York." MMNY, AAS.

183. WILLIAM L. PIERCE. A680. Fm., illus. p. 65. Shield with three black birds, surmounted by swan. Sig.: "Maverick Sculpt." About 1785–1790. AAS, DC, MMNY, NYHS.

184. JOHN PINTARD. A686. Fm. Festooned armorial, oval shield with three stars and three roses. Sig.: "Maverick Sct." About 1795 or earlier. AAS, DC, MMNY, NYHS Landauer, NYHS.

185. CARLILE POLLOCK. Fm. Chippendale. Sig.: "Maverick Sct."

186. WILLIAM POPHAM. In A. supplementary list. Fm. Festooned. Sig.: "Maverick Sct." Shield with two stag heads, backed by crossed branches. Crest a stag head. About 1790. Indication of erasure at top of copy seen. NYHS, AAS.

187. HALCOTT B. PRIDE. A701. Fm. Festooned armorial. Shield with star and three crescent moons. Crest a dragon. Sig.: "Maverick Sculp." About 1790–1795. AAS, MMNY, NYHS.

188. SAML. PROVOOST, ESQR. Coll: Pet: Cant. A708. Armorial Chippendale. Unsigned, but A. says "undoubtedly" by Maverick; I doubt it very much, as Allen did later. AAS, NYHS Landauer, DC, MMNY, NYHS.

189. SAML. PROVOOST. A709. Fm. See *Ex Libris Journal*, vol. III, p. 157. Festooned armorial, with a bishop's mitre as crest. Sig.: "Maverick Sculpt." About 1787–1790. AAS, NYHS, DC, MMNY, NYHS Landauer.

190. WILLIAM SETON. A775. Fm. Festooned armorial. Sig.: "Maverick Sculpt." About 1790. AAS, MMNY, NYHS. St.M. 87, and his wife, 328, American founder of the Sisters of Charity.

191. PETER SILVESTER. Fm. I can find no Silvester plate except that in the DePeyster book given to the NYHS, which is by Child.

192. JOHN SITGREAVES, of New Bern. Armorial type, but no arms. Name

in center where shield would be. Below frame, books and writing material. Sig.: "Maverick Sct. New York." About 1790. AAS, DC, MMNY.

193. JAMES SCOTT SMITH. A792. Fm. Festooned shield, and below it trees, books, inkstand, etc. Sig.: "Maverick Sculpt." About 1790–1795. AAS, DC, NYHS, NYHS Landauer, MMNY.

194. THOMAS SMITH JUNR. A801. Fm. Similar to the preceding, not same copper. Sig.: "Maverick Sculpt." About 1790–1795. AAS, DC, MMNY, NYHS Landauer.

195. THOMAS J. SMITH. A802. Fm. A. says, "Armorial, signed by Maverick."

196. WILLIAM SMITH. A804. Fm. Festooned armorial. Similar to J. S. S. and T. S. Jr. above, but no landscape. Sig.: "Maverick Sculpt." About 1790–1795. AAS, NYHS.

197. WILLIAM STEPHENS. A821. Fm. Jacobean armorial. Mantling. A. says "possibly" by Maverick. Not in his usual style. NYHS.

198. JOHN STURGES. A836. Fm. A. says this is armorial and signed by Maverick. The sig. is in fact "R. M. sculp." and the plate is apparently the work of Robert Mountaine, an English engraver. AAS, MMNY.

199. WILLIAM TAYLOR. A849. Fm. Festooned armorial. Sig.: "Maverick Sct." Shield with two lions, three rings on chevron. Crest a unicorn. About 1785–1790.

200. JOHN C. TEN BROECK. A851. Festooned armorial. Unsigned, with evidences of an erasure in lower left corner. A says "very probably" by Maverick; it looks so, resembling work of about 1790. AAS, DC, MMNY, NYHS, NYHS Landauer.

201. JAMES THOMSON. A855. Fm. Plain armorial. Crest a rampant lion, with lions and birds on shield. Sig.: "P. Maverick, Durand & Co." 1818–1820. AAS, DC, MMNY.

202. JOHN TILLOTSON. Fm. Not in A. No copy found.

203. THOMAS TILLOTSON. A861. Fm. Festooned armorial, sheaves of wheat on shield, and an antelope for the crest. Motto: "Virtus et natale meum." Sig.: "Maverick Sculpt. New York." About 1790–1795. AAS, DC, MMNY, NYHS.

204. P. J. VAN BERCKELL. A878, illus. p. 294. Fm. Arms supported by fig-leafed savages armed with bludgeons. Sig.: "Maverick Sct." About 1790. AAS, NYHS.

205. K. K. VAN RENSSELAER. A883. Fm. Festooned armorial, the crest a

flaming basket. Sig.: "Maverick Sc." About 1790. AAS, NYHS Landauer, DC, MMNY. St.M. 438.

206. STEPHEN VAN RENSSELAER. A885. Mantled armorial. A. says "probably" by Maverick; if so, it is quite different from the usual designs of either the father or the son. AAS, MMNY, St.M. 55.

207. J. A. VANDEN HEUVEL. Armorial, three mountains and vertical sword on shield, helmet above. Name in caps. below. Sig.: "P. Maverick sc." NYHS.

208. B. WALKER. Armorial. Crest only, head and forelegs of tiger, jessant, holding flowers. Sig.: "P. Maverick sc. Newark." 1809–1817. AAS, NYHS Landauer, MMNY.

209. PROSPER WETMORE. A925. Fm. Festooned armorial. Landscape background. Sig.: "Maverick Sculpt." NYHS. Recut by Doolittle for Dr. C. H. Wetmore, and used by his son, Prosper M. Wetmore, as a gift plate to Ohio State University Library.

210. POLYDORE B. WISNER. A952. Fm. Festooned armorial. Sig.: "Maverick Sculpt." Shield with two bust portraits divided by plume. Crest a rampant lion. NYHS. In blue, AAS.

211. YALE COLLEGE, BROTHERS IN UNITY. A., in list of signed plates, p. 321, gives one for this group signed "P. R. Maverick Sct. No. 3 Crown Street, N.Y.," but does not have it in his numbered list. It may have been a reworking of the Pelton plate. A966. From the sig., the date was about 1793.

C. Peter Maverick

GENERAL WORKS

301. MLLE. ADELINE, BROADWAY THEATRE. Lith., by P. Maverick, 61 Grand St., noted by Harry Peters in *America on Stone*, p. 274.

AKENSIDE, MARK. *The Pleasures of Imagination*. N.Y.: R. M. McDermut and D. D. Arden, 1813. AAS, NYPL. (Item 302.)

302. Front. Line vign., 2.11 x 2.7. Three standing young women in flowing robes, four cherubs above holding floral festoon. Sig.: "T. Stothard del. P. Maverick sct. Newark." NYHS.

AKENSIDE, MARK. *The Pleasures of Imagination and other Poems*. N.Y.: R. & W. A. Bartow, 347 Pearl Street, Franklin Square, 1819. (Items 303 and 304.)

303. Title-page, line 3.11 x 2.11, data as given above. No sig. AAS.

304. a. Frontispiece. Line rect., 3.4 x 2.8. Man facing urn in burying-ground. Inscription: "P. Maverick, Durand & Co. / -silent and unseen / To pay the mournful tribute of his tears. / Pleasures of Imagination Book—— Line——"
    b. With "Drawn by Durand" added before signature. AAS.

ALDEN, TIMOTHY. *Collection of American Epitaphs and Inscriptions,* etc. 5v. N.Y., 1814. (Item 305.)

305. Title page, vol. I, sometimes used in other volumes. Line vign., 2.7 x 2.6, in design 4 x 2.6, showing man seated in graveyard under willow. Two-line prose quotation. Sig.: "P. Maverick sc." AAS.

306. ALEXANDRIA. Line rect., 2.14 x 3.12. Officer on horse in sword battle with foot-soldier. Flag and soldiers in background. Ins.: "Burney del. P. Maverick sculpt. / The Battle of Alexandria / March 23, 1801."

307. IN *The Analectic Magazine.* Line vign., 3.8 x 3.6, of Milton dictating to his daughter, in design 7.14 x 4.4. Ins.: "The / Analectic Magazine / Vol. 4. / Published by / Moses Thomas / No. 52 Chesnut [*sic*] St. / Philadelphia. / G. Fairman script. 1814. P. Maverick sculpt." Sig. on vign.: "Sully pinxt. P. Maverick sct."

IN *Annals of the Lyceum of Natural History of New York.* N.Y.: Printed for the Lyceum by J. Seymour and sold by G. & C. Carvill, 108 Broadway, N.Y. AAS, NYHS. vol. I, Part the First, 1824 (items 308 through 313); vol. I, Part the Second, 1825 (items 314 through 322); and vol. II, 1826–1828 (items 323 through 327).

308. . . . Pl. I. Line, 6.8 x 3.12. Four drawings of cellular fabric. Sig.: "Halsey del. P. Maverick sc."

309. Pl. II. Stip. vign., 7 x 4.12. Three fish. Sig.: "P. M. sc."

310. Pl. III. Line vign., 5.4 x 3.12. Four plant and flower drawings. Sig.: "A. Halsey del. Peter Maverick sc."

311. Pl. IV. Line drawings, 6.2 x 2.8. Eel and eel head. Sig.: "P. M. sc."

312. Pl. X. Inscription: "Pleuraphis Jamesii / J. Torrey del. P. Maverick sc."

313. Pl. 13. Lith. Sig.: "P. Maverick's Lithog. p."

314. . . . Pl. XIX. Line vign., 2.10 x 7.4. Inscription: "Chlamyphorus Truncatus / W. W. Wood del. Peter Maverick sc."

315. Pl. XX. Seven detail views of preceding. Same sig.

316. Pl. XXII. [Amphiuma Means.] Stip., 7.2 x 4.8. Sig.: "P. Maverick sc."

317. Pl. XXIV. Carices of North America. Inscription: "Annals Lyceum Nat. Hist. Pl. XXIV / C. Arida C. Cristata P. Maverick."

318. Pl. XXV. [More carices.] Same sig.

319. Pl. XXVI. [More carices.] Sig.: "P. Maverick del. et sc."

320. Pl. XXVII. [More carices.] Same sig. as prec.

321. Pl. XXVIII. [More carices.] Sig.: "P. Maverick sc."

322. Pl. XXIX. [More carices.] Sig.: "P. Maverick del. et sc."

323. Pl. II. Prosopis Glandulosa. Line vign., 8.8 x 5.4. Sig.: "Peter Maverick sc."

324. Pl. III. Phacelia Integrifolia. Line and stip. vign., 7 x 4.4. Sig.: "P. Maverick sc."

325. Pl. IV. Quercus Undulata. Line and stip. vign., 8 x 5.4. Sig.: "Peter Maverick sc."

326. Pl. V. Diodon, etc. Five details. Lith. vigns. in rect. 7.12 x 4.8. Sig.: "Lith. P. Maverick."

327. Pl. VI. Bison skull. Three lith. vigns. in rect 7.12 x 4.8. Sig.: "Swett Del. Lith. of P. Maverick."

Note: Consult check lists of Emily and Maria Ann Maverick (pp. 176 and 177) for plates done by them for this series.

ARABIAN NIGHTS. Publication not found. In the 1831 sale 13 plates, 6 x 9.8, sold for $95.00. (Items 328 and 329.)

328. . . . Old Man of the Sea. Line rect., 5.1 x 3.14. Man on another's shoulders. Sig.: "R. Smirke R. A. pinx. Peter Maverick dirix." with title as given.

329. . . . Zobeide. Line rect., 5.1 x 3.14. Woman on knees, winged snake above her, another on ground. Ins.: "R. Smirke R. A. pinx. Peter Maverick dir x [sic] / Zobeide After Rescuing the Fairy." A form is reported with "dir. sc."

330. ARCADE. 1831 sale, 68 for 51¢.

331. ARE YOU MISCHIEVOUS? 1831 sale, 160 for $1.60.

ARIOSTO, LUDOVICO. *Orlando Furioso,* trans. by John Hoole. Phila.: Henry Hudson, 1816. 6 vols. AAS, NYPL, BA. (Items 332 through 334).

332. Frontispiece, vol. IV. St2207. Line oval portrait, 3.4 x 2.9. Bust, almost profile to left. Inscription: "P. Maverick sculpt. / John Hoole."

333. Frontispiece, vol. V. Line rect., 3.11 x 2.9. Woman with sword, man in armor, woman with spear. Inscription: "Vol. V . . . Book 36, line 399 / P. Maverick sc."

334. . . . . Frontispiece, vol. VI. Line rect., 3.10 x 2.9. Youth, soldiers, monk with cross on shoulder, mountain background. Inscription: "Vol. 6. / Book 44, line 134. / P. Maverick s."

ARLINCOURT, VICTOR VISCOUNT D'. *The Solitary*, translated by an American lady, 2 vols. in one. N.Y.: Henry Durell, 1822. C. S. Van Winkle, printer. NYPL. (Item 335.)

335. . . . . Frontispiece, line rect., 3.12 x 2.13. Warrior in cloak, woman in white. Inscription: "C. Chasselet del . . . Peter Maverick sc. / New York Published by H. Durell." 1831 sale, plate $1.13.

336. ASTRONOMY. 1831 sale, 4 plates for $2.00. One plate 8 x 16 for 80¢. See also, Solar System.

337. BAINBRIDGE, WILLIAM. St2183. Line rect., 8.13 x 7.9. Half length in uniform, face front. Inscription: "Painted by J. Jarvis. Engraved by Peter Maverick. / Commodore Bainbridge. / Published by P. Maverick, New York, 1820." 1831 sale, 600 for $12.05, plate for $17.

[BARRELL, GEORGE.] *Letters from Asia;* written by a Gentleman of Boston. N.Y.: A. T. Goodrich & Co., 1819. AAS. (Item 338.)

338. Title page. Line, 4.5 x 2.12, with vign. of crescent moon. Sig.: "P. Maverick Durand & Co."

BELL, BENJ. *A Treatise on Gonorrhea Cirulenta* etc. Albany: E. F. Backus, 1814. 2 vols. AAS. (Items 339 through 343.)

339. Plate I. 4 stip. vigns., 6.8 x 4.8 overall. Sections of penis. Sig.: "P. Maverick sc."

340. Plate II. 4 stip. vigns., 6.8 x 4.10 overall. Penis, etc. Same sig.

341. Plate III. 1 stip vign., 5.12 x 3.10. Womb. Same sig.

342. Plate IV. 9 stip. vigns., 6.4 x 4.8 overall. Penis and surg. instruments. Same sig.

343. Plate V. 7 catheters, etc., 13.12 x 4.2. No sig.

BELL, JOHN AND CHARLES. *The Anatomy and Physiology of the Human Body* etc. by John Bell and *The Anatomy and Physiology of the Brain and Nerves* etc. by Charles Bell. N.Y.: Collins & Perkins, 1809. (Also subsequent editions. Positions of engravings vary in various editions.) AAS, UV, AMMNJ.

344. Vol. II, p. 23. Line vign., 4.8 x 4.9. Inscription: "Drawing of the Eustachian Valve. . . . I. Bell delt. P. Maverick sct." GC.

345. Vol. II, p. 29. Two line vignettes, upper 3.1 x 3. lower 3.3 x 3.2. Inscription: "Sketches. . . . of the Heart. I. Bell delt. P. Maverick sct." GC.

346. Vol. IV, p. xi. Line vign., 4 x 4.8. [Third-month uterus] Sig.: "Chas. Bell delt. P. Maverick sct. Published by Collins & Perkins 1810."

347. Vol. IV, p. xii. Line vign., 4 x 5.10. [Third-month uterus, section.] Sig.: "Chas. Bell delt. P. Maverick sct. Published by Collins & Perkins 1810."

348. BERTHIER. St2236. Line rect., 3.7 x 5.14. Landscape, sailboats; 3 figures, 2 in foreground fishing. Ins.: "Drawn by Alexr. Robertson Engraved by P. Maverick, N.Y. / Near Berthier on the St. Lawrence." In *The Port Folio*, New Series, by Oliver Oldschool, Esq., 2: facing p. 265, Sept. 1809. Used also in P. S. Palmer's *History of Lake Champlain*, Albany, 1866. AAS, NYPL, BA, WMFA, GC.

IN *The Holy Bible Abridged . . . for the Use of Children.* N.Y.: Hodge, Allen & Campbell, 1790. AAS, NYPL. (Item 349.)

349. . . . Relief-block print, 2.15 x 2.1. Adam and Eve, tree, serpent. Sig.: "P. Maverick Sct. AE 9 Years." Peter Maverick's famous first print.

IN *The Holy Bible.* Boston: R. P. & C. Williams, 1818. Stereotyped by B. & J. Collins. (Item 350.)

350. . . . Line vign., 2.10 x 2.4. Angel in clouds, eyes aloft. Lyre in right hand, scroll in left. Ins., with appearance of attempt to erase or leave unprinted the final line: "W. Hamilton d. P. Maverick sc. / New York. / Published by Henry I. Megarey."

BIBLE (COLLINS'S). For the series of Quarto Bibles issued by the Collins firm and its successors, Peter Maverick participated in the second edition, 1806, of Collins & Perkins; in the editions of 1814, 1816, and 1821 of Collins & Co. (all of New York); and in the Philadelphia edition of 1823 by Kimber & Sharpless which was kept in print until the sale to Jacob Harding in 1844. The extent of Maverick's work is not always clear, though from the succession of signatures, as shown below, it would seem that sometimes his plates were reworked by other engravers when they became worn, and that sometimes he was engaged to restore the work of others. The editions and the signature—if different from the description given—are indicated for each print below. In other editions many will be found which I have omitted merely because the volumes which I could examine did not contain them, such pictures being often removed for framing. (Items 351 through 359.)

351. Murder of Abel. Line rect., 4.9 x 6.14. Abel slain, Cain fleeing. Ins.: "Engraved for Collins's Quarto-Bible, Third Edition, 1814. / A. Sacchi pinxt. P. Maverick sculpt. / The Murder of Abel." Front.

1814, Front. 1816. Signed by Kearny in 1823. NYPL, GC, WMFA.

352. Elisha. Line rect., 4.12 x 6.1. Ins.: "Engraved for Collins's Quarto-Bible, Third Edition, 1814. Painted by West. Engraved by P. Maverick, Newark. / Elisha restores the Shunammite's Son to Life. / II Kings IV. 37." 1814, 1816, 1823. GC, WMFA.

353. Good Samaritan. Line rect., 4.12 x 5.10. Man and boy carrying man into courtyard. Ins.: "Engraved for Collins's Quarto Bible, Stereotype Edition, 1816. / Rembrandt Pinx. Kearny & Maverick Sculp. / The Good Samaritan. / Luke X. 34." 1814 Kearny, 1816, 1821, 1823. GC.

354. Holy Family. Line rect., 7.10 x 5.13. Mary holding infant Jesus, John the Baptist kneeling, Joseph seated at table. Ins.: "Engraved for Collins' Quarto Bible, Second Edition. / Painted by Annibal Carrache. Engraved by Peter Maverick / The Holy Family. / New York, Published by Collins, Perkins & Co. 1807 [sic]." NYPL, GC.

355. Jacob. Line rect., 4.10 x 5.15. Ins.: "Engraved for Collins's Quarto Bible, Fourth Edition, 1816. / Rembrandt . . . Fairman & Maverick s. / Jacob blessing the Sons of Joseph." 1814 Fairman, 1816.

356. Joseph. Line rect., 5.7 x 6.3. Ins.: "Engraved for Collins's Quarto Bible, Fourth Edition, 1816. / Guercino pinxt. Boyd & Maverick sc. / Joseph interpreting Pharaoh's dream. / Gen. XLI. 25. 32." 1814 Boyd, 1816, 1821, 1823.

357. Moses Rescued by Pharaoh's Daughter. Line rect., 7.8 x 5.14. Sig.: "L. Simond del. W. S. Leney and P. Maverick sc." and quot., Exod. 52:6. 1816.

358. Saint Paul. Line rect., 7.14 x 5.12. St. Paul seated on rock, arm on book, soldiers in background. Ins.: "Kimber & Sharpless Quarto Bible Stereotype Edition. / Tiebout & Maverick s. / St. Paul." 1807 Tiebout, 1816, 1823.

359. a. Virgin Mary. Stip. rect., 5.10 x 4.9. Raphael's Madonna of the Chair. Sig.: "Raphael Pinxt. Edwin & Maverick sc." 1816.

b. Same, except complete inscription is: "P. Maverick Sculpt. / Madona [sic] & Child."

BIBLE, DR. SCOTT's. N.Y.: Whiting & Watson, 1810. Note that some of these, at least, are found marked: "Engraved for W. W. Woodward's quarto edition . . ." with title and date as given. The title of each map is in an oval panel, the publisher's line above, and the engraver's line below. (Items 360 through 365.)

360. Asia Minor. Line rect., 13.10 x 17.6. Sig.: "by Peter Maverick, Newark, N.J." NPL.

361. a. Egypt. Line rect., 17.12 x 13.8. Arabia and Ethiopia in inset. Sig.: "by Peter Maverick, Newark, N.J." NPL.

   b. Same engraved for Woodward edition. AAS.

362. . . . Greece and Italy. Line rect., 13.3 x 17.11. Sig.: "by P. Maverick, Newark N. Jersey." NPL. 1831 sale, 2 plates, maps of Greece, for $4.20.

363. . . . Palestine. Line rect., 16.7 x 13.4. Map of the tribes in inset. Pub. and eng. line below oval, sig.: "Peter Maverick Newark."

364. . . . Persia. Line rect., 13.14 x 18. Sig.: "by P. Maverick, Newark, N. Jersey." NPL.

365. a. World. Line rect., 13.4 x 20.4. Sig.: "by P. Maverick, Newark." NPL.

   b. Same engraved for Woodward edition. AAS.

366. BIRDS. 1831 sale, 300 for $3. [Is this the woodcock or snipe lith., or another?]

367. BLACKBURN, GIDEON. St2184. Stip. vign., 3 x 1.12. Bust, profile left. Ins.: "The Evangelical Intelligencer. / J. Jarvis del. P. Maverick sculpt. / Rev. Gideon Blackburn. / Engraved for W. P. Ferrand [Farrand], & Co. No. 170 Market Street, Philadelphia." From *Evangelical Intelligencer, or General Assembly's* Missionary Magazine, New Series, 2: facing p. 97. Phila., Mar. 1808. AAS, NYPL, BA.

368. BLAIR, HUGH. St2185. Stip. rect., 3.12 x 3.3. Bust, robed, ¾ left. Ins.: "P. Maverick, sc. Newark / Hugh Blair. D. D." Front., *Lectures on Rhetoric and Belles Lettres* by Hugh Blair. Morristown, N.J.: Peter A. Johnson, 1814. NYPL. Apparently used also in N.Y. edition of R. & W. Bartow.

369. BOLIVAR, SIMON. St2186. Stip. circ., diam 2.4. Bust in uniform, face ¾ right. Ins.: "P. Maverick / Genl. Bolivar." 1831 sale, 321 for $3.57; plate 25¢. NYPL.

370. a. BROWN, JACOB. St2187. Stip. vign., 4.8 x 3.13. Bust in uniform, face direct. Ins.: "J. Jarvis pinxt. P. Maverick sculpt. / Major Genl. Brown. U.S. Army. / Engraved for the Analectic Magazine / Philadelphia, Published by M. Thomas / 1815." In *The Ana-*

lectic, New Series, 5: facing p. 265, April 1815. NYPL, AAS, GC, MMNY.

    b. Title changed to "Genl. Brown."

    c. With "Engraved . . ." line erased.

371. . . . BUNKER HILL PORTRAITS. Line, 8.14 x 11. Seventeen separated heads of officers at Bunker Hill. Ins.: "No. 1: [list of portraits] Bunker's Hill. / P. Maverick sct." Apparently key to Trumbull's Bunker Hill painting. AAS, NYPL. See also Harry Peters's *Currier & Ives,* Plate 128. J. N. Gimbrede engraved both picture and key for the *N.Y. Mirror,* 1842. AMNNJ.

BUNYAN, JOHN. *Pilgrim's Progress,* ed. by T. Scott. Hartford, Conn. Edition not further identified. Item 372 and perhaps others below.

372. Title page, trimmed of all data but those given above. Line vign., 2.8 x 2.2, on design 4 x 2.2. White-clad woman at church door. Three-line inscription. Sig.: "H. Corbould. P. Maverick." NPL.

373. Probably intended for same vol. Line rect., 2.5 x 3.2. Three women and man seated at table, man's hand upraised. Two-line inscription. Sig.: "H. Corbould. Peter Maverick." NPL.

374. BUNYAN, JOHN. St2188. Line rect., 3 x 2.3. Full bust, face slightly right. Ins.: "P. M. / John Bunyan." NYPL, GC.

375. [BUNYAN, JOHN.] Line vign., 2.12 x 2.4, on design 3.10 x 2.4. Vign. shows Jesus on cross, landscape background. Complete ins.: "Grace Abounding; Hearts [*sic*] Ease; / The World to Come, &c. / [vign.] /P. M. / He hath made peace by the Blood of his Cross." GC, NYPL.

376. BURGOIN [*sic*], J. 1831 sale, 24 for 36¢. Possibly 1705.

BURNS, ROBERT. *Works,* etc. 4 vols. N.Y.: R. & W. A. Bartow and also Richmond, Va.: W. A. Bartow & Co., 1821. AAS. (Items 377 and 378.)

377. a. Title-page, vol. II. Line vign., 2.6 x 2.4, on design 4.4 x 2.4. Burns's birthplace, woman with bundle and another with bucket on head, child. Sig.: "T. Stothard, R. A. del. Peter Maverick sc." Bibliog. data for only the N.Y. publication on engraved title page.

    b. Same vign., illustrating "The Methodist's Story" in *The Hyacinth.* N.Y.: J. C. Riker, 1831. AAS.

378. a. Title page, vol. III. Line vign. 2.4 x 2.8, of workman with spade approaching cottage. Reversed view of frontispiece in 1815 ed. *infra.* N.Y. bibliog data and "Peter Maverick sc. / The Cotter's Saturday Night."

    b. Same vign., with "The Cotter's" erased, used to illustrate the poem "Saturday Night." *The Hyacinth.* N.Y.: J. C. Riker, 1831. AAS.

BURNS, ROBERT. *The Works of Robert Burns.* Baltimore: F. Lucas Jr. & J. Cushing, 1815. G. Palmer, printer. AAS. (Item 379 through 381.)

379. . . . Title page, vol. 3. Line. Data as given above and design of bee-hive, sickle, plow, etc., with scroll inscribed, "The Mountain Daisy." Sig.: "P. Maverick."

380. . . . Frontispiece. Line rect., 4.1 x 2.7. Worker approaching home, woman in doorway, child. Ins.: " 'At length his lonely Cot appears in view.' / Cotters [*sic*] Saturday night. / Engd. by P. Maverick, Newark N.J. / Printed by Dainly & Finn No. 236 Market St. Baltimore."

381. . . . Portrait. St2189. Stip. vign., 3.15 x 4.2. Half length, seated, almost profile left. Ins.: "P. M. / Robert Burns." Used also as front. in *The Works of Robert Burns in Prose and Verse,* N.Y.: Wm. Borradaile, 1826. NYPL. Used also in *Works,* Phila.: J. Crissy, 1827 and also Phila.: J. Crissy & J. Grigg, 1831.

BYRON, LORD. *The Works of* . . . N.Y.: Wm. B. Gilley, 1820. Date not included in engraved title pages. Note also the Philadelphia publisher's line on one title page, *infra.* AAS. (Items 382 through 390.)

382. . . . Title page, vol. I. Line vign., 2.2 x 2.7, on design 4.10 x 2.7, of woman in white with cavaliers seated at her feet. Title: "Childe Harold" and two-line quotation. Sig.: "Corbould del. P. Maverick, Durand & Co."

383. . . . Title page, vol. II. Line vign., 2.2 x 2.3, on design 4.11 x 2.8, of woman with head resting on man's breast. Title: "Corsair" and two-line quotation. Sig.: "Corbould del. P. Maverick, Durand & Co. sc."

384. Title page, vol. III. Line vign., 2.1 x 2.4, on design 4.15 x 2.9, of man leaning over reclining boy. Title: "The Prisoner of Chillon" and two-line quot. Sig. as for vol. I.

385. a. Title page, vol. IV. Line vign., 2.6 x 2.8, on design 4.15 x 2.8, of flying angel with sword. Title: "Hebrew Melodies" and one-line quot. with source. Sig. as for vol. I.

   b. Same, except for pub. line: "Philadelphia, Published by R. W. Pomeroy." GC.

386. Front., vol. I. Line circ. with orn., 4.13 x 3.4. Two women and four children, child in canopy above, with ref. to "Childe Harold." Sig. as for vol. II title page.

387. Front., vol. II. Line circ. with orn., 5.2 x 3.4. Man supporting woman, table with pistol and goblet. Ref. to "The Bride of Abydos." Sig.: "P. Maverick, Durand & Co. sc."

388. Front., vol. III. Line circ. with orn., 4.10 x 2.14. Man and woman, woman pointing to sky. Ref. to "The Siege of Corinth." Sig. as for vol. I title page.

389. Front., vol. IV. Line circ. with orn., 4.8 x 2.14. Man with small girl beside him. Ref. to Poem 20. Sig.: "P. Maverick, Durand & Co."

390. Giaour. vol. II, p. 247.

BYRON. Edition unidentified except for data as here given (Items 391 and 392.)

391. Giaour. Line rect., 3.4 x 2.7. Swordsman standing over body, horse and men in background. Ins.: "Painted by T. Stothard R. A. Engraved by P. Maverick. / Giaour. / [Three-line quot.] / Pub. by Eastburn, Kirk & Co. N. York and M. Thomas Phila."

392. . . . Corsair. Swordsman carrying off woman. Man in background, dead man between swordsman's feet. Ins.: "Painted by T. Stothard R. A. Engraved by P. Maverick. / Corsair. / [Two-line quot.] / Pub. by M. Thomas Phila. and Eastburn, Kirk & Co. N. York."

393. a. CALMADY. Lith. vign., 9 x 8. Two young girls. Ins.: "Sir Thos. Lawrence P. R. A. pinx. Peter Maverick delt. 1829. / The Daughters of Charles B. Calmady Esqr. / Lithy. P. Maverick. N. York." 1831 sale lists "Sisters, 8 for 50¢." AAS.

  b. As above, with "Sir Thos." and "1829" erased.

CALMET, AUGUSTIN. *Great Dictionary of the Holy Bible*. Charlestown, Mass.: Edited by Charles Taylor, printed and sold by Samuel Etheridge Jr. Vol. I, 1812; vol. II, 1813; vol. III, 1813; vol. IV, 1814. The first English translation of this had been in 1732. Then, beginning in 1797, Charles Taylor brought out three editions in England prior to his American edition. Maverick's work was the engraving of new plates of illustrations in Taylor's English editions, illustrations engraved by Taylor or under his direction, and sometimes taken from sources quite unrelated to Biblical times or lands. An American edition of 1837 (Boston: Crocker & Brewster, and New York: Leavitt, Lord & Co.) used relief cuts of many of these pictures. AAS, BA, NYPL. (Items 394 through 431.)

394. . . . Agriculture. Line rect., 8.10 x 7. Eight implements. Ins.: "P. Maverick sc. / Agriculture." Vol. III, facing p. 324. Perhaps Durand's first apprentice work; see text of biography.

395. Altars. Line rect., 7.15 x 6.15. Perspective and side elevation, with

scale, of large altar, including altar ministrants in ceremony. Two small altars with fires, attendants, and birds. Ins.: "P. Maverick sct. / Altars." Vol. III, facing p. 144.

396. Animals. Line drawings, 7.12 x 6.8. Six numbered sheep and goats. Ins.: "P. Maverick sct. / Syrian Animals." Vol. III, facing p. 191.

397. Ark. Line rect., 8.10 x 6.9. Six numbered plans and perspective views. Ins.: "P. Maverick sct. / Construction of Noah's Ark." Vol. III, facing p. 270.

398. Armor. Line rect., 8.9 x 6.11. Thirteen figures illustrating armor. Ins.: "P. Maverick sc. / Armour. Plate II." Vol. III, facing p. 312. Plate I done by F. Kearny and his sig. later erased.

399. Baal. Line rect., 7.15 x 6.4. Seven representations of Baal, with Greek inscriptions. Ins.: "P. Maverick sc. / Baal." Vol. III, facing p. 122.

400. Behemoth. Line rect., 6.3 x 8.11. Three mythical animals. Ins.: "Fragment No. LXV page— / P. Maverick sc. / Behemoth from Egyptian Representations." Vol. III, facing p. 83.

401. Books. Line rect., 6.4 x 8. Scrolls, stylus, etc. in two numbered groups. Ins.: "Fragment LXXIV p. 129. / P. Maverick sct. / Ancient Books. Plate II." Plate I unsigned, probably not Maverick's.

402. Cherubim. Stip. rect., 7.14 x 6.10. Four cherubim. Ins.: "P. Maverick sc. / Cherubim from Calmet." Vol. III, facing p. 193.

403. Cherubim. Line vign., 8.5 x 6.11. Cherubim, ark of covenant. Ins.: "P. Maverick sc. / Cherubim. Plate II." Vol. III, facing p. 199.

404. Cherubim. Line rect., 8.2 x 7. Nine man-animal figures. Ins.: "P. Maverick sc. / Cherubim. Plate III." Vol. III, facing p. 200.

405. Cherubim. Line rect., 8.7 x 6.14. Nine cherubim. Ins.: "P. Maverick sc. / Cherubim. Plate IV." Following preceding plate.

406. Dagon. Stip. oval, 4 x 5.1. Male and female figures, half fish. Ins.: "P. Maverick sc. / Dagon." Vol. III, facing p. 182.

407. Dagon. Line rect., 8.2 x 6.8. Ins.: "P. Maverick sc. / Plate II, Dagon Derketos, Jonah." Following preceding plate.

408. Faith. Line rect., 7 x 5.7. Figure kneeling; woman standing points at flying cherubs. Ins.: "R. Smirke R. A. pinxt. P. Maverick, Newark, sculpt. / Faith. / The Evidence of things not seen./ [Same in Greek and Latin, two lines] / Hebr. Ch XI ver 1. / Charlestown Massats. Published by S. Etheridge Junr." Front, vol. II. WMFA.

409. Hades. Line rect., 8.7 x 6.10. Two diagrams and half-opened door. Inside, man with staff. Greek and Latin inscriptions. Ins.: "P. Maverick sct. / Gates of Hades: Hell."

410. Innocence. Line rect., 7.3 x 5.9. Seated woman, waterfall, lamb. Ins.:
"R. Smirke R. A. pinxt. Peter Maverick sculpt. / Innocence. / I
will wash my hands in innocency. / [same in Latin] / Psalm
XXVI. ver 6. / Charlestown: Massachts. Published by Saml.
Etheridge, Junr. 1813." Vol. III, front.

411. Jackall and Fox. Line vignettes in rect. border, 5.2 x 3.11. Ins.: "P.
Maverick sc. / Jackall. Fox."

412. Mercy and Truth. Line rect., 7.1 x 5.4. Two female figures, one
with crown. Ins.: "Angelica Kauffman R. A. pinx. P. Maverick
sculp. Newark N. Jersey. / Mercy and Truth. / Mercy and Truth
are met together. / [same in Latin] / Psalm LXXXV, ver 10. /
Charlestown, Massats. Published by S. Etheridge junr." Vol. I,
front. Used earlier as front. to Dr. Thomas Scott's Bible, N.Y.:
Williams & Whiting, 1810. NPL.

413. Miscellanies. Line drawings in rect. 8.5 x 7.1. Four views, Assyrian
man-lion, etc. Ins.: "P. Maverick sct. / Miscellanies Plate III."

414. Musical instruments. Line drawings in rect. 8.6 x 6.5. Fifteen instruments, various types. Ins.: "P. Maverick sct. / Musical instruments. Plate I."

415. Musical instruments. Line drawings in rect. 8.5 x 6.4. Nine stringed
instruments; in center Oriental with banjo-type instrument. Ins.:
"P. Maverick sc. / Musical Instruments. Plate II."

416. Musical Instruments. Line and stipple in rect. 8.5 x 6.4. Ten instruments, various types. Horizontal stipple panel, three cherubs with
harp, clappers, and pipes. Ins.: "P. Maverick sc. / Musical Instruments. Plate III."

417. Ostrich. Line vignettes in rect. 7.8 x 6.3. Two ostriches. Ins.: "P.
Maverick sc. / The Ostrich." Vol. III, facing p. 179.

418. Pectoral. Line rect., 8.6 x 6.8. Pectoral with corner rings and ribbon
ties. Ins.: "The High Priest's Pectoral. / P. Maverick sc."

419. Plants. Line rect., 6. x 8.8. Five lettered illustrations of plants. Ins.:
"Camphire, Cypress; Ai-henna: Solomon's Song. Plate I. / P.
Maverick sct." Vol. III, facing p. 476. Plate II not by Maverick.

420. Priest. Stip. rect., 8.3 x 6.7. Priest in robes. Ins.: "P. Maverick sct.
/ The High Priest, in his Robes; from Calmet." Vol. III, facing
p. 344.

421. Sepulchre. Line rect., 7.14 x 6.7. Plans and details with scale, and
perspective view with seated angel at side and city in the distance.

Ins.: "P. Maverick sc. / Sepulchre of Jesus Christ." Vol. III, facing p. 166.

422. Sepulchre. Line rect., 6.12 x 8.4. Plan of church and perspective details. Ins.: "P. Maverick sc. / Sepulchre of Jesus Christ. Plate II." Following preceding plate.

423. Serpents. Line and stip. in rect. 8.9 x 6.10. Six numbered views of serpents or details. Ins.: "P. Maverick sc. / Serpent's Head."

424. Shew-bread. Line in rect. 6.8 x 8.7. Nine groups, shew-bread, tables, utensils. Ins.: "P. Maverick sc. / Table of Shew-Bread."

425. Ships. Line rect., 8.8 x 6.4. Seven numbered ships and parts. Ins.: "P. Maverick sc. / Ancient Ships." Vol. III, facing p. 286.

426. Ships. Line rect., 8.7 x 7. Nine ships. Ins.: "P. Maverick sc. / Ancient Ships Plate II." Vol. III, facing p. 301.

427. Ships. Line rect., 6.6 x 8.11. Trireme, parts lettered, scale below. Ins.: "P. Maverick sc. / Ancient Ships. Plate III." Vol. III, facing p. 307.

428. Ships. Line rect., 6.8. x 8.10. Numbered cross-sections, with scale. Ins.: "P. Maverick sct. / Ancient Ships. Plate IV." Vol. III, facing p. 306.

429. Ships. Line rect., 6.6 x 8.12. Six small, one large; Greek inscriptions. Ins.: "P. Maverick sc. / Ancient Ships, Plate V." Vol. III, facing p. 388.

430. Tombs. Line rect., 8.2 x 5.12. Three panels, group of tombs, tombs in cliff, and interior with explorers. Ins.: "P. Maverick sc. / Tombs."

431. Wheat. Line vign. in rect. 8 x 6.9. Ear of wheat. Ins.: "Fragment No. . . . / Species of Egyptian Wheat. / P. Maverick sct." Vol. III, facing p. 190.

CAMPBELL, THOMAS. *The Pleasures of Hope and Other Poems.* N.Y.: R. & W. Bartow, 1820. Also Richmond, Va.: W. A. Bartow, 1820. (Item 432.)

432. Title page. Lettered design, 3.2 x 2.5, no vign. N.Y. bibliog. data only on engr. design. Sig.: "P. Maverick sc." Front. done by Durand.

CARDELL, WILLIAM SAMUEL. *Jack Halyard the Sailor Boy, or the Virtuous Family,* [ca.1825]. (Item 433.)

433. Title page. Line vign., 2.6 x 3.12, in design 5.9 x 3.12, showing boatman rescuing children from water. N.Y., 4th ed., no pub., no date. Sig.: "Drawn by H. Inman. Engrd. by P. Maverick." 1831 sale, Jack Halyard, plate 8 x 5 for $1. GC.

434. CATALINI. 1831 sale, 1 for $1.

435. CERVANTES, MIGUEL. (Edition not found. Probably N.Y.: Bartow, *ca*.1818.) Line rect., 4.12 x 3.9. Nearly half-length; face ¾ right. Ins.: "Engrd. by Peter Maverick. / Miguel De Cervantes Saavedra." 1831 sale, 216 for $1.58, plate $2. 4 plates Don Quixote for $4. NYPL.

CHEETOPE. *A Selection of Ballads Legendary and Pathetic.* Baltimore: E. I. Coale. (Items 436 and 437.)

436. Title page. Line, very ornately lettered.

437. Front. Line rect., 3.11 x 2.1. Woman on knees before old man; young man in background. Three-line quotation from "Amyntor & Theodora." Ins.: "R. Westall R. A. del. P. Maverick sc. Newark, N.J. / Publish'd by E. I. Coale." NYHS.

CHEMISTRY. (Work not found. Probably N.Y.: Eastburn, 1818.) Plates showing chemical apparatus. 1831 sale, 4 plates, 10 x 8, for $1.80. Since the following discovered plates were made in pairs, there are three as yet unaccounted for. (Items 438 through 445.)

438. Plate I. Ten line drawings of chemical vessels, etc., in rect. 6.8 x 3.13. Sig.: "P. Maverick & Durand sc."

439. Plate II. Graduates, furnace, etc., in rect. 6.9 x 3.13. Same sig.

440. Plate III. Tongs, vessels, etc. Rect. 6.10 x 3.13. Same sig.

441. Plate IV. Retorts, coils, etc. Rect. Same size and sig.

442. Plate V. Complex distilling apparatus, etc. Rect. 3.13 x 6.6. Sig.: "P. Maverick & Durand s."

443–45. Plates VI to VIII. Unseen.

446. CHILD SAYING PRAYERS. 1831 sale, plate for 63¢.

447. CHRIST AND GROUP. Line rect., 3.15 x 3. Christ seated, child at side, three men and two women. Ins.: "Peter Maverick sculpt." NYHS.

448. CHRIST AND GROUP. Line vign. 2.13 x 3.6, trimmed, same view as preceding, with ins.: "Peter Maverick sc. / Suffer the little Children to come unto me and forbid them not." NYHS.

449. a. CHRIST BLESSING LITTLE CHILDREN. F1037. Line rect., 13.4 x 16.9. In oval panel, Jesus with four children. Sig.: "Charles Ingham delt. Peter Maverick sculpt." 1831 sale, 570 for $28.75. Plate $47.

    b. With line: "Published by Willis Thrall, Hartford, Ct. 1832." WMFA.

450. CHRIST AND DISCIPLES ON THE WAY TO EMMAUS. Line, circle in rect., ornamented, 4.11 x 2.14. Ins.: "Gonzales pinx. P. Maverick sculp.

Newark N.J. / 'He took Bread and blessed it, and brake, and gave to them; / and their eyes were open and they knew him.' " Said to be from *The Book of Psalms with Hymns*, Phila.: Moses Thomas, 1812. GC.

451. CHRIST WAS PRESENT. 1831 sale, plate $3.25.

452. CHRIST ECCE HOMO. 1831 sale, 230 for $3.45. This and the two preceding items may relate to the same print.

453. CHRISTMAS PRESENTS. 1831 sale, 79 for 99¢.

CLARKE, MRS. BEULAH ALLEN. *Sermon on the Death of*——. N.Y.: J. P. Haven, 1827. (Item 454.)

454. Portrait. St2193, F. 1024. Stip. vign., 4.8 x 3.8. Ins.: "Painted by Ames. Engrd. by Peter Maverick / Mrs. Beulah Allen Clarke. / Utica, N.Y." NYPL.

CLARKE, MCDONALD. *The Gossip, or a Laugh with the Ladies.* N.Y., 1823. NYPL. (Item 455.)

455. a. Port. front. Stip. vign., 3.3 x 2.12. Bust to left, face ¾ right. Ins.: "H. Inman del. Peter Maverick sc. / Mc. Donald Clarke / Entered according to Act of Congress Octr., 1823."

  b. St. 2194. As described, with "27" inserted after "Octr." NYPL.

  c. Autograph title, engraved, and date "Oct. 25th 1823. NYHS.

  d. As described, with "Born June 18, 1798" above copyright line. Front. *Poems of Mc Donald Clarke*, N.Y.: J. W. Bell, 1836. HU.

CLARKSON, THOMAS. *Portraiture of Quakerism.* N.Y., 1806. AAS, NYPL, WMFA. (Item 456.)

456. Port. St2191. Stip. oval, 4.8 x 3.9. Bust. Ins.: "Engd. by P. Maverick, 84 Nassau Strt. N. York / Thomas Clarkson, A. M." NYPL, GC.

457. a. CLAY, HENRY. Line rect., 13.13 x 10.13. Face ¾ right, ½ length, seated. Scroll in hand. Ins.: "Painted by Charles King. Washington City: Published by Benjamin O. Tyler, 1822. Engraved by Peter Maverick / New York. / Henry Clay." NYPL, PAFA.

  b. St2192. As described, with added long Spanish inscription and title in both English and Spanish. Added copyright line and printer's line. "Printed by P. Maverick." HU Fogg.

  c. Same, inscribed only "Henry Clay."

458. CLINTON, DEWITT. Line orn. circ., diam. 2.6. Bust, face front. Ins.: "DeWitt Clinton. / Born March 1769. Died Feb. 11th, 1828. / Peter Maverick Sc." 1831 sale, 108 for $3.86. NYPL.

459. a. CLINTON, GEORGE. St2195. Line rect., 5.5 x 4.5. Full bust, ¾ right. Ins.: "Painted by Ames. Engraved by P. Maverick. / Pub-

lished by Joseph Delaplaine. / George Clinton. / Printed by Porter and Harrison." Used facing p. 19 of the second part of Delaplaine's *Repository of Lives and Portraits of Distinguished Characters*, Phila., 1815. NYPL, AAS, MMNY, HU.

   b. Publisher's line erased.

   c. Printer's line erased.

   d. Like state a above, except printer's line "Printed by Harrison & Porter [*sic*]" is found above the name of Clinton.

460. COAL-BLACK ROSE. Lith. music, two sheets each 12 x 9.10. At top of first, three roses, middle rose containing Negro face. Ins.: "The Coal-Black Rose / Compd. by Snyder and Sung by / Mr. G. Dixon, the celebrated / American Buffo Singer. / Sold by P. Maverick 61 Grand Street, N.Y. / P. Maverick's Lithogry." 1831 sale, 187 for $4.29.

461. COINS, VALUE OF. Book? Chart? 1831 sale, 24 for $1.08.

462. a. COLDEN, CADWALLADER D. St572, the work of Durand. Line vign., 7.7 x 5.14. Bust to left, face front. Sig.: "Painted by Waldo & Jewett. Eng. by P. Maverick, Durand & Co."

   b. "Eng. by A. B. Durand." "Mayor" & ff. erased.

463. a. COLUMBUS, CHRISTOPHER. Line rect., 5.4 x 4.5. Bust in armor, face slightly left. Ins.: "M. Maella pinx. P. Maverick sculp. Newark, N.J. / Columbus. / Published by Joseph Delaplaine." In Delaplaine's *Repository of the Lives and Portraits of Distinguished American Characters*. Phila., 1815.

   b. As described, except "Rogers & Esler Printers" in place of Delaplaine line.

   c. Publisher's line erased.

   d. "P. Price, Printer."

   e. Printer's line replaced by "Published by S. C. Atkinson for the Casket." Phila., Dec. 1829.

464. CONSTANCE. Lith. vign., in rect. 6.15 x 5.5. Young woman, comb in hair. Ins.: "Lithography. / Peter Maverick, 61 Grand st. N.Y. / Constance." AAS.

COWPER, WILLIAM. Portraits possibly made for the Huntington edition below, but not found *in situ*. (Items 465 and 466.)

465. William Cowper. St2198. Stip. oval, 4.1 x 3.5. Face half left. Sig.: "Romney del. P. Maverick sct." NYPL.

466. Mrs. Cowper. St2199. Stip. oval, 4.1 x 3.4. Bust, face front. Ins.:

"D. Heins pinx. P. Maverick sculp. / Mrs. Cowper. / Mother of the Poet." NYPL.

COWPER, WILLIAM. *Poems.* 2 vols. N.Y. David Huntington, 1814. HU. (Items 467 and 468.)

467. Title page, vol. I. Line vign., 1.15 x 2.8, on design 3.14 x 2.8. Angel painting flowers and rainbow. Ref. to "Table Talk." Sig.: "G. Fairman del. P. Maverick sc."

468. Front., vol. I. Line rect. 3.7 x 2.1. Angel, Father Time, and woman with sculptor's chisel. Ref. to "The Historic Muse." Sig.: "G. Fairman del. P. Maverick sc." Engravings in vol. II are by Leney.

COWPER, WILLIAM. *Poems.* 2 vols. N.Y.: R. & W. A. Bartow, 1819. NYPL. (Items 469 through 475.)

469. Title page, vol. I. Line, 3.11 x 2.13, no vign. No sig.

470. Title page, vol. II. Same desc.

471. Front., vol. I. The Rose. Line rect., 3.1 x 2.7. Man seated, two women standing, rose on ground between them. Quot. beginning, "This elegant rose . . ." Sig.: "Westall R. A. del. P. Maverick & Durand sc."

472. a. Front., vol. II. "The Task." Line rect., 3.5 x 2.10. Man, woman, three children at cottage hearth. Three-line quotation. Sig.: "R. Westall R. A. del. P. Maverick & Durand sc."

   b. Same, with title changed to "Domestic Comfort on a Stormy Night." used as front. in *The Hyacinth.* N.Y.: J. C. Riker, 1831. Quot. and Bartow pub. line erased.

473. Illus. The Lily and the Rose. Line vign., 2.13 x 2.8, of girl in white, rose bush at right, lilies at left, Four-line quot. Sig.: "Drawn by Rich. Westall, Eng. by P. Maverick & Durand, N. York." Reported in volume dated 1818. Used as front, vol. III, Bartow ed. of 1821.

474. Illus. Night. Line rect., 3.12 x 2.10, of woman running in night. Quot. from "Night I." Sig.: "Drawn by T. Uwins. P. Maverick & Durand sc."

475. a. Illus. On His Mother's Picture. Line vign., 3 x 2.6. Man at table looking at picture. Four-line quot. beginning: "O that those lips . . ." Sig.: "Drawn by Richd. Westall. Eng. by P. Maverick & Durand."

   b. Same, without Bartow pub. line, used to illustrate Cowper's poem in *The Hyacinth.* N.Y.: J. C. Riker, 1831. AAS.
   1831 sale entry, 2 plates Cowper's Poems, 6 x 7, for $2.

476. CRISTIANI, STEPHEN. St2200. Stip. vign., 4.8 x 3.1. Half-length, writ-
ing music, face left. Ins.: "L. Persico del. P. Maverick sc. / Stephen
Cristiani / Master and Composer of Music; of the Theatre of the
Spanish Court." NYPL, NPL.

[DARWIN, ERASMUS.] *The Botanic Garden,* 2 vols., N.Y.: T. & J. Swords,
1807. AAS. (Item 477.)

477. Line rect., 4.14 x 3.11. Anubis astride the Nile. Ins.: "H. Fuseli,
R. A. del. P. Maverick sculp. / Fertilization of Egypt." Vol. I,
facing p. 81. GC.

DEAN, HENRY. *Large Text Words.* N.Y.: Hopkins & Baird, 1808. This
book was made by cutting the lettering plates of the following books in
two, and binding them to make a small volume. CU Plimpton.

DEAN, HENRY. *Universal Penman* etc. N.Y.: George F. Hopkins, 1808.
This book used all the sheets of models which appear in the following book.
Some of them are dated 1808, a fact which has caused the predating of the
Analytical Guide. CU Plimpton.

DEAN, HENRY. *Analytical Guide to the Art of Penmanship.* N.Y.: Published for the author and sold by many listed persons. Copyright June 27,
1810. J. B. & A. G. Reynolds, copperplate printers, J. Seymour typo-
graphic printer. NYPL, GC, CU Plimpton. (Items 478 through 490.)

478. Title page. Eng. script lettering. No sig.

479. a. Front. St2241. Line rect., 8.8 x 5.4. Standing woman offers writing materials to woman seated, with book, globe, map. Ships in
background, sails draped above, box and barrel at left, swan at
right. Ins.: "Drawn by Archbd. Robertson. Engraved by Peter
Maverick. / The Genius of Penmanship / offering her aid to Science
& Commerce. / two lines of Ovid." At top "Frontispiece."
b. Same, inscription erased except for signatures and word "Frontispiece."

480. Chancery alphabets. Letters, with man on horse stabbing dragon with
pen. This and other illustrations done in pen scroll work. 9.8 x 7.8.
Sig.: "P. Maverick sct."

481. Square-text alph. Angel with horn and wreath above, winged dragon
below. 9.8 x 7.8. Sig.: "P. Maverick sct."

482. Italian alph. Eagle. 9 x 7.8. Sig.: "P. Maverick sct. New York."

483. Round-text alph. 9.4 x 7.4. Sig.: "P. Maverick sculpt."

484. Round-text alph., cont. 9.4 x 7.4. Sig.: "P. Maverick sct."

485. Business forms. Note, etc., written by Phebe and Sarah Johnson. Sig.: "Engrd. by P. Maverick."

486. Plate called Industry. Specimens of penmanship as written by Phebe Johnson. Angels at top. 7.8 x 8.12. Sig.: "Engraved by P. Maverick."

487. Plate of large-text mottoes. 7.12 x 7.8. Sig.: "P. Maverick sculpt."

488. Another. Same size and sig.

489. Another. Same size and sig.

490. Another. 8.12 x 7.4. Same sig.

Related plate. Though not found in situ, *the following may have been made for this or a similar book. See also, Jenkins.*

491. Old English alph. Winged dragon below. 6 x 7.4. Sig.: "P. Maverick sct."

492. DECLARATION OF INDEPENDENCE. Line rect., 29.6 x 22.10. Text in ornate script, signatures in facsimile. Copied from the original and published by Benjamin O. Tyler, 1818. Certificate of accuracy by Richard Rush, Acting Secretary of State, dated Sept. 10, 1817. Signed "Engraved by Peter Maverick, Newark, N.J." and apparently done just before the partnership with Durand began. 1831 sale, one for 80¢. BPL, NYHS, NJHS, EI. See Dard Hunter, *Papermaking*, N.Y.: Knopf, 1943, pp. 18 and 353.

493. DISMAL SWAMP. St2239. Line rect., 2.15 x 4.4. Swamp scene. Ins.: "H. Inman, N. A. Pinx. Peter Maverick, N. A. sculp. / Dismal Swamp." Facing p. 255 of *The Talisman* for 1829, N.Y.: Elam Bliss, 1828. NYPL.

494. DISTRESS. 1831 sale, 128 for 64¢.

495. DIXON. [Is this Coal Black Rose?] 1831 sale, 14 for 23¢.

496. DOG AND MONKEY. Lith. vign., trimmed size 8 x 7. Girl holds dog barking at monkey held by boy. Cert. in family scrapbook as lith. by Peter Maverick. NPL.

DRAWING BOOKS. Maverick published several books for students in portrait and figure, with no text but with graded designs illustrating the geometrical base of the head, then details of feature or figure, and then a few completed studies. Engravers' names are not given; the plates were probably apprentices' exercises, turned to profit during Maverick's lean years after 1820. The 1831 sale has these pertinent items: *Rudiments of Drawing*, 83 for $6.23; *Drawing books*, 462 for $27.62; *Book of heads*, 27 for $1.89;

Drawing Plates (probably loose sheets) 400 for $1; 60 plates, 7 x 10, for $39. (Items 497 through 501.)

497. *Rudiments of Drawing*. N.Y.: Peter Maverick, 1822. Cover label 1.4 x 3.15. Page size 8.13 x 11.4, plate size about 6 x 7. Fourteen pages of details, four large male heads, two large female heads, and one copy of Ribera Spagnoletto's The Flaying of Marsyas (source not acknowledged). BPL.

498. *Figures*. N.Y.: Peter Maverick, n.d. (Penciled price, $1.25.) Seven unnumbered plates, page size 8 x 11.8, with cover label 2 x 3.8. Plate 1, seated nude male figure holding tablet (abacus?) signed "C. Vanloo del." No other signatures in book. Plate 2, a gladiator. Plate 3, John the Baptist (?). Plate 4, Marcus Aurelius. Plate 5, Venus de Medici. Plate 6, the Farnesian Hercules. Plate 7, seated man gazing at tomb. NPL.

499. CARACCI, ANNIBAL. *Principles of Design*. N.Y.: P. Maverick, Durand & Co., 1820. (Penciled price, $3.) Cover label, 4 x 6. Twenty-seven plates of portrait and figure work, details and wholes, introduced by geometrical analysis. Page size, 8 x 11.8. Most plates give outline drawings accompanied by same drawings shaded. Page 7 unnumbered and unsigned, others signed with artist's name only, given variously as "Anib." or "A.," "Caracci" or "Carrache" or "Carracche," followed by "in." or "del." or "d." NPL.

500. CIPRIANI, G. B. *Rudiments of Drawing*. "Engraved for and published by P. Maverick, New York." No date. Six unnumbered plates, page size 8 x 11.8, of eyes, ears, hands, feet, and lower face, with t. p. showing three cupids and seated woman with palette and brushes, and final page, signed "G. B. Cipriani del." showing bearded man and two women. Cipriani sig. on two exercise plates. A cover label, line oval, 2.12 x 5, with Old English lettering "Cipriani's Rudiments" exists, and may be for this collection. NPL.

501. Drawing book (?) decoration. Line oval, 4.6 x 5.6. Seated man, woman tracing his shadow on wall, cupid hovering near. No lettering on trimmed copy in Maverick family scrapbook, attested in pencil as P. Maverick's. NPL.

502. a. DREAM OF YOUTH. Line rect., 2.13 x 4.3. Landscape, woman reclining on arm in foreground, birds in tree. Ins.: "Dream of Youth / Eng. by Peter Maverick from a sketch by H. J. Morton." NYPL.

b. As above, title "Dream of Papantzin." *The Talisman for 1829*. N.Y.: Elam Bliss, 1828.

503. EAST RIVER. Line rect., 3.11 x 6.4. Two fishers in boat off shore right, large vine-covered tree left, point of land in middle distance with house and outhouses. Ins.: "Engrd. by P. Maverick, Newark / View of East-River or Sound, taken from Riker's Island, with a distant view of the Seat of Joshua Waddington Esqr." From *The Port Folio*, New Series, vol. IV, facing p. 621, Dec., 1810. Illus. etc., in C. W. Drepperd's *American Pioneer Arts and Artists*, Springfield, 1942. NYPL, MCNY, GC.

In *The Echo, with Other Poems*. Copyrighted by Noah Bailey in 1807. "Printed at the Porcupine Press by Pasquin Petronius." (Item 504.)

504. Title page. Lettering, and perhaps vign. of porcupine, done by Maverick, the sig. being "P. Maverick sc." Chief vign. sig.: "Tisdale delt. Leney Sct." 6 x 3.10 overall.

505. a. ELLSWORTH, OLIVER. St2201, F1025. Stip. oval, 3.14 x 3.2. Bust, face front. Ins.: "Painted by Ino. Trumbull. Engrd. by P. Maverick, Newark. / The Hon. / Oliver Ellsworth Esqr." From *The Recorder*, N.Y.: D. Longworth for Wm. Dunlap, 1813. 1831 sale, plate for 65¢. NYPL, WMFA, MMNY.

   b. "Newark" erased and "late Chief Justice of the United States" and "Printed by Andw. Maverick" added.

   c. Printer's line omitted. WMFA.

506. EMMETT, THOMAS A. 1831 sale, 165 for $9.07, plate for $10.25.

ENCYCLOPEDIA PLATES. In the American edition of the *Edinburgh Encyclopaedia*, edited by Abraham Rees and published by Samuel F. Bradford and Murray Firman Co. in Philadelphia, 1810–1842, occur in some copies and in various places the following plates by Maverick. AAS, NYHS. (Items 507 through 509.)

507. Aeronautics. Four line drawings of balloons, 8.10 x 5.2 overall. Sig.: "Engrd. by P. Maverick, Newark, N.J."

508. Sheep. F1055. Two groups of South Down Polled sheep, line vigns. in rect. 9 x 7.2. Sig.: "Sydm. Edwards delt. P. Maverick sculpt. N. York."

509. a. Oxen. Line vigns. in rect. 9 x 7.2. Wild ox of Scotland, and cow and calf. Sig.: "Syd. Edwards delt. P. Maverick sculpt. / Printed by H. Charles." NYPL, AAS.

   b. Without printer's line.

510. ERIE CANAL. F1058. Line rect., 2.13 x 4.7. Boat on canal, mountain at right. Ins.: "H. Inman del. Peter Maverick sc. / Travelling on the Erie Canal. / N. York Pub. by Wilder & Campbell 1825."

Facing p. 29 in *The Northern Traveller* etc. pub. as given. Used also in *The Northern Traveller and Northern Tour* etc., N.Y.: J. & J. Harper, 1831. AAS, NYPL.

ERSKINE, THOMAS. *Speeches of . . . connected with the Liberty of the Press.* N.Y.: Eastburn, Kirk & Co., 1813. (Item 511.)

511. Front., vol. I. Line oval, 3.2 x 2.11. Bust, ¾ right. Ins.: "R. Cosway R. A. pinxt. P. Maverick sct. Newark. / The Honble. Thos. Erskine. / now / Lord Erskine. / [Pub. line as above] NYPL, AAS, WMFA.

EYE, ANATOMY OF. Publication unidentified. See also Emily and Maria A. Maverick for plates in this group. (Item 512.)

512. Plate I. Seven three-color three-copperplate line drawings of diseased eyes. Copperplate size, 8.14 x 5.8. Sig.: "Drawn by H. Thomson. Eng. print & col. by Peter Maverick." NPL.

513. FAMILY REGISTER. Line rect., 22.13 x 18.5. Pillars and female figures at sides. Above, swan with young. Sig.: "Ransom Hinman inv. H. Williams del P. Maverick sculp. Newark, N.J." Also "Copyright secured." 1831 sale, 1100 for $31.15. NYHS.

514. FANCY HAT. 1831 sale, 7 for $3.15. Also Hat, 6 plates for $2.70.

515. FASHIONS, LONDON. 1831 sale, 21 for $2.10 and "balance" for $3.57.

516. LE FIDELE AMI. Lith. in rect. 5.1 x 4.7. Girl with dog. Ins.: "Drawn by C. Toppan. Lith. of P. Maverick, N.Y. / Le Fidele Ami." 1831 sale, 31 for 31¢. AAS.

517. FIDELITY. 1831 sale, 90 for $1.93.

518. FELICITY, PERFECT. 1831 sale, 460 for $6.55.

FESSENDEN, THOMAS GREEN. (Christopher Caustic). *Terrible Tractoration!! A Poetical Petition against Galvanising Trumpery* etc. First American, from second London edition. N.Y.: Samuel Stansbury, 1804. Southwick & Hardcastle, printers. AAS. (Item 519.)

519. Facing p. 57. Line circ., diam. 2.10, in orn. pattern 5.12 x 3.2. Old man in bed, surgeon piercing vein, men and women about. Two-line quotation beginning, "He comes!" Sig.: "A. I. Stansbury del. P. Maverick sct."

520. FLOWERS. 1831 sale, 6 plates for 48¢.

521. A FOOT. 1831 sale, 18 for 36¢.

FOX, JOHN. *An Abridgement of the Book of Martyrs.* N.Y.: Samuel Wood, 1810. AAS. (Item 522.)

522. Front. Line rect., 6.7 x 3.14. Martyrdom by mutilation of seven

brothers. Sig.: "Archb. Robertson del. P. Maverick sc. Newark."
GC, NYHS.

Fox, John. *Fox's Book of Martyrs* revised and improved by Rev. John
Malham; re-edited by Rev. T. Pratt, D. D. Phila.: J. J. Woodward, 1830.
2 vols. in one. AAS. (Items 523 and 524.)

523. Front., vol. I. Line rect., ornamented, 7.10 x 6.8. Panel of 9 views,
8 martyrdoms and the "comprehensive conflagration." Sig.: "Eng.
on steel by Peter Maverick." NYPL, WMFA.

524. Front., vol. II. F1041. Line vign., 6.4 x 6.4; overall 9.8 x 6.4. Burning of Ridley and Latimer. Sig.: "On steel by P. Maverick."

525. Franklin, Benjamin. F1026. Line rect, 6.14 x 7.6. Bust to left.
Ins.: "Drawn by Iohn R. Smith. Engraved by Peter Maverick. /
No. ——." On cert. of The Society for the Encouragement of
Faithful Domestic Servants.

526. Franklin, Benjamin. Line vign., 6.13 x 5.4. Bust, profile left, fur
cap. Diverging rays from head. Ins.: "Printed & Published by S.
Maverick, New York / P. Maverick & Durand sc."

Franklin, Benjamin. See also Tapping Reeve.

527. Franklin's Art of Making Money. 1831 sale, 1000 for $4.45.
Plate, 8 x 11, for $7.35. I have not found one of these, but it is
almost undoubtedly the rebus that N. Dearborn engraved (F. 338)
and that Currier lithographed. (Reproduced in Harry Peters's
Currier & Ives, Plate 27.)

528. Galatea. 1831 sale, 168 for $2.52.

529. Gano, Rev. Stephen. 1831 sale, 9 for 36¢. Plate, 9 x 13, for $5. See
St2443.

530. Gentle Tooth Drawer. 1831 sale, 309 for $3.84.

531. a. Lake George. St2243. Line rect., 2.12 x 4.7. Lake, mountains,
clouds. Ins.: "Peter Maverick sc. / Lake George. / N. York. Pub.
by Wilder & Campbell. 1825." In *The Northern Traveller* etc.
pub. as stated. NYPL, AAS, HU, GC.

b. With pub. line erased, used in *The Northern Traveller* etc. N.Y.:
J. & J. Harper, 1831.

532. Lake George. St2244. Line rect., 4.1 x 7. Ins.: "P. Maverick sc.
Newark N.J. / View of Lake George." NYPL. Used H. G. Spafford's *Gazetteer*, *q. v.*

Goldsmith, Oliver. *Miscellaneous Works*. 6 vols. N.Y.: Wm. Durell &
Co., 1809. HU. (Item 533.)

533. Front., vol. III. Line rect., 3.15 x 2.12. Beggar on crutches, man in

top hat, man in oriental costume. Woman and child in background. Sig.: "Stothard del. P. Maverick sculp." WMFA.

534. a. GRACES. Line rect., 4 x 3. Three graces, with three satyrs in background. Ins.: "W. Hamilton R. A. delt. Peter Maverick sculpt. / The Graces stand in sight . . ." etc.
   b. Last line omitted, NYHS.

535. GRAFTING. Line vign., 4.8 x 3.10, as part of larger design. Man inserting twigs in tree trunk. Calvary with empty crosses in distance. Inscription above: "God is able to graff them in again. Romans XI, 23." At left, remnant "-ke" and below it "TO" are left from trimming. Sig.: "Inman del. Peter Maverick sc." NYPL.

536. GRANDFATHER'S WIG. 1831 sale, 240 for $3.27.

537. GRANDMOTHER'S CAP. 1831 sale, 200 for $4.

538. HARRIS, REV. J. 1831 sale, plate for $2.75.

HAYLEY, WILLIAM. *The Triumphs of Temper*. N.Y.: David Longworth, Printed by D. & G. Bruce, 1809. Engravings impressed upon the same pages as the letterpress, heavier paper being used for the pages containing engravings. Many unsigned plates, not included in this list. All the plates listed are 1 x 2.6 in size, and signed "Engrd. by P. Maverick." AAS, NYPL, HU. (Items 539 through 542.)

539. Page 40. Woman lying in prow of narrow boat. Four-line quot. beginning: ". . . the obedient maid."

540. Page 42. Woman with spear and helmet leading another woman. Seated woman and children in background. Four-line quot. beginning: "High on an ebon throne . . ."

541. Page 43. Fire at left, two women at right. Three-line quot. beginning: "And, as she spoke . . ."

542. Page 52. Woman with helmet holds another. Fiends at right. Four-line quot. beginning: "And now his livid lips . . ."

HENRY, ALEXANDER. *Travels and Adventures in Canada* etc. N.Y.: I. Riley, 1809. AAS, NYPL. (Item 543.)

543. Portrait. F1027. Stip. oval, 3.6 x 2.10. Half length. Ins.: "Engraved by P. Maverick from an Original miniature. / Alexander Henry. / [Pub. as given above.]"

HERVEY, JAMES. *Meditations and Contemplations* etc., 2 vols. in one. N.Y.: Richard Scott, 1824. (Items 544 and 545.)

544. a. Title page. Line rect., 4.6 x 3. Ruled background. Bibliog. data as given above.

b. Title page. Second state of 1824 title page, with change of publisher for 1830 edition below.

545. Front. Line rect., 3.12 x 3. Woman kneeling before another. Ins.: "R. Westall R. A. del. Peter Maverick sc. / Hervey's Meditations. / Let their loins bless you for comfortable cloathing. / Winter piece." GC.

HERVEY, JAMES. *Meditations and Contemplations* etc., N.Y.: S. & D. A. Forbes, 1830. 1831 sale, plate, $9.50. AAS. See 544b. (Item 546.)

546. a. Front. Line rect., 3.10 x 2.14. Two women, two children, and seated man in churchyard. Ins.: "Peter Maverick sc. / Let the poor as they pass my Grave point at the little spot." BMFA, GC.

b. Ins.: "My Mother's Grave. / For The Ladies' Companion III 185. N.Y. Sept. 1835" Sig. erased.

547. HICKS, ELIAS. St2205. Stip. vign., 5.6 x 5.2. Bust, face ¾ right. Ins.: "Drawn by H. Inman. Engrd. by Peter Maverick. / Elias Hicks / Published by Edward Hopper / No. 420 Pearl St. New York. / Entered According to Act of Congress the 18th day of the Sixth Month 1830, by V. Seaman of the State of New York." 1831 sale, 140 for $5.78. NYPL.

548. HILSON, THOMAS. Lith. vign., 5.14 x 4.12, on cover of music, *The Adventures of Paul Pry* as sung by Mr. Hilson, N.Y.: Dubois & Stodart, n.d. Hilson with hat in arm, umbrella, and spectacles. Sig.: "From Mr. Gear. P. Maverick's Lith." Harvard Theatre Collection.

549. HISTORICAL CHART. 1831 sale, 47 for $1.21.

550. HOBART, [BISHOP JOHN HENRY?]. 1831 sale, 34 for $2.38. Another item, "Stone Hobart" may indicate that this was a lithograph, and that the stone was still capable of further printing.

551. HOHENLOHE. Stip. rect., 4.3 x 3.5. Half length, clerical garb., eyes upraised. Ins.: "His Serene Highness the very Revd. / Prince Alexr. Hohenlohe / A Canon of the Noble Chapter of Olmutz & Knight of Malta / Engrd. in New York by Peter Maverick from a copy of the original done in Bamberg." NPL.

HOMER. *The Odyssey*, Pope's translation. N.Y.: W. Durell, 1812. (Some of these items may have been made for an earlier edition.) (Items 552 through 555.)

552. a. Front., vol. II. Line rect., 3.3 x 2.5. Man in boat, woman bending over him. Two-line quot. beginning: "This heavenly scarf . . ." Sig.: "J. Thurston del. P. Maverick sc." NYPL, BMFA.

b. With "Published by W. Durell, 1809."

553. Illustration. Line rect., 3.5 x 2.3. Man seated on beach, woman near him. Three-line quot. beginning: "Him pensive . . ." Sig.: "J. Thurston del. P. Maverick sc." BMFA.

554. Portrait. St2206. Line oval, 3.5 x 2.8. Bust on pedestal, half left. Ins.: "P. Maverick sc. / Homer."

555. Andromeda. Line rect., 4.5 x 2.14. Andromeda chained, Cupid at her feet. Perseus and Gorgon in background. Ins.: "Peter Maverick sc. / Perseus and Andromeda."

556. HUMPHREYS MEDAL. St2258. Line engraving of two faces of medal, each oval 2.10 x 2.1, awarded to David Humphreys, late minister to Spain, for importing merino sheep. Award by Mass. Soc. for Promoting Agriculture in 1802. Sig.: "Engd. by P. Maverick." AAS, NYPL, GC. Illus. in F. L. Humphreys's *Life and Times of David Humphreys*, N.Y.: Putnam, 1917.

INNES, JOHN. *A Short Description of the Human Muscles*, etc. N.Y.: Collins & Co., 1818. AAS, NYHS, AMNNJ. (Items 557 through 573.)

557. . . . Plate 1. Line vign., 4.15 x 3.10. Surface muscles, front of body. Sig.: "Mogdridge Del. P. Maverick & Durand Sc."

558. . . . Plate 2. Line vign., 4.14 x 3.9. Muscles next underlying. Same sig.

559. . . . Plate 3. Line vign., 4.14 x 3.10. Muscles next underlying. Same sig.

560. . . . Plate 4. Same type, size, and sig. The fourth underlying group, with bones and ligaments.

561. . . . Plate 5. Same type, size, and sig. Outer muscles of back.

562. . . . Plate 6. Same type, size, and sig. Muscles next underlying.

563. . . . Plate 7. Same type and size. Muscles next underlying. Sig.: "P. Maverick & Durand Sc."

564. . . . Plate 8. Line vign., 5 x 3.10. Innermost muscles of the back. Sig.: "P. Maverick & Durand sc."

565. . . . Plate 9. Line vign., 4.12 x 3.6. External muscles of the side. Sig. same as preceding.

566. . . . Plate 10. Five line vigns., 6.2 x 3.10 overall. External muscles of front of feet, head, and hands. Sig. same as preceding.

567. . . . Plate 11. Five line vigns., 6.4 x 3.12 overall. Next underlying muscles. Sig. same as preceding.

568. . . . Plate 12. Five line vigns., 6.4 x 3.8 overall. Next underlying muscles. Sig. same as preceding.

569. . . . Plate 13. Five line vigns., 6 x 3.8 overall. Next underlying muscles. Sig. same as preceding.

570. . . . Plate 14. Five line vigns., back views of items in Plate 10, external muscles, 6.2 x 3.10. Sig. as in Plate 1.

571. . . . Plate 15. Five line vigns., 6 x 3.10. Next underlying muscles. Sig. as in Plate 1.

572. . . . Plate 16. Five line vigns., 6 x 3.8. Innermost muscles. Sig. as in Plate 1.

573. . . . Plate 17. Five line vigns., side views of items in Plate 10. Sig. as in Plate 1.

574. JACKSON & PALM TREE. 1831 sale, 31 for 47¢.

575. JACKSON, ANDREW. St2208. Line vign., 8.4 x 6.8. Half-length in uniform, face ¾ left. Ins.: "S. L. Waldo pinxt. P. Maverick sculpt. / Maj. Gen. Andrew Jackson." NYPL, BMFA.

576. JACKSON, ANDREW. Lith. mentioned by Harry Peters, *America on Stone*, p. 274. (Perhaps same, size 15 x 11, reported in sale, Bristol, Eng.)

577. JACKSON, ANDREW. St2209. Stip. and line vign., 3.5 x 2.11. Bust, face ¾ right. Ins.: "J. Wood pinx. Peter Maverick sc. / Maj. Gen. Andrew Jackson." Front. to *The Civil and Military History of Andrew Jackson* by "an American officer." N.Y.: P. M. Davis, 1825. NYPL, BA, HU, GC.

578. JACKSON, ANDREW. F1028. Stip. circ., diam. 1.9 in line frame, diam. 2.5. Bust in uniform, face right. Sig.: "P. M. sc."
Andrew Jackson items, 1831 sale. 800 for $10.08 and 47 for $2.94, perhaps different prints. Also plate, 7.8 x 4.8, for 50¢.

579. JACKSON, JAMES. St2210. Line rect., 11.8 x 8.12. Half-length standing, uniformed, face front. Ins.: "Painted by Archd. Robertson, No. 79 Liberty St. Engraved by Peter Maverick, N. York. / His Excellency / Major General James Jackson." NYPL (halftone reprod.) 1831 sale, 12 for 36¢. Two plates listed, one for $2 and one, 13 x 10, for $7.

580. JAY, JOHN. St2211. Stip. oval, 3.6 x 2.9. Bust, face ¾ right. Ins.: "G. Stuart Pinxt. P. Maverick Sct. / John Jay." 1831 sale, plate for 60¢. NYPL.

581. JEFFERSON, THOMAS. St2212. Stip. vign., 3.10 x 2.12. Bust, face ¾ left, Hands holding Decl. of Independence. Sig.: "I. R. Smith del. P. Maverick sct." Part of policy of the Jefferson Insurance Co. 1831 sale, 29 for 23¢, 41 "in board" for 72¢. UV.

582. JEFFERSON, THOMAS. Lith vign., 5 x 3.12. Bust, body and face left. Sig. partly erased in unique copy in Maverick family scrapbook, but name of Maverick is decipherable. Added pen-written sig.: "P. Maverick del." NPL.

583. JEFFERSON AND ADAMS. Line circ., diam. 2.4. Ins.: "Died July 4, 1826 / Jefferson & Adams / Born Apr. 2, 1743—Born Octr. 19, 1735 / P. Maverick sc."

JENKINS, JOHN. *The Art of Writing*. First ed., 1791, no Maverick work. Second ed., Cambridge, printed at Andover for the author by Flagg & Gould, 1813, title page and port. front. as given below. Third ed., Elizabethtown, N.J., J. & E. Sanderson, 1816, same eng. except change on title page as given. Eds. 1 and 2, MMNY and CU Plimpton Coll. Ed. 3, CU Plimpton Coll. Port., NYPL. (Items 584 and 585.)

584. a. Title page. Engr. script with title and author only, other bibliog. data from copyright. No sig, but plate continuous with port.
     b. With added "E. Shepherd Scr." in 1816 ed.

585. Port. front. St2213. Stip. oval, 4 x 3.3, on penmanship design 6.8 x 4.8. Nearly half length, face slightly right. Four-line quot. from Bickham. Sig.: "J. Jenkins scr. P. Maverick sc."

JOHNSON, SAMUEL. *Works*, 15 vols. N.Y.: William Durell, 1809–1812. Also, vols. I & II, Boston: Etheridge Hastings & Bliss, 1809. AAS.

586. Front., vol. I. St2214. Stip. oval port., 3.4 x 2.10. Full bust, face to right, manuscript in hands. Sig.: "Drawn by W. H. Brown. Engraved by P. Maverick." WMFA.

587. Front., vol. V. Line circ. with orn., 4.13 x 2.12. Girl at table with pen, woman standing tearing letter. Ref. to "Rambler." Sig.: "Wholley del. P. Maverick sct. Newark."

JOSEPHUS. *Works*, 7 vols. N.Y.: David Huntington, 1815. HU. (Items 588 through 590.)

588. Front. *port.*, vol. I. St2215. Stip. rect., 4.2 x 3.3. Bust, face front, oriental dress. Sig.: "P. Maverick sc."

589. Josephus (?) Unidentified. Line rect., 3.10 x 3.2. Man in coat of mail addressing crowd from platform. Ins.: "Engrd. by Peter Maverick. / The speech of Agrippa, to dissuade the Jews from a war with the Romans. / pa. 509."

590. Josephus (?) Unidentified. Line rect., 3.4 x 2.11 in rules 4 x 3.6. Men stabbing selves and others. Pillars and fire in background. Ins.: "Drawn by H. Inman. Engraved by Peter Maverick. People of Masada." NYHS.

JOSEPHUS. *The Works of Flavius Josephus,* translated by William Whiston. Phila.: J. Grigg, 1829. AAS, NYPL, RU. (Items 591 and 592.)

591. Front., vol. I. Line rect., orn., 4.15 x 4.2. Man at bridge-head beneath palms awaits caravan. Ins.: "P. Maverick sc. / Isaac & Rebeka." GC.

592. Front., vol. II. Line rect., orn., 4.15 x 4.3. Lightning striking pillar, crowned man and prophet in foreground. Ins.: "P. Maverick sc. / Jeroboam & the Prophet Jadon." GC.

JUNIUS. *The Letters of Junius.* Baltimore: Fielding Lucas Jr. and Joseph Cushing, 1814. L. Robinson Printer. AAS. (Items 593 and 594.)

593. Title page. Line, 3.3 x 1.15. Bibliog. data as given. Unsigned.

594. Front. Line rect., 3.8 x 2. Two winged figures, one with spear, one falling. Triangle inscribed "King, Lords, Commons" Ins.: "R. Cooke del. P. Maverick sc. / The Genius of Patriotism driving / Corruption from the Constitution."

595. KITTENS. Lith. rect., 11.8 x 16. One upright, the other lying with paw upraised to hit ball. Sig.: "Drawn by I. Herring. Printed at P. Maverick's lith. p. Published by M. Bancroft, 403 Broadway." AAS.

596. KNICKERBOCKER. 1831 sale, 100 for 75¢.

597. KIRWAN. Stip. rect., 4.12 x 3.12. Bust, body right, head front. Ins.: "M. A. Shee pinxt. P. Maverick sct. / The Revd. Walter Blake Kirwan, / Dean of Killala. / Published by Eastburn, Kirk & Co. 1814." NPL.

598. KOUTOUSOFF. St2216. Stip. vign., 4.6 x 4. Half length in uniform, face ¾ left. Ins.: "P. Maverick sc. / Prince Koutousoff." NYPL, GC, WMFA.

599. LADY. 1831 sale, 25 for 63¢, and "1 lith. stone lady" for $5.

600. LA FAYETTE. Port., stip. oval 1.2 x .14, in line wreath of lilies, roses, and foliage. Whole design 1.12 x 2.12. Above: "The Friend of Washington." Below: "r. at N. York Aug. 15th 1824. / P. Maverick sc." NPL.

601. a. LA FAYETTE. St.2217. Stip. port. (after A. Scheffer) in orn. circle, diam. 3.6. Eulogistic inscr. on circ. and sig.: "Engr. & Print. by P. Maverick, 342 Broadway." MMNY.
    b. Same in elaborate orn. embossed circle, diam. 8.5. Sig. (partly illegible): "Engd. by . . . sted. Embd. by P. Maverick. N. York." AAS.

602. LAPLAND. St.2245. Line rect., 5.7 x 7.10. Tepee, man on skis, rein

deer, sled, trees. Ins.: "Engraved by Peter Maverick, Newark, 1810. Scene in Lapland." NYPL, WMFA.

LARDNER, DIONYSIUS. *Popular Lectures on the Steam Engine*. N.Y.: Elam Bliss, 1828. Engravings are copies of those done by H. Adlard for the London editions, of which HU has the sixth. In the second American edition (Phila.: E. L. Carey & A. Hart, 1836), and later, Plate XII has been reëngraved with changes and is unsigned. HU. (Items 603 through 615.)

603. Plate I. Line, 5.6 x 3.4. Drawings of vessels and pipes. Sig.: "Engr. by P. Maverick."

604. Plate II. Line vign. and diagram, 5.14 x 3.4. Savery's steam engine. Sig.: "Engr. by P. Maverick."

605. Plate III. Line drawings, 6 x 3.6. Sectional views of steam boilers and pistons. Sig.: "Drawn by the Author. Engr. by P. Maverick."

606. Plate IV. Line drawings, 5.12 x 6.12. Sectional and detail views of Watt's single-acting steam engine. Sig. as for III.

607. Plate V. Line drawings, 6 x 6.12. Sectional views, Watt's double-acting steam engine. Sig.: "Drawn by J. Clement. Eng. by P. Maverick."

608. Plate VI. Line drawings, 5.12 x 3. Gears, cranks, cylinders. Sig.: "Drawn by the Author. Engr. by Peter Maverick."

609. Plate VII. Line drawings, 5.12 x 2.14. Cylinder assemblies, pistons, and valves. Sig. as for VI.

610. Plate VIII. Line drawings, 5.12 x 3.4. Cylinders, valves, and floats. No sig.

611. Plate IX. Line drawings, 5.12 x 3.4. Cylinder assemblies, etc. No sig.

612. Plate X. Line drawing, 5.12 x 3.8. Sectional view of engine. Sig.: "Engr. by P. Maverick."

613. Plate XI. Line drawings, 5.6 x 3.4. Various details of engine. Sig. as for X.

614. Plate XII. Line drawings and diagrams, 6 x 3.4. Sig.: "Drawn by the Author. Engr. by P. Maverick."

615. Plate XIII. Line drawing, 6.6 x 6.4. American high-pressure engine. Sig.: "Drawn by H. Brevoort. Engr. by P. Maverick."

616. a. LEE, RICHARD HENRY. St2218. Stip. rect., 4 x 3.5. Nearly half-length, face ¾ right. Ins.: "Richard Henry Lee. / Engr. by P. Maverick & J. B. Longacre from an original miniature." From vol. IX, *Biography of the Signers of the Declaration of Independence*. Phila.: R. W. Pomeroy, 1827. (See also William Paca.) NYPL.

b. Name in autograph. BMFA.

617. LUNA. 1831 sale, 12 for 36¢.

618. a. LUTHER. Line rect., 5.4 x 3.5. Luther, left, before Diet of Worms. German and English versions of title and his declaration. Sig.: "I. H. Ramberg del. P. Maverick sculpt." Front. *The Blessed Reformation* by Frederick Christian Schaeffer. N.Y.: Kirk and Mercein, 1817. AAS, NYPL.

b. F1042. With added "Printed by Saml. Maverick N.Y." In pamphlet, NYHS.

MACPHERSON, JAMES. *The Poems of Ossian*. Morristown, N.J.: Peter A. Johnson, 1813 (see also 1823 ed.); printed by Lewis Deare, New Brunswick, N.J. 2 vols., NYPL. Also, 1815, same pub. and print., sometimes lacking copperplates. (Items 619 through 621.)

619. Title page, vol. I. Line vign. 2.2 x 1.12 on design 4 x 2.5. Uncasqued warrior seated at water's edge. Publisher as given, with "Cuthullin sat by Tura's wall" and source. Sig.: "Singleton pinx. P. Maverick sc." NYHS.

620. a. Title page, vol. II. Line vign. 2 x 2.5 on design 3.14 x 2.5. Vign. shows charioteer. Publisher as given, quotation, "Within the Car . . ." etc., and sig.: "H. Singleton, pinx. P. Maverick sc. Newark."

b. With source for quotation added, not quite on the line, "Fingal. Vol. II, p. 16."

621. Front., vol. I. Line rect., 3.13 x 2.2. Old man blessing armed warrior. Ins.: "Crothar rose, stretched his aged hand, and / blessed the son of Fingal. / Croma. Vol. I., p. 267. / Painted by H. Singleton . . . Engraved by P. Maverick, Newark." NYHS.

MACPHERSON, JAMES. As above, except date 1823. (Items 622 through 624.)

622. Title page, vol. I. Vign. 2 x 2.8 on design 4 x 3.7. Bibliog. data as given. RU.

623. Title page, vol. II. F1053. Vign. 2 x 2.6 on design 4 x 2.8. This vign. exists in proof state before lettering.

624. Front., vol. II. (Found also in some 1813 and 1815 editions) Line rect., 3.14 x 2.2. Aged man with staff, woman, ghostly vision. Ins.: "Grey, at his mossy cave, is bent the aged / form of Clonmal. / Temora, Vol. 2, p. 307. / H. Singleton pinx. P. Maverick sculp." NYHS.

625. MAID AND MILK PAIL. 1831 sale, 350 for $3.

626. MARATHON. Line rect., 4 x 2.14. Battle on shore and ships. Ins.:

"Burney del. P. Maverick sct. / The Battle of Marathon." NYHS.

627. MATERNAL AFFECTION. 1831 sale, 100 for $2, and plate for $3.25. Not found. Trumbull had a painting with this title, Emily Maverick a lithograph.

628. McDonough, Com. 1831 sale, "30¢, 4 pictures at 10¢ each" meaning perhaps that besides the four prints, a plate sold for 30¢. A lithographic stone would have brought more, the price being usually ten cents a pound, or higher if it had a drawing from which more impressions could be taken before resurfacing. This might be Jarvis's portrait, in the N.Y. City Hall group, of Commander Thomas MacDonough.

629. MERIT AWARD FOR UNIDENTIFIED GIRL'S SCHOOL. Stip. vign., 2.14 x 3.12 on design 6.4 x 3.14 certifying excellence in English and French. Goddess of Wisdom, seated, places crown on kneeling girl. Sig.: "I. R. Smith del. Peter Maverick sc." NPL.

630. MERIT AWARD. Stip. vign., probably cut from certificate like preceding. Goddess points girl's way to shrine on hill. Sig.: "I. R. Smith del. Peter Maverick sc." NPL.

631. MILNOR. Line rect., 8.10 x 6.14. Port., face front, body right. Ins.: "Painted by Waldo & Jewett. 1819. Eng. by P. Maverick, Durand & Co. / Rev. James Milnor D. D. / Rector of St. George's Church, N. York." NYHS. Perhaps Durand's work.

MILTON. *The Poetical Works of John Milton*. Baltimore: F. Lucas Jr. and I. Cushing, 1813. AAS. (Items 632 through 634.)

632. Title page, vol. I. Vign. 1.10 x 2.4 on design 3.11 x 2.4. Vign. shows youth with lyre, hand raised. Bibliog. data as given, quotation from Gray, and sig.: "P. Maverick sc., Newark." NYHS.

633. Title page, vol. II. Like the preceding, except for volume number.

634. a. Front., vol. I. Line rect., 3.13 x 2.2. Kneeling angel in sun's rays. Ins.: "—— a voice, / From midst a golden cloud, thus mild was heard: / Servant of God well done—— Book VI. / J. Thurston del. P. Maverick sc. Newark. / Published by F. Lucas Jr. & I. Cushing."

  b. Without pub. line. NYPL.

MILTON. *Milton's Poetical Works*. N.Y.: R. & W. A. Bartow, 1822. Also Richmond, W. A. Bartow, on type title page. AAS, HU. (Item 635.)

635. a. Title page, vol. III. Line vign. 2.13 x 2.14 on design 4.10 x 2.14. The three wise men. Bibliog. data as given, quotation, "See how far upon the eastern road / The star-led wizards haste with

odours sweet. / Ode on the Nativity." and sig., "Drawn by R. Westall. Engr. by Peter Maverick." Title pages of vols. I and II by Durand. NYHS.

b. Vign. and inscription, publisher's name erased, used facing p. 66 of *The Hyacinth*. N.Y.: J. C. Riker. 1831. AAS.

636. MITCHELL, EDWARD. St2219. Line rect., 8.7 x 6.10. Half length, seated at right, chair and curtain in left background. Ins.: "Waldo & Jewett pinxt. Peter Maverick sculpt. / Revd. Edwd. Mitchell / Published by Peter Maverick New York 1820." 1831 sale, 600 for $8.25. Plate, 13 x 10, for $10. NPL.

637. MOHAWK RIVER. St2237. Line rect., 3.8 x 7. Ins.: "Ch. Loss del P. Maverick sc. Newark / A View of the Boats & manner of navigating on the Mohawk River. / Published by I. Riley July 1810."

MONTGOMERY, JAMES. *The Wanderer of Switzerland*. Morristown, N.J.: Peter A. Johnson, 1811. Printed by Lewis Deare, New Brunswick, N.J. Found also without engravings. RU. (Item 638.)

638. In vol. II. Line rect., 3.3 x 2.3. Man carrying unconscious youth. Above, "The Wanderer" and below, "Tisdale del. P. Maverick sc. / Then with desperation bold, / Albert's precious corpse I bore / On these shoulders weak and old, / Bow'd with misery before." Used in edition of Montgomery's work, Boston: Leonard C. Bowles, 1821. Used as vol. I front. of Johnson's edition of the complete works printed at Salem, N.Y. in 1817. AAS.

MONTOLIEU, MRS. *The Enchanted Plants; Fables in Verse*. N.Y.: David Longworth, 1803. NYPL. (Item 639.)

639. Front. Winged man, with scarf about body, kissing flowers. Light streaming through trees at right. Sig.: "W. Hamilton R. A. Delt. P. Maverick Sculpt."

640. MONT ROSA. St2248. Line rect., 4.15 x 6.14. Mountains, snow-capped, in distance. Trees and houses in foreground, two figures in path. Ins.: "Engraved by Peter Maverick, Newark, N.J. / Mont Rosa, / as seen from Macugnaga." GC, NYPL.

641. a. MOORE, RICHARD CHANNING. St2220. Line rect., 13.12 x 11.11. In robes, seated. Ins.: Painted by Wm. Dunlap. Engraved by Peter Maverick. / The Right Reverend Richard Channing Moore D. D. / Bishop of the Protestant Episcopal Church in the State of Virginia. / New York 1823 Published by Peter Maverick and William Dunlap." NYPL, PAFA. 1831 sale, 200 for $15.13. Plate, 19 x 15, for $54. See Dunlap's Diary, Jan. 12, 1820.

b. Publication line changed to "New York 1832 Published by Monson Bancroft 389 Broad Way."

c. Pub. line erased.

MOORE, THOMAS. *Works of* . . . 5 vols. N.Y.: W. B. Gilley, 1821. Albany ed., same pub. and date, without engravings. (Items 642 through 651.)

642. Title page, vol. I. Line vign., 2.6 x 2.8, on design 4.13 x 2.8. Man in foreground holding unconscious woman. Soldiers in background. Sig.: "Corbould del. Peter Maverick sc."

643. Title page, vol. II. Line vign., 2.4 x 2.14, on design 4.2 x 2.14. Warrior with wreath, woman at side, child on edge of shield. Sig.: "Silvester del. P. Maverick sc."

644. Title page, vol. III. Line vign., 2 x 2.8, on design 4.6 x 2.8. Woman with stick and jug, boy in background, in moonlight. Sig.: "Silvester del. P. Maverick sculp."

645. Title page, vol. IV. Line vign., 1.12 x 2.10, on design 4 x 2.10. Harp on river bank. Sig.: "P. Maverick sculp."

646. Title page, vol. V. Line vign., 2.2 x 3, on design 4.8 x 3. Helmeted woman, shield, lyre, ship. Shamrock on shield. Sig.: "Peter Maverick sc."

647. Front., vol. I. Line rect., 3.4 x 2.8, in orn. design 4.6 x 2.8. Man and girl beside stream. Ins.: "Lalla Rookh / Veiled Prophet / R. Corbould del. Peter Maverick sct."

648. Front., vol. I in some sets, elsewhere in others. St2221. Line oval, 3.2 x 2.8. Bust, face slightly left. Ins.: "Peter Maverick s. / Thomas Moore, Esqr."

649. Front., vol. II or elsewhere. Line rect., with added orn., 3.5 x 2.10. Cupid in boat, woman on shore. Ins.: "Love & Hope. / Stothard del. Peter Maverick sc."

650. Front., vol. IV. Line rect., 3.5 x 2.10, with orn. extra. Temple in background, Cupid joining hands of man and woman. Other figures. Ins.: "The Sale of Loves / J. Mitan del. Peter Maverick sc." NYHS, NPL.

651. a. LALLA ROOKH. Line rect., 3.10 x 2.13. Hinda awakening on ship's deck. Ins.: "Drawn by R. Westall R. A. Engraved by P. Maverick. / Lalla Rookh. / [three-line quot.] / I. Porter, Printer." In *Lalla Rookh*, Phila.: M. Thomas, 1817. BMFA, GC.

b. Same, printer's line erased, used as front. in the 1821 N.Y. Gilley ed. here being described.

    c. Used also in *Lalla Rookh*, Phila.: Thomas De Silver, 1821.

    d. Used also in *Lalla Rookh*, Phila.: James Crissy, 1821. AAS.

MOORE, THOMAS. Edition unidentified. (Item 652.)

652. a. Line rect., 3.4 x 4.8. Man on shore, r. hand resting on harp, l. hand upraised to sea and sun. Hill and trees in background. Spear. and shield with shamrock, lower r. Ins.: "Ino. R. Smith del. Peter Maverick sct." and two lines beginning, "The day star. . . ." "Published by Wm. Bayley." NYHS.

    b. Apparently same plate but with "Dear Harp of my Country" replacing the couplet, illustrates Moore's poem of that title in *The Ladies' Scrap Book*. Hartford: S. Andrus & Son, 1845.

653. a. MOUNT BLANC. St2246. Line rect., 5 x 6.15. Ins.: "Engraved by P. Maverick, Newark N.J. / Mount Blanc / from the Valley of Chamouny, on the Side ascended by Soussure." NYPL.

    b. With: "Published by P. Price, Jr. 66 Lombard St. Philada. for the *Atlantic Souvenir*, Dec. 1827."

654. MOUNT JOLIET. St2247. Line rect., 3.1 x 6. Ins.: "H. Inman del. / Peter Maverick sc. / Mount Joliet" NYPL, BMFA. Used in *The Ladies' Companion*.

MOUNT ROSA. St2248. See Mont Rosa.

655. MUSIC. 1831 sale, 4 plates for 40¢.

656. NAPOLEON. F1029. Stip. rect. in border 4.1 x 3.3. In uniform, body left, face front. Ins.: Vauthier pinx. Peter Maverick sculp. / Napoleon Buonaparte." Front. *The Life of Napoleon Buonaparte*. By an American. Elizabeth-town, N.J.: Samuel C. Allen Jr. and John T. Bryant, 1820. J. & E. Sanderson, printers.

657. a. NEW YORK. Line rect., 2.14 x 4.9. Ins.: W. G. Wall pinxt. Peter Maverick sct. / New York." This is the same view, with changes, as one published by Wall, eng. by I. Hill, in 1823 (Plate 92, vol. 3, of Stokes's *Iconography of Manhattan*). It was used in *The Atlantic Souvenir* (Phila.: H. C. Carey & I. Lea, 1827), in *Presente de las damas* (Phila.: 1829), and in *The Traveller's Guide* (N.Y.: 1833). NYPL, MCNY, AAS, GC.

    b. With traces of a border. NYPL.

    c. With added work, upper left corner. "New York" erased, one-line border at top and right, two at left and bottom. NYPL.

658. a. NIAGARA FALLS, St.2251. Line rect., 4.6 x 2.13. Ins.: "Peter Maverick sc. / Niagara, from below" NYPL, AAS.

    b. With added line, "N. York. Pub. by Wilder & Campbell, 1825" used in Theodore Dwight's *The Northern Traveller,* same pub. and date, and later editions 1826, 1828, 1830, 1831, 1834. HU.

659. NIAGARA FALLS. F1052. Ins.: "P. Maverick sc. Newark N.J. / General View of The Falls of Niagara." In H. G. Spafford's *Gazetteer of the State of New York,* Albany, 1813. q. v. NYPL. Niagara Falls items. 1831 sale.

4 "Falls Niagara" [prints?] for $3.20, 2 plates for $2.70.

OBOOKIAH. *Memoirs of Henry Obookiah.* Elizabeth-town, N.J.: Edson Hart, 1819. Printed by J. & E. Sanderson. NYPL, AAS. (Item 660.)

660. Front. St2223. Stip. vign., 3.2 x 2.13. Bust, face ¾ left. Ins.: "P. Maverick Durand & Co. sc. / Obookiah. / a native of Owhyhee." GC.

661. a. O'CONNELL, DANIEL. St2222. Stip. vign., 8.14 x 7.6. Standing, ¾ length, face ¾ left. Right hand extended, left hand holding scroll inscribed "Catholic Rent." Ins.: "Peter Maverick sc. / Daniel O'Connell / Hereditary Bondsmen know you not / Who would be free . . . / Themselves must strike the blow." NYPL.

1831 sale, 73 for $2.19. Plate, 11 x 9, for $6.

b. As above, but with sig. erased. BMFA.

662. ORIGINAL DRAWING. Pencil, 3.12 x 3. Hand holding block of wood. In family scrapbook, attested as P. Maverick's. NPL.

663. ORIGINAL DRAWING. Pencil, six vigns. of hands. Cert. in family scrapbook as done by Peter Maverick. NPL.

664. ORIGINAL WASH DRAWING. 10.8 x 7.8. Copy of Farnese Hercules. "Peter Maverick del." added in pencil on this in family scrapbook. NPL.

665. OWEN, ROBERT. Lith. vign., 4.8 x 5. Ins.: "Lambdin Px. / Robert Owen / Peter Maverick Lith. 149 Broadway, N.Y." AAS. The address is almost illegible in the AAS copy, the only copy found, and this print may be the work of young Peter after his father's death. The 1831 estate inventory has no mention of this item.

666. PACA, WILLIAM. St2225. Line rect., 4.1 x 3.6. Bust, face ¾ right. Ins.: "William Paca. / Engd by P. Maverick from a drawing by J. P. Longacre from Copley." In vol. 8, *Biography of the Signers of the Declaration of Independence.* Phila.: R. W. Pomeroy, 1827. (See also R. H. Lee portrait by Maverick.) NYPL, AAS.

667. PARKINSON, WILLIAM. St2226. Stip. oval, 2.12 x 2.3. Bust, profile right. Ins.: "Drawn by L. Lemet. Engd. By P. Maverick. / Wm. Parkinson / Minister of the Gospel." NYPL.

668. PETALESHAROO. St2227. Line vign., 5.8 x 3.11. Standing, full length. Arms wrapped in blanket. Feather headdress. Face ¾ left. Ins.: "Engrd. by Peter Maverick from a sketch in oil by Ino. Neagle. / Petalesharoo / Son of Latelesha, Knife Chief of the Pani-Loups: in full dress" In John D. Godman's *American Natural History.* Phila.: Stoddart & Atherton, 1831. (2nd ed.) Copyright 1826. Port. also in 3rd ed., 1846, not as front. 1831 sale, "Indian chief" 12 for 21¢. NYPL, AAS, HU, GC.

669. a. SAINT PETER. Lithograph vign., 3.12 x 3.8 (or more, copy trimmed). Head and neck, almost profile left. Open mouth, bald head. Sig.: "P. Maverick del." 1831 sale, 420 for $5.70. WMFA, NPL.

b. With "From West" on left shoulder. No sig.

670. PHANETTE DES GANTELMES. Line rect., 3.14 x 3.1. Woman at window with book, looking at sea. Ins.: "Robert W. Weir pinxt. Peter Maverick sculpt. / Phanette des Gantelmes." In *The Talisman* for 1830, facing p. 238. N.Y.: Elam Bliss, 1829. NYPL, GC.

671. PHEASANT, RUSSIAN. 1831 sale, one for 21¢. (This may be a household picture, not a product of the shop.)

672. PHILOSOPHY. 1831 sale, 14 plates, 7 x 5.8, for $5.25.

PONS, F. R. J. DE. *A Voyage to the Eastern Part of Terra Firma, or the Spanish Main* etc. N.Y.: I. Riley & Co., 1806. AAS. (Item 673.)

673. a. MAP OF CARACAS. Line rect., 16.3 x 25. Title in oval, upper right, and sig.: "Dressee par J. B. Poiron Ingenieur Geographe en 1805. / [scales, 3 lines] / Engd. by P. Maverick, New York." Below oval, "Water by R. Tanner."

b. With line: "Published by I. Riley & Co. April, 1807."

674. PRAYER BOOK, SPANISH. 1831 sale, 4 engravings for $3.50.

675. PSALMS. Not found. A front. eng. by P. Maverick after W. Hamilton, is reported in *The Whole Book of Psalms, in Metre,* 1820, second part of *Book of Common Prayer.* N.Y.: Henry I. Megarey, 1820. This may be the plate used in the Bible pub. by Williamses in Boston, q. v.

676. PUPPIES. Lith. rect., 11.6 x 15.4. Two puppies, lying down but alert for play. Sig.: "Drawn by I. Herring. Printed by P. Maverick." AAS. 1831 sale, for this or other item, "Spanish Puppies" 145 for $5.57 and "one stone & drawing, Puppies" for $5. Also "2 Puppies" for 38¢.

677. QUAILS. In 1831 sale, a lith stone, so labeled, sold for a shilling

(12½¢) a pound, the usual price in this sale for blank stone being 10¢. This may have been a companion piece to the pictures of Woodcocks and Snipes.

678. RABBITS. 1831 sale, 49 for $1.23.

679. REEVE, TAPPING. St2228. Line rect., 5.1 x 4.4. Seated, ¾ length, book on lap, glasses in hand. Ins.: "Geo. Catlin pinx. Peter Maverick sculp. / The Hon. Tapping Reeve. / Published by George Catlin from the only portrait of him in existence; New York, 1829" NYPL, NPL.

In the 1831 sale 193 copies were sold for $1.51, and the plate for $4.25, under the name of Reeve. A later owner of the plate erased the name and the last line and substituted the name of Benjamin Franklin, selling the print as a portrait of Franklin. (St2203)

680. REFLECTION. 1831 sale, 15 for 23¢.

681. ROCK FORT. St2254. Line vign. 3.12 x 6.10. Ins.: "H. Inman del. Peter Maverick sc. / Rock Fort, on the Illinois." NYPL, BMFA. Used in *The Ladies' Companion*.

ROGERS, SAMUEL. *The Pleasures of Memory and other Poems*, and *The Pains of Memory* by Robert Merry. N.Y.; R. & W. A. Bartow, and W. A. Bartow, Richmond, 1820. NYPL. (Item 682.)

682. Title page. Line, 4.3 x 3.7. No vign. No sig.

683. ROYALIST. 1831 sale, 12 for 48¢.

684. RUSH, BENJAMIN. 1831 sale, plate for 70¢.

685. a. SARATOGA. St2255. Line rect., 2.12 x 4.6. Ins.: "H. Inman del. Peter Maverick sc. / Saratoga / N. York, Pub. by Wilder & Campbell 1825." NYPL, AAS, WMFA, GC.

b. Without pub. line, found in *The Northern Traveller* etc., same date and pub. as in a, above. HU. See Niagara.

SCHULTZ, CHRISTIAN, JR. ESQ. *Travels on an Inland Voyage.* 2 vols., N.Y.: Isaac Riley, 1810. AGS, AAS. (Items 686 through 689.)

686. Map, apparently St2242. Line rect., 7.7 x 13. Ins.: "A Map / of the Hudson and Mohawk Rivers" etc., with sig.: "C. Schultz, Jr. del. P. Maverick s. Newark. NYPL.

687. Plan. Line rect., 7.11 x 7.11. Ins.: "A Plan / of the Ruins / of the Ancient Fortifications / at Marietta" etc., with sig.: "C. Schultz, Jun. del. P. Maverick sculp. Newark."

688. Map. St2252. Line rect., 8.9 x 15.13. Ins: "A Map / of the Ohio River and part / of the Mississippi" etc., and sig.: "C. Schultz Jr.

del. P. Maverick sc. Newark." NYPL. Not in AGS copy of book. AAS.

689. Map. Line rect., two sections, one 9.11 x 7.6, the other 9.11 x 5.8. Ins.: "A map / of the / Mississippi River" etc. and sig.: "C. Schultz jun. del. P. Maverick sct. Newark N.J." AAS.

690. SCOTCH BEAUTY. 1831 sale, plate for $4.25.

SCOTT, WALTER. *Poetical Works.* N.Y.: James Eastburn & Co., 1819. 1831 sale, "Waverly" 53 for 80¢. and 7 plates for $20.30. (Items 691 through 702.)

691. Title page, vol. I. Line vign., 1.2 x 2.8, on design 4.4 x 2.9. Harp on closed book, tree, distant castle and mountains. Sig.: "Westall del. P. Maverick & Durand sc." Two-line Latin quot.

692. Title page, vol. II. Line vign., 2.8 x 2.12, on design 4.9 x 2.12. Koran open on altar, cross broken down. Two-line quot. from Don Roderick. Sig.: "R. Westall R. A. Del. P. Maverick & Durand Sc."

693. Title page, vol. III. Line vign., 1.13 x 2.8, on design 4.5 x 2.9. Cross on altar, armor, mountains. Four-line quot. from Leyden. Sig.: "P. Maverick & Durand sc."

694. Title page, vol. IV. Line vign., 2.1 x 2.9, on design 4.3 x 2.9. Harp on tree, deer in background. No quot. Sig.: "P. Maverick & Durand, s." This found dated 1818.

695. Title page, vol. V. Line vign., 2.1 x 2.8, on design 4.3 x 2.8. Stream and castle in moonlight. No quot. Sig.: "P. Maverick & Durand sc."

696. Title page, vol. VI. Line vign., 2.4 x 2.4, on design 3.14 x 2.8. Man on rock, hands upraised, beside flag. Fleet and volcano in distance. No quot. Sig.: "R. Westall del. P. Maverick & Durand s."

697. Front., vol. I (?). Line vign., 3.9 x 2.10. Woman in black seated, man in armor standing before her, others about. Ins.: "R. Westall R. A. del. P. Maverick & Durand sc. / Lay of the Last Minstrel / [two-line quot. and ref. to Canto I.]"

698. Front., vol. II. Line vign., 4 x 2.10. Youth on cliff guarded by dog. Ins.: "Drawn by Richd. Westall, R. A. Engd. by P. Maverick & Durand / Helvellyn. / [two-line quot.]"

699. Front., vol. III. Line vign., 3.8 x 2.10. Black-clad man with staff facing seated knight. Ins.: "R. Westall R. A. del. P. Maverick & Durand sc. / Marmion. / [three-line quot. and ref. to Canto I; and pub. line, which appears sometimes on others of the frontispieces.]

700. Front., vol. IV. Line vign., 3.9 x 2.10. Seated woman in white and

old man in plaid, with harp. Ins.: "Drawn by Richd. Westall R. A. Engd. by P. Maverick & Durand / Lady of the Lake. / [two-line quot. and ref. to Canto II.]"

701. Front., vol. V. Line vign., 3.9 x 2.9. Scott, full length, seated on stone, dog at feet. Ins.: "H. Raeburn del. P. Maverick & Durand sc. / Walter Scott, Esq. / New York, Published by James Eastburn & Co. 1819."

702. Front., vol. VI. Line vign., 3.10 x 2.11. Knight kneeling beside fallen youth. Ins.: "Westall pinxt. P. Maverick & Durand sc. / Lord of the Isles. / [two-line quot., ref. to Canto V, and pub. line.]"

703. SHAKESPEARE, WILLIAM. Line rect., 4.8 x 2.11. *Tempest.* Caliban. Sig.: "Stothard del. P. Maverick sc." Very likely the front. for vol. 1, next item, made by Maverick before the Durand partnership began, but not found *in situ*. NPL.

SHAKESPEARE, WILLIAM. Dramatic Works, 10 vols., N.Y.: Henry Durell, 1817, except vols. VII and X are dated 1818. AAS. See also "Stereotype Edition" *infra*. (Items 704 through 713.)

704. Front., vol. I. Not found. See item 703.

705. Front., vol. II. *Merchant of Venice.* Line rect., 4.7 x 2.12. Lorenzo and Jessica in moonlight on bank of stream. Sig.: "Thurston del. P. Maverick sc."

706. Front., vol. III. *Comedy of Errors.* Line rect., 4.8 x 2.14. Antipholus of Syr., Dromio, Adriana, & Luciana. Sig.: "Singleton pinx. P. Maverick dir. [*sic*]" This and next probably early work of Emily or Maria Ann.

707. Front., vol. IV. *All's Well.* Line rect., 4.8 x 2.14. Countess and Helena. Sig.: "Thurston del. P. Maverick dir."

708. Front., vol. V. *King John.* Similar to the others, but not signed.

709. Front., vol. VI. *Henry VI, Part III.* Line rect., 4.10 x 2.14. Clifford & Rutland, swordsman standing over kneeling boy. Sig.: "Porter del. P. Maverick & Durand sc."

710. Front., vol. VII. *Richard III.* Line rect., 4.5 x 2.9. Richard and the ghosts. Sig.: "Thurston del. P. Maverick sc."

711. a. Front., vol. VIII. *Antony and Cleopatra.* Line rect., 4.4 x 2.9. Cleopatra and weeping attendants. Sig.: Uwins del. P. Maverick, Durand & Co. sc."

b. With added "P.M." after "Uwins del." to indicate Maverick as engraver.

712. Front., vol. IX. *Cymbeline.* Line rect., 4.9 x 2.14. Group, Belarius,

Guiderius, Averagus, and Imogen. Sig.: "Westall del. P. Maverick & Durand." NYHS.

713. Front., vol. X. *Hamlet*. Line rect., 4.5 x 2.14. Ophelia seated in willow tree. Sig.: "Smirke del. P. Maverick, Durand & Co. s."

SHAKESPEARE, WILLIAM. *Dramatic Works, Stereotype Edition*. AAS, NYPL. Same title, publisher, date, and pagination as the preceding, but the engravings are different, and greater in number. In volumes I–VIII the engravings are by Tanner, Vallance, Kearny & Co. The Maverick firm did the following. (Items 714 through 720.)

714. Vol. IX, p. 9. *Troilus & Cressida*. Line rect., 4.6 x 2.9. Man and woman kneeling, old man in background. Sig.: Thurston del. P. M. P. Maverick & Durand sc." This unusual sig. is another attempt to distinguish between the work of the two partners.

715. Vol. IX, p. 105. *Cymbeline*. Line rect., 4.5 x 2.11. Imogen kneeling beside Posthumus. Sig.: "Drawn by J. Thurston. Eng. by P. Maverick & Durand.

716. Vol. IX, p. 209. *King Lear*. Line rect., 4.5 x 2.10. Lear carrying Cordelia. Sig.: "Drawn by Thurston. Eng. by P. Maverick & Durand."

717. Vol. IX, p. 314. *Romeo & Juliet*. Line rect., 4.6 x 2.11. Romeo and Juliet seated on a bench. Sig.: "Drawn by Uwins. Eng. by P. Maverick & Durand."

718. Vol. X, p. 9. *Hamlet*. Line rect., 4.8 x 2.13. Hamlet and his father's ghost. Sig.: "Drawn by Loutherbourg. Eng. by P. Maverick & Durand."

719. Vol. X, p. 122. *Othello*. Line rect., 4.6 x 2.11. Othello and sleeping Desdemona. Sig.: "Drawn by Thurston. Eng. by P. Maverick & Durand."

720. Vol. X, p. 216. *Pericles*. Line rect., 4.7 x 2.11. Leonine and kneeling Marina. Sig.: "Drawn by R. K. Porter. Eng. by P. Maverick & Durand."

721. SHAKESPEARE, WILLIAM. Theater ticket. Stip. oval portrait, 2.2 x 1.9, in orn. symbolical design 4 x 2.12. Bust, face slightly left. Above: "Theatre." Below: "1st Box. / P. Maverick sc."

1831 sale, 5 plates Shakespeare for $10 and one plate Shakespeare for $30.

[SHARPE, RICHARD SCRAFTON.] *Theodore, or the Gamester's Progress*. A Poetic Tale. London: 1799, 1802 NYPL. American edition not found, except AAS without t. p. (Item 722.)

722. Front. used for Amer. ed. Line rect., 4.3 x 2.10. Two old men holding masks, young man who has just dropped dice box. Sig.:
"Thurston Del. P. Maverick Sculpt. 68 Beekman St." and two-
line quotation: "Curse not thy father . . ." etc. Work of Maverick's earliest independent period. NYHS, quot. trimmed.

723. SHEPHERD [E.?]. *American Geographical Copies.* No given name on
title page. N.Y.: Pub. for the author, 1801. Apparently a book
about 7 x 8, with engraved title page and 20 unnumbered plates,
each containing a geographic view or a map in the upper half, and
in the lower a title and three lines of information in model penmanship. The only copy I have been able to find, that in the George A.
Plimpton collection at Columbia University, contains the complete
title page but only the script part of the other pages. Plates 4, 5,
and 6 are signed "P. Maverick Sculpt." The sigs. for the others
may have been cut off. Probably all are Peter's work, and they are
very early in his career. There is no letterpress.

[SIMON, MRS. BARBARA ANNE]. *A View of the Human Heart,* etc. By
the author of *The Hope of Israel.* Other bibliog. data of American edition
not available. Each print 8 x 5, design in line vign, about 5 x 3, exclusive
of legends. Maverick probably did the unsigned plates also. (Items 724
through 732.)

724. Plate I. The heart of man before regeneration. The heart encloses
pictures of peacock, snake, pig, etc., each labeled with its significa-
tion. Sig.: "Sketched by Mrs. Simon. Drawn by J. R. Smith. Engrd.
by Peter Maverick."

725. Plate 2. The heart just impressed by a view of death. Animals fleeing
away. Sig. only: "Peter Maverick sc."

726. Plate 3. The heart which has tasted the word of God. A dove within
the heart. Sig. as in Plate 1.

727. Plate 4. The heart which has been regenerated. No sig.

728. Plate 5. The heart in which the laws of God are engraven. No sig.

729. Plate 6. The heart which resists temptation. No sig.

730. Plate 7. The heart with the form of religion but denying its power.
Sig. as in Plate 1.

731. Plate 8. The heart which has relapsed into sin. Sig. as in Plate 1.

732. Plate 9. The heart with its passions subdued by philosophy. Sig. as
in Plate 1.

The same, English edition. London: Erasmus H. Simon et al., 1832.
Same Maverick plates, in order 1, 2, 3, 7, 8, 9, 4, 5, 6. NPL.

SMOLLETT, TOBIAS. *The History of England*. Albany: B. D. Packard, 1816. (Items 733 and 734.)

733. a. Queen Anne, St2181., front., vol. I. Line, orn. oval, 7.13 x 4.8. Bust, face front. Ins.: "Queen Anne / P. Maverick sculp. (Newark)" and pub. as given. NYPL, WMFA.

   b. Pub. line: "Published by Edward Parker, Philada. 1822."

   c. No. pub. line.

734. George I. St2204. Vol. I, facing p. 60. Line, orn. oval, 7.1 x 3.10. Bust, face front. Title and pub. as for Queen Anne, with sig.: "P. Maverick sculp. Newark N.J." WMFA.

735. SNIPES. A companion piece to the lithograph of Woodcocks, drawn by J. Herring and lithographed by Peter Maverick. No copy available. See Woodcocks.

736. SOLAR SYSTEM. 1831 sale, 12 for 96¢. Plate for $2.50.

SPAFFORD, HORATIO GATES. *A Gazetteer of the State of New York*. Albany: H. C. Southwick, 1813. (Item 737.)

737. Map. Line rect., 7.13 x 9.8. State of New York. Sig.: "Drawn by Mrs. B. C. Spafford. Engrd. by P. Maverick, Newark N.J." Same, in border line 8.12 x 9.9, also noted. AGS, RU, AAS, HU. See also Lake George and Niagara, general view.

SPAFFORD, HORATIO GATES. *Some Cursory Observations on . . . Wheel Carriages*. Albany: E. E. Hosford, 1815. (Item 738.)

738. Line vign., 6.13 x 4.3. Vertical section of axle and body, and perspective view of wheel and frame. Sig.: "P. Maverick." AAS. Also in Spafford's *American Magazine*, 1815. Found also without sig.

STERNE, LAWRENCE. *Works*, 6 vols. N.Y.: William Durell & Co., 1813. HU (copy imperfect; supplemented by loose prints). (Items 739 through 742.)

739. Sermon Illus. Line rect., 4.1 x 2.10. Turbaned and bearded man giving alms. Man in background with trumpet. Ins.: "T. Stothard del. P. Maverick sc. / Sermon XVII. / Pub. by W. Durell & Co."

740. Letter Illus. Line rect., 4.1 x 2.10. Periwigged man, two women, carriage outside. Ins.: "T. Stothard delt. P. Maverick sc. / Letter CXVIII, Page 105. / Pub. by W. Durell & Co."

741. TRISTRAM SHANDY. Line rect., 4.2 x 2.10. Man standing before chair, one foot on stool, arm outstretched holding walking-stick. Another man beside him, and a third behind door. Ins.: "P. Maverick sct. / Tristram Shandy. Ch. 53. / Published by W. Durell & Co."

742. SENTIMENTAL JOURNEY. Line rect., 4.1 x 2.10. Man and woman,

small dog. Ins.: "P. Maverick s. / Sentimental Journey, Maria. / Pub. by W. Durell & Co."

743. STEWART [*sic*], GILBERT. 1831 sale, 6 plates for $1.85.

SWIFT, JONATHAN. *Works*, 24 vols. N.Y.: William Durell & Co., 1812–1813. NYPL, AAS. (Items 744 through 749.)

744. . . . Front., vol. II. Line rect., 3.7 x 2.8. Men dueling, one run through. Sig. "Engrd. by P. Maverick, from a sketch by W. S. Leney," with a two-line prose quot. beginning: "Ah, poor Creed . . ."

745. Front., vol. IX. Line circ. in orn. design 4.7 x 2.14. Gulliver among Lilliputians. Sig.: "Engraved by P. Maverick, Newark."

746. Front., vol. XII. Line circ., diam. 2.6, in rect. 4.10 x 2.13. Sick scholar in bed, another in academic gown beside him. Two-line quot. from Cassius & Peter beginning; "And yet I dare . . ." Sig.: "P. Maverick sct. Newark." GC.

747. Front., vol. XX. St2182. Bishop Atterbury. Stip. oval, 3.4 x 2.8. Bust in robes, face half left. Sig.: "Peter Maverick sc. Newark." NYPL, GC. 1831 sale, plate for 75¢.

748. Front., vol. XXI. Earl of Oxford. St2224. Line oval, 3.3 x 2.9. Bust, slightly right. Sig.: "P. Maverick sc. Newark, N.J." NYPL, GC.

749. . . . Front., vol. ? Line rect., 3.14 x 2.11. Scene from Gulliver. Giant woman and midget warrior defying king before battlemented gate. Sig.: "M. Rooker del. P. Maverick sc." Not seen *in situ*. GC.

750. TASSO. Publication unidentified. Line rect., 5.2 x 3.6. Woman in white on knees before tree, man in armor with raised sword. Children in background. Ins.: "Vol. 2. / Stothard del. P. Maverick sc. Newark N.J. / Published by E. Little & Co. 1810."

751. TELESCOPE. Line rect., 8.3 x 9.9. Perspective of instrument, ladders, revolving platform. Ins.: "P. Maverick sc. Newark. / View of Herschell's Forty-foot Reflecting Telescope." In vol. I, facing p. 287, of *The Emporium of Arts and Sciences*, New Series, conducted by Thomas Cooper. June 1813–April 1814. NYPL.

752. TELL, WILLIAM. Publication unidentified. Line rect., 3.15 x 3. Scene in mountains, small child with apple on head, Tell and horseman in foreground. Ins.: "Vol. 18. / Engd. by P. Maverick / William compelled to shoot at / an apple on the Head of his Son."

THOMSON, JAMES. *The Seasons; with the Castle of Indolence*. Georgetown: Richards and Mallory, 1814. Wm. Fry, printer. (Engraved t.p. by G. Fairman gives also P. H. Nicklin of Phila. as a publisher, and spells the author "Thompson." Vol. contains life by Patrick Murdoch and essay on poem by J. Aiken.) CU. (Item 753.)

753. Front. Line rect., 3.10 x 2.6. Man with sickle and sheaf approaching stile. Church in distance. Two-line quot. beginning, "Breathe your still song . . ." Sig.: "Drawn by Hamilton R. A. Engraved by P. Maverick, Newark."

THOMPSON, JAMES. *The Seasons*. N.Y.: R. & W. A. Bartow, 1819. (1820 on printed title page.) (Engravings probably Durand's work.) AAS. (Items 754 through 759.)

754. Title page. Line, 3.3 x 2.6. Data as given, with street address of pub.

755. a. Autumn. Line rect., 3.7 x 2.8. Woman seated before cottage. Three-line quotation: "The news . . ." etc. No sig. GC.
     b. Two-line quot.: "While pierced . . . Lavinia's fate." In autograph album, n. p., n. d., *c.*1832. RU.

756. Winter. Line rect., 3.8 x 2.8. Horse falling, rider, wolf, in snow. Sig.: "P. Maverick, Durand & Co. sc." Two-line quotation: "They fasten . . ." etc. GC Used also in album noted above.

757. Spring. Line rect., 3.8 x 2.9. Youth reclining under tree. Sig.: "P. Maverick, Durand & Co." One-line quotation: "Or lie reclin'd . . ."etc. Used also in album noted above.

758. Summer. Line rect., 3.6 x 2.8. Draped girl kneeling, book in hand. No sig. Two-line quotation: "But when . . ." etc.

759. Autumn. Line rect., 3.8 x 2.9. Woman with sheaf on head, seated child. Field workers in background. Two-line quot. beginning: "The gleaners . . ." Sig.: P. Maverick, Durand & Co. sc." Used as front. in some copies, with no other engravings. AAS.

760. "THYSELF." Line vign., 4.14 x 4. Man and woman beside varied colonnade, man pointing to capital lying on ground. Dome and swans in background. Ins.: "A. Smith delt. P. Maverick sculpt. / It is Thyself." NYHS. Front. for Isaac D'Israeli, *Romances*, N.Y.: D. Longworth, 1803. NYPL.

761. a. TICONDEROGA. St2256. Line rect., 2.15 x 4.9. View westward across Lake Champlain to fort ruins. Ins.: "W. G. Wall pinxt. Peter Maverick sct. / Ticonderoga." In *The Atlantic Souvenir* (Phila.: Carey, Lea & Carey, 1828) and also *Presente a las damas* (Phila., 1829). NYPL.
     b. Without title.

TRUMBULL, JOHN (the poet). *The Poetical Works of John Trumbull, LL.D.* Hartford, Conn.: Samuel G. Goodrich, 1820. AAS. (Item 762.)

762. a. Front. St2229, Line rect., 4 x 3.3. Half-length, face almost front. Ins.: "Painted by John Trumbull, [i.e., the artist] 1793. Eng. by P. Maverick, Durand & Co.; John Trumbull Esq. / Printed by D. Russell. NYPL, GC.

  b. Without printer's line.

763. VASE. Line vign., 3 x 4.6. Vase, flowers, lyre, pipes, mask, etc. Sig.: "F. Herbert del. / Peter Maverick sc." Facing p. 5 in *The Talisman* for 1828. N.Y.: Elam Bliss, 1827. GC.

764. a. VIRGIL. Publication not found. Line vign., 2.2 x 2.4, on title page design 3.12 x 2.4. Infant Hercules strangling serpents. Ins.: "Virgil's Aeneis. / Translated / by / John Dryden. / [vign.] / T. Uwins del. P. Maverick sc. / Newark N.J. / The serpents strangled with his infant hands. / Aeneis Book VIII. / Philadelphia. / Published by John Conrad." WMFA.

  b. Without pub. line, NYHS.

765. VIRGIN MARY & CHILD. 1831 sale, one plate for $3.75 and also one plate 10 x 7.8, Virgin Mary, for $3.25.

766. a. VIRGINIA. Plan of the University of Virginia. Line rect. 16.6 x 18.10. Jefferson's designs for the buildings and grounds in 1822. See pages 62–64 of this volume for further details. Sig.: "Peter Maverick sct. N.Y." U. Va. Art Library. Reprod. in 1923 supp. to Fiske Kimball's *Thomas Jefferson, Architect*. Boston: Riverside Press, 1916.

  b. The same with changes, winter of 1824–1825. Dormitories now numbered, in addition to the two-story pavilions which were numbered in 1822 edition. Sig.: "John Neilson delt. Peter Maverick sct. N.Y." Reprod., without sigs., in *Reise Sr. Hoheit des Herzogs Bernhard zu Sachsen-Weimar-Eisenach durch Nord-Amerika in dem Jahren 1825 und 1826*. Herausgegeben von Heinrich Luden. Weimar, Wilhelm Hoffmann, 1828. Engraving, UV. Book, UV, NYPL. See also *Proceedings*, Amer. Philos. Soc., vol. 90, No. 2 (1946) pp. 81–90.

767. a. WASHINGTON. St2232. Stip. oval port., 3.13 x 3.3, in elaborate script design 16.8 x 20.7. Port. in lower center, half-length in uniform, face ¼ left. Various national and Masonic emblems, 28 lines of verse, etc. Sig.: "Designed / Written / and Published / by / Benjamin O. Tyler / Professor of Penmanship. / New York. / 1815" and "Engraved by P. Maverick, Newark, N. Jersey." Also:

"Penmanship . . . Taught . . . by Benjn. Owen. Tyler—" etc.
NYPL.

b. "Benjn." changed to "Benjamin."

c. Date changed to 1817, and Washington's name in script.

1831 sale, plate, "portrait Washington" $14, may be this item or the
following.

768. WASHINGTON. St2230. Line oval in oak leaf border, 1.11 x 1.7. Sig.:
"P. Maverick" NYPL.

769. WASHINGTON. St2231. Two festooned medallions, overall 3.2 x 5.4.
On one flag: "shington" and sig: "Peter Maverick Sc."

770. WASHINGTON. Line rect., 10.1 x 7.12. Ins. "from G. Stuart's painting. / George Washington / New York. Published by P. Maverick,
Durand & Co." NPL.

771. LADY WASHINGTON. 1831 sale, 214 for $6.92.

772. WATTS. 1831 sale, plate 6.8 x 5.8 for $2.

WHITMAN, BENJAMIN JR. *Heroes of the North*. Boston: Barber Badger,
1816. AAS, NYPL, BA. (Items 773 and 774.)

773. . . . Battle of Erie. Line rect., 4.3 x 8. Sailing ships in conflict. Ins.:
"Printed by Saml. Maverick N.Y. Engraved by P. Maverick,
Newark, N.J. / Battle of Erie." Used also in *The Naval Temple*,
same date and pub. AAS.

774. a. Battle of Erie, II. Line rect. 4.2 x 8. Fifteen ships in full sale. Ins.:
"P. Maverick sc. Newark N.J. / Printed by Saml. Maverick New-
York. / Battle of Erie, 2d View." Also used in *The Naval Temple*.
AAS.

b. Without printer's line.

WIRT, WILLIAM. *The Letters of the British Spy*. Balt.: Fielding Lucas Jr.,
Seventh ed. [1818–1819?] Editions of 1813 and 1817 have title page
signed by Edwin and front. view of Richmond unsigned. Eighth ed., after
1820, has engravings as here described. Maverick here was reproducing
a damaged or lost plate, and he made a plate which shows his clean technique at its best, as compared with the competent and attractive, but different, technique of Edwin or the unnamed engraver. The view of Richmond which A. W. Weddel reproduces in *Richmond, Virginia, in Old
Prints* (Richmond: Johnson Pub. Co., 1932), and which he says was "drawn
by Peter Maverick," is not Maverick's but the earlier anonymous view. As
to the date of Maverick's plate for the 7th ed., the sig. seems to point to a
date no later than September or October of 1817, when the Durand partnership began; of course Durand may have cut this plate. Editions: 1813, BA;

NYPL; 1817, NYPL; 1818–1819 (?) after 1820, AAS, NYPL. (Items 775 and 776.)

775. Title page. St2233. Stip. vign., 2.1 x 1.13, on line design 3.13 x 2.12. Vign. is the profile, left, of William Wirt, done in Richmond in 1808 by St. Mémin. (Orig. circ. port. illus. in Fillmore Norfleet's *St. Mémin in Virginia*, Richmond: Dietz Press, 1942.) Also St. M. 581.

776. Front. St2253. Line rect., 2.6 x 4.5. (Earlier plate 2.4 x 4.3) Richmond from across the James River. Ins.: "P. Maverick sc. / Richmond."

777. WISDOM. Line rect., 3.12 x 2.15. Woman with helmet and shield, lamb and two cherubs. Ins.: "Corbould del. P. Maverick sct. Wisdom. [Two-line quot., Prov. 3:17.] New York, Pub. Augt. 1, 1803 by Burnton & Darling." NYHS.

778. WOMAN. Lith. vign., 7.6 x 5.14 (trimmed). Almost profile right, eyes downcast, shoulders bare. In family scrapbook, with sig. "P. M." added. NPL.

779. WOODCOCKS. Colored lith., 12.8 x 16.6. Two woodcocks at pool, hill and trees in background. Ins.: "Drawn by J. Herring. Printed by P. Maverick. / Woodcocks / Published by M. Bancroft, 403 Broadway." NYHS.

WOODWORTH, SAMUEL. *Melodies, Songs and Ballads*. N.Y.: James M. Campbell, 1826. HU, NYHS. (Items 780 and 781.)

780. Title page. Line vign., 2 x 2.12, on design 4.8 x 2.12. Family picknicking under willow on bank of stream. Sig.: "Drawn by I. R. Smith. Engr. by Peter Maverick."

781. Front. The Bucket. Line rect., 3.10 x 2.11. House, well, and sweep in foreground; man drinking from bucket. Sig.: "Drawn by I. R. Smith. Engraved by Peter Maverick." Two-line quot. beginning: "How sweet from its green mossy brim . . ." 1831 sale, 362 for $4.52. Plate for $4.50.

782. YAMODYNE. 1831 sale, plate 9.8 x 7.8 for $1.75. This might be plate Durand made for J. W. Eastburn's *Yamoyden*, N.Y.: Eastman, 1820.

783. YOUNG ARTISTS. 1831 sale, 300 for $3.75.

YOUNG, EDWARD. *Night Thoughts* etc. N.Y.: R. & W. A. Bartow, 1821. Sigs. suggest use of plates in earlier eds. (Items 784 through 786.)

784. Title page. Script lettering, no vign. Sig.: "P. M. sc."

785. Front. Line rect., 3.3 x 2.6. Man kneeling beside bed, ray of light

from above. Ref. to "The Complaint," Night VIII. Three-line quot. Sig.: "Peter Maverick sc." GC.

786. a. Illus. Line rect., 3.13 x 2.9. Woman in white walking in garden. Sig.: "Drawn by T. Uwins. P. Maverick, Durand & Co. sc." Quot. and ref. to Night I. GC.

b. As above, but firm name is "P. Maverick & Durand." NYHS.

c. Proof of partly completed plate, Durand Collection, NYHS.

787. ZAIDE. 1831 sale, 44 for $1.37.

Unidentified items—titles and uses not known. (Items 788 through 793.)

788. Academic design. Line rect., 3.4 x 1.14. Female figure with scroll, pointing to hilltop shrine surmounted by angelic figure. Three youths in academic robes. Ins. in Greek characters: "I 'na kleos esthlon 'agoito" at top, and below "Philokleos." Sig.: "Peter Maverick s." NPL.

789. Stabbing. Line rect., 4.4 x 2.13. Man stabbing woman in forest, tri-cornered hat on ground, another man running to rescue. Three copies, NYHS, one proof before letters, one proof of partially engraved plate, and one with ins.: "Vol. VIII P. Maverick sc."

790. Allegorical design. Line rect., 7.2 x 4.13. Above, dove and cherubs. Background, cherubs on ark. Foreground, man with tables of commandments, one with harp and crown, one with scroll, and others. On scroll, "Threni Aleph." Below, "Spiritu Sancto . . ." etc. from II Peter 1:21. No sig., but in early scrapbook of Maverick prints, NYPL.

791. Homer or other Classic? Line vign., 2 x 2.15, trimmed. Man with helmet and armor, Diana at left, Cupid perching on his shield at right holding laurel wreath. Sig.: "Silvester del. P. Maverick sc." NYPL.

792. Domestic Scene. Line rect., 3.8 x 5.10. Young man, older man seated, two standing women, one with rosary. Desk at left, books and window rear, globe right. No lettering except "p. 52." Copy trimmed. NYPL.

793. Domestic Scene. Line rect. Seated woman with book, man, disheveled, pulling another man away. Other figures in background. Costumes, etc., of 18th century English upper classes. Sig.: "M. Rooker del. P. Maverick sc."

794. CALEDONIAN BALL TICKET. Line vign., 2.15 x 3.11, with "Ladies' ticket" etc. in circle surrounded by figures. Sig.: "A. del. P. Maverick sc."

CERTIFICATES AND EMBLEMATIC DESIGNS

COLUMBIA COLLEGE. (Items 901 through 905.)

901. Peitho-Logian Society. Cert., 12.3 x 13.14. Latin script and ornate lettering, no vign. Sig.: "Written & Engraved by P. Maverick." NYHS, CU.

902. Philolexian Society, Cert., Latin script and ornate lettering. At top, line vign. 3.8 x 5.3, man kneeling before altar, Minerva in clouds, temple on distant hill. Sig.: "Engraved by P. Maverick, Newark, N.J. / Printed by Saml. Maverick, New York." Sig. on vign: "Archibald Robertson del. Peter Maverick Sculp." CU.

903. Ticket. F1038. Line vign., 3.10 x 2.9. Woman seated on clouds places wreath on boy's head. Latin motto and "Alma Mater" above. Below: "Archbd Robertson del. P. Maverick Sct. Newark. / Columbia College / Commencement, 1813." CU, NYHS.

904. Ticket. F1039. Line vign., 4.2 x 2.12. Minerva crowning gowned youth with laurel. Latin motto and "Peter Maverick sc. / Columbia College, / Commencement. / 1822." NYPL.

905. Ticket. St2238. Line vign., 2.9 x 4.5. Gowned student and woman with harp. Greek motto and "Drawn by I. R. Smith. Engrd by Peter Maverick. / Columbia College Commencement, 1826." NYPL, CU.

906. DUMFRIES AND GALLOWAY SOCIETY. Line rect., 13.5 x 11.9, overall, 15.11 x 11.9. Above, flying eagle. Below, woman and children. Town, bridge, ruins in background. Ins.: "Engraved by Peter Maverick from a Painting by J. James. / This is to certify that _____ was duly / admitted . . ." etc.

907. FIREMEN. St2257. Line rect., 13.8 x 9.15. Circular picture of Triton chaining Vulcan, with Cerberus in background. Below, a fire-fighting scene. Sig.: "Engraved by Peter Maverick, from a Drawing by Archibald Robertson. / March, 1807." MCNY, NYPL, NYHS.

908. HIGH SCHOOL. Line vign., 1.14 x 3.12. View of building. Ins.: "N.Y. High School. / Crosby Street, between Grand & Broom. / I. R. Smith del. Peter Maverick sc." NYPL.

909. JUVENILE DELINQUENTS. Line circ., diam 2.6. Entrance, with man welcoming ragged boy. Ins., on border, "Society for the Reformation of Juvenile Delinquents." Below: "Inman del. Peter Maverick sc." MCNY.

910. MANUMISSION OF SLAVES, NEW YORK SOCIETY FOR PROMOTING THE. Membership cert., line script, 11.12 x 13.9. Sig.: "Written & Engraved by Peter Maverick."

911. MASONIC CERTIFICATE. George Cupples, M.D., in address in October, 1870, before the Alamo Literary Society of San Antonio, Texas, on the life of Samuel A. Maverick said, "I have in my possession a diploma or certificate issued to a master Mason . . . in English, Spanish, and French . . . handsomely engraved on parchment, by Peter Maverick, and published by Bro. Samuel Maverick of New York." This may be the line and stipple certificate, 11.12 x 15.10 within borders, used in 1823 by Adelphia Lodge of New York City. Masonic symbols, pillars at side, altar lower center, figures above. In the three languages the certificate of membership and "Published by Brother Samuel Maverick, New York," and in English only "Drawn by Br. Jno. R. Smith, N.Y. Engraved by Peter Maverick." Library, Grand Lodge of New York.

912. MONTREAL, NATURAL HISTORY SOCIETY OF. Line membership certificate, plate size 9.6 x 12.12. Top, vign. of owl with small tree, and motto "Tandem Fit Surculus Arbor." Sig.: "Peter Maverick sc. N. York." J. J. Audubon's copy now owned by Amer. Mus. of Nat. Hist., N.Y.

913. a. NEW YORK TYPOGRAPHICAL SOCIETY. Line 5.4 x 8.12, with oval port. of Franklin, .12 x .9. Printing press, Liberty with scepter and crown at her feet Eagle with ribbon. Sig.: "P. Maverick, Durand & Co." NYPL.

b. With legend on ribbon: "The Art Preservative of all Arts."

914. RUTGERS COLLEGE. Diploma, line lettering, no vign., 13.14 x 15.10. Sig.: "Peter Maverick script. et sculpt. N. York, 1829." Used by Rutgers, 1829–1932. Plate with Am. Bank Note Co. RU.

915. HEBREW BENEVOLENT SOCIETY OF CHARLESTON, SOUTH CAROLINA. Cert. reported but no copy found.

TRADE CARDS AND BUSINESS FORMS

1001. ADDY, JNO., Hatter, 215 Greenwich Street, New York. Line vign., 2.9 x 3.1. Justice, eagle, ships in background, name and hat on scroll. Sig.: "Peter Maverick sc." NYHS.

1002. ASH. F1061. Line vign., 2.8 x 3.12. Carter unloading chairs. Thomas Ash, chair manufacturer, 33 John St., N.Y. Sig.: "P. Maverick &

Durand sc." About 1818. NYPL, WMFA, MMNY. Reprod. in G. F. Dow, "Trade Cards," *Old Time New England* 27:11. July, 1936.

1003. a. BLEEKER, FREDK. D., 164 Broadway, New York. Line circ. watch paper, diam. 1.15. Sig. "P. Maverick Sct." MCNY.

b. With address blanked out, and "24 Maiden Lane" added in pen.

1004. BOUREAU. Stip. rect., 3.2 x 4.11. Name in oval surrounded by three cupids, silverware, jewelry. Boureau & Co., jewellery and hardware, 169 Pearl St., N.Y. Sig.: "P. Maverick Sculpt. 1801."

1005. Brewster. Line vign., 4 x 2.7. Seated woman with spear, eagle, shield, boxes, ship in background. J. & L. Brewster, hatmakers, 102 Broadway, N.Y. Sig.: "P. M. s. N.Y." Also in *U.S. Directory*, Phila., Joshua Shaw, 1822. MMNY.

1006. BREWSTER. Line vign., 4.5 x 2.8. View similar to preceding on square pillar. J. Brewster, 102 Broadway. Sig.: "Engraved by P. Maverick." NYHS.

1007. CHEAVENS. Watch paper, line circ., diam. 1.14. Neptune and lady in shell barge. Above, Time holds out watch. Ins.: "Henry Cheavens / Watch Maker / No. 121 Cherry Street, / New York." No sig., but in a collection of Peter Maverick material given to NYHS, and the style is Maverick's.

1008. CLARK. Line vign., 4.2 x 4.8. Ins. on square pedestal, with woman at left leaning against it, holding sword and scales. Horn of plenty, boxes, top hats, rose bush, and badger. In background, ship in full sail. Theodore Clark, hatmaker, Chatham & Pearl Streets, N.Y. Sig.: "P. Maverick Durand & Co. Sc." About 1819–1820. NYHS. Landauer.

1009. CLARK & RAYMOND, Hatters, 77 Maiden Lane, N.Y.C. Line rect., 3.15 x 4.11. View of Maiden Lane. Sig.: "I. R. Smith del. Peter Maverick sc." NYPL.

1010. DYER & EDDY's. 49 Marlboro St., Boston. Line rect., 3 x 4.10. Jewelry store upper center, women at sides, large eye above. Sig.: "P. Maverick sculpt. New York." WMFA.

1011. FRENCH REPUBLIC. F1040. Line vign., 3.12 x 6.8. Seated woman, wreath at left, liberty cap on pole at right. Ins.: "République Francaise. / La Loi. / Liberté, Egalité / Drawn & Engraved by Peter Maverick / Commissariat de New York, et New Jersey." NYPL.

1012. HAMILTON & BRUSH, hatmakers, New Haven, Conn., and Charleston, S.C. Line vign., 3.14 x 4. On stone foundation, hat with Liberty and Justice on either side. Ocean and ships in background. Sig.: "P. Maverick sc." NYHS.

1013. HARRAL, GEORGE, Savannah, Ga. Druggist's trade card, line rect., 3.2 x 4.10. Boy seated on ground with mortar, pestle, retort, etc. Sig.: "P. Maverick Sct. N. York."

1014. HINTON, NATHANIEL B., hat manufacturer, 333 Broadway, N.Y. Trade card, line vign., 5.2 x 4.8. Flowers, beehive, boy chasing butterfly. Sig.: "Peter Maverick sc." MCNY.

1015. INGLESBY & STOKES, merchant tailors, 30 Wall Street, N.Y. Trade card, sig.: "P. Maverick, 1801." AAS.

1016. IVES & WHITE, trade card. Spread eagle surmounting oval which bears name. Ribbon in beak, thirteen stars above. I. Ives and O. White, "American Manufactures," 83 Chatham and 144 Water Streets, N.Y. Sig.: "P. Maverick sct." AAS.

1017. JOHNSON. Line vign., 4.2 x 2.7. Ins. on face of pedestal, Columbia above, eagle, shield, shipping. John Johnson & Sons, hat makers, Main St., Norfolk, Va. Sig.: "P. Maverick & Durand, N. York." About 1817– 1818.

1018. Maverick. F1033. Line vign., 2.10 x 4.12. Andrew Maverick, copper-plate printer and agent for Peter Maverick, 21 Liberty St., N.Y. Sig.: "P. M. sc." 1816–1820. NYPL.

1019. MAVERICK. Line vign., 2.10 x 4.12. Three children holding prints. Andrew Maverick, as above, except 27 Liberty St. On front cover of Longworth's N.Y. directory, 1815. AAS, NYHS. Also trade card, NYHS.

1020. MAVERICK. Line vign., oval wreath, 1.10 x 2.8, containing ins. Andrew Maverick, as above, 34 Liberty St., N.Y. Sig.: "P. Maverick sc." 1808–1810. AAS (in bookplate collection).

1021. MAVERICK. Line vign., 2.4 x 4.4. Woman in boat, anchor at side. Motto: "J'espere d'avoir Succes." Andrew Maverick, 21 Liberty St. This design, with variations in the wording, used as a trade card, inside the cover of Longworth's N.Y. Directory, and per-haps elsewhere. It was unsigned, but evidently the work of Peter. Reprod. in G. F. Dow's "Trade Cards" in *Old Time New Eng-land*, 27:14. July, 1936.

1022. MAVERICK. Line vign., oval wreath containing ins. Peter Maverick, 65 Liberty St., N.Y. This is probably Peter's trade card before he left his father's shop. NYHS.

1023. MAVERICK. Line script, 9.8 x 12.7. Peter Maverick's trade announcement, *N.Y. Mirror*, Nov. 15, 1828. Address, 149 Broadway. Reproduced in Harry Peters's *America on Stone*. NYHS Landauer.

1024. MAVERICK. Line vign., 3.15 x 2.12. Engraving press and worker. Samuel Maverick, copperplate printer, 73 Liberty St., N.Y. Sig.: "P. Maverick sc. Newark, N.J." 1813–1817. NYHS Landauer.

1025. MAVERICK. Trade announcement, Samuel Maverick. Line vign., 7.4 x 4.2, with vign. of Franklin, in fur cap, in center. Used on back cover of Mercein's N.Y. directory, 1820. Used also on cover of Longworth's directory with the sig.: "P. Maverick & Durand Sculp."

1026. NEW YORK LOAN CO. 1831 sale, "2 plates and 2 policy of insurance" for $3.

1027. NOTE FORM, Script, 3.7 x 7.6. Simple cross-hatching at left end. Sig.: "P. Maverick sc. Newark."

1028. NOTE FORM. Lith., 2.14 x 7.9. Eagle and scroll design at left end. Sig.: "Peter Maverick, Lithography, N.Y." and "Sold by Bonine & Co., Cor. of Wall and Water St." This might be the work of young Peter; the one in the Landauer Collection, NYHS, was used in 1837. NYHS.

1029. RANKIN. F1034. Line vign., 3.12 x 4. Ins. on pedestal: "Andrew Rankin / Hat Manufacturer / opposite State Bank / Newark, N.J. / P. Maverick."

1030. RANKIN. Line vign., 4.2 x 2.6. Design like John Johnson's above. Andrew Rankin, same wording as the preceding except the sig.: "P. Maverick, Durand & Co." 1818–1820.

1031. RANKIN. Line vign., 4.12 x 3.11. Label on silk lining for beaver hat. Pedestal, hatter at right, Indian hunter at left. Columbia, eagle, hemlock tree, sunrise, ship in background. William Rankin, hat manufacturer, opposite the church, Newark, N.J. Sig.: "Peter Maverick sc." NJHS.

1032. RANKIN. Line vign., 4.6 x 3.6. Except for size and absence of ship in background, the description of the preceding item fits this exactly. NPL, NYHS.

1033. RANKIN. F1062. Line vign., 4.10 x 3.12. Franklin bust, eagle, ships. Rankin & Fowle, hat manufacturers, 122½ Market St., Philadelphia. Sig.: "P. Maverick, Durand & Co. sc. New York." About 1818–1820. NYPL.

1034. THOMAS A. RONALDS. Bus. card, 3.14 x 2.9. Bookseller, stationer, and account-book manufacturer, at the Sign of the Ledger, 188 Pearl St. Sig.: "P. Maverick sc. Newark, N.J." NYHS Landauer.

1035. P. H. TAYLOR, professor of music. Line vign., 3.10 x 2.10. Column, harp above, lion at base. Sig.: "Charles Canda del. Peter Maverick sct." NYPL.

1036. SECOND OF EXCHANGE. Top center, Mercury with caduceus. Left end, panel with "Second" in oval. Sig.: "Peter Maverick sc." GC.

1037. THORBURN. F1057. Line vign., 2 x 3.5. Hot houses, garden implements, etc. Bill head, G. Thorburn & Sons, seedsmen and florists, 20 Nassau St., N.Y. Sig.: "Peter Maverick sc."

1038. WASHINGTON BLEACH WORKS. 1831 sale, lot for 18¢. This may well be the engraving signed by William Dodd (F343). See Dodd in reference to Newark engraving family, p. 42.

1039. a. WEST-POINT FOUNDERY AND BORING MILL. Line vign., 3.14 x 4.14 in printed broadside 16 x 9.13 with printed list of wheel patterns. Mill flanked by spray of leaves, cannon and gears in foreground. Sig.: "P. Maverick Durand & Co. Sc." NYHS.

    b. As described, with "West-Point Foundery" in arc above, and two ventilating cupolas added to roof. NYHS. Landauer.

1040. WILLIAMS. Line vign., plate 5 x 3.2. Corner shop, men inside and men and woman in front. John Williams, clothier, 212 Broadway, N.Y. Penciled note on copy seen says "Engraved by Maverick 1816." No sig.

1041. BOURNE's DEPOSITORY OF ARTS, 359 Broadway, N.Y., with inserted panel "Peter Maverick, Engraver, etc., 51 Grand St." NYHS Landauer.

MAPS AND RELATED MATERIAL

1101. ATLAS. No title page. Ins. on engraved cover label, 1.2. x 2. "Published by / P. Maverick, Durand & Co. / New York." Map of world dated 1816, but signature shows 1819 or 1820 as date for the book. LC. (Items 1101 through 1106.)

1102. Plate 1. Line, plate size 4.10 x 6.8. Two hemispheres. Ins.: "The World 1816."

1103. Plate 2. Ins.: "North America." Line rect., 4.9 x 5.15.

1104. Plate 3. Ins.: "Europe." Line rect., 4.10 x 5.15.

1105. Plate 4. Ins.: "Asia." Line rect., 4.8 x 6.

1106. Plate 5. Ins.: "Africa." Line rect., 4.10 x 5.15.
1831 sale, Outline Atlas, 250 for $13.

1107. I. B. CHURCH. Line rect., 14.12 x 19. A map showing a tract of
100,000 acres belonging to I. B. Church on the Geneseo River 22
miles south of Williamsburgh, etc. Sig.: "Jos. Fr. Mangin del.
Peter Maverick sculp. / 26 Nassau Street, N-York." NYPL ms.
div., NYHS.

1108. CONNECTICUT. 1831 sale, map unsold and unappraised.

1109. a. DELAWARE & RARITON [sic] CANAL. Line rect., 8.10 x 9.13. No
sig., no engraved title, but contemporaneous annotation as Maverick's, with price of 1100 copies for $76. RU.
b. Like above, dated 1826, with engraved title and added profile of
altitudes, town names, etc. No sig. RU.

1110. KEY WEST. 1831 sale, a lot by this title sold for 6¢. It might have
been a map of a "Key West lot" or tract.

1111. LONG ISLAND SOUND. Navigation chart. Line vign., 19.8 x 63.8. Ins.:
"A / New, and Correct Chart / of / Long Island Sound /
From / Montauk Point to Frogs Point, includings / Fisher's
Island Sound, and Watch Hill Reef / Published June 1st 1805
/ by / John Cahoone, Newport / and / N. Fosdick, New London.
/ Entered [same date and persons] / Engr'd by P. Maverick,
N. York." With scale and rose. AAS.

1112. MEDITERRANEAN AND REGION. Line rect., 8.12 x 14.4 plus (end
trimmed.) Sig.: "P. Maverick sc." In Richard V. Morris, *Defense
of the Conduct of Commodore Morris*, N.Y.: I. Riley & Co.,
1804. NYHS.

1113. NEW YORK CITY, 1803. F1045. Line rect., 35.12 x 40.5. Plan of
the city, by Casimir Th. Goerck and Joseph Fr. Mangin, city
surveyors. New York, Nov. 1803. Sig.: "Jos. Fr. Mangin Del. /
Engraved by Peter Maverick." Reprod. in I. N. Phelps-Stokes's
Iconography of Manhattan, 1:454, Plate 70. NYPL, NYHS, LC.

1114. NEW YORK CITY, 1807. St2250. Line rect., 12.6 x 12.15. Ins.:
"Plan of the City of New York / with the recent and intended
improvements. Drawn from / actual survey by William Bridges,
City Surveyor, A. D. 1807. / Published by / Isaac Riley / New
York 1807. / Engraved by Peter Maverick." In Samuel L.
Mitchill's *The Picture of New York*, 1807. NYPL, NYHS, LC,
MMNY.

1115. NEW YORK CITY, 1811. F1044. Line rect., 24.14 x 92. Map of the

City of New York and Island of Manhattan. Sig.: "Wm. Bridges / City Surveyor. / Engraved by P. Maverick." Entered, etc., Nov. 16, 1811. Numerous references and certifications. NYHS, RU, LC, NYPL, AGS. Reprod. in I. N. Phelps-Stokes's *Iconography of Manhattan*, 3:542–549, Plate 80b.

1116. a. NEW YORK CITY AND THIRTY MILES AROUND. Line circ., diam. 20.12, in rect. border 22.4 x 22.4. Ins.: "Map of the country thirty miles around the city of New York. Designed & drawn by I. H. Eddy, 1812. Engraved by P. Maverick, Newark, N. Jersey. [New York:] Prior & Dunning." LC, NYHS, NYPL, AGS. Reprod. in I. N. Phelps-Stokes's *Iconography of Manhattan*, 3:551, Plate 82.

    b. New edition, W. Hooker and E. Blount, 1828. Sig. unchanged. Also, without Maverick sig., editions in 1839, 1846, 1850, 1851, and 1855.

1117. NEW YORK AND SURROUNDING TERRITORY, 1821. Line rect., 22 x 33. The city of New York as laid out by the commissioners, with the surrounding country, by their secretary and surveyor, John Randel, junr. Entered, etc., Feb. 13, 1821. Sig.: "P. Maverick sculpt. 342 Broadway, N.Y." Engraved as if superimposed on other maps, with bits of Philadelphia, Rhode Island, Connecticut, etc. showing. Surveying instruments part of decoration. NYPL, LC, NYHS.

1118. a. NEW YORK CITY, 1821. Line rect., 26.4 x 22.12. Plan of the City of New York etc., by Thomas H. Poppleton. N.Y.: Prior & Dunning, 1821. Sig.: "P. Maverick sc. Newark." Sig. indicates earlier state, between 1809 and 1817. NYHS.

    b. F1046. New edition by Wm. Hooker, pub. by Prior & Bowne, with additions to 1829. Maverick sig. and place unchanged. NJHS, NPL.

1119. NEW YORK STATE, WESTERN PART. Line rect., 11 x 21. Ins.: "Map / of the / Western Part / of the State of New York / Showing the route of the proposed canal from Lake Erie to Hudson's River / Compiled by John H. Eddy from the best authorities / 1811. [below] Profile of Levels on the Route of the Canal. Engraved by P. Maverick, Newark." LC.

1120. NEW YORK STATE, NORTHERN PART. Line rect., 29.8 x 49. Sig.: "Compiled from actual survey by Amos Lay, 1812. Engraved by P. Maverick, Newark, N.J." LC.

1121. a. NEW YORK STATE, SOUTHERN PART. Line rect., 23 x 28. Map of the southern part of the state of New York including Long Island, the Sound, the state of Connecticut, part of the state of New Jersey and islands adjacent. Done, 1815, by Wm. Damerum, general surveyor, New York. Sig.: "P. Maverick, sct." LC, AGS.

b. Later state, though with date unchanged. Many revisions. The earlier, to give one example, has "John Schyler's copper mines" on the Passaic River above Newark. In the later state the word "John" is erased. LC, NYHS.

BANK NOTES

Colombia, Republica de. (Items 1201 through 1204.)

1201. 1 peso. Rotary lathe panels at ends, with denominations. Center vign. fasces bound with bow and arrows, flanked by horns of plenty and topped by word *Bolivar*. Sig.: "Peter Maverick, New York." 1820–1830. CNB.

1202. 2 pesos. As above, except for denomination. CNB.

1203. 3 pesos. As above, except for denomination. CNB.

1204. 5 pesos. As above, except for denomination. CNB.

Georgia

AUGUSTA. BANK OF AUGUSTA. (Items 1211 thru 1213.)

1211. $1. Line. Columbia at left, Justice right. Above, center vign. of Plenty. Rotary-lathe work, 1820–1831. Sig.: "Peter Maverick sc. N.Y."

1212. $2. Line. Above center, vign of Franklin. Left rect. Justice. Right rect. Columbia. Sig.: "Peter Maverick N. York." Rotary-lathe work, as above.

1213. $3. Line, with stip. for Franklin port. Above center, Liberty seated, with eagle. Right oval, Washington. Left oval, Franklin. Sig.: "Peter Maverick N. York." Rotary-lathe work, as above. AAS, GC, CNB.

1831 sale, "1 lot Augusta Ga. notes, 30¢."

Michigan

MONROE. BANK OF MONROE. (Items 1221 through 1223.)

1221. $1. Top center, vign. of deer and cattle. Rotary-lathe white-on-black panels at ends, with port. of Gov. Cass at left and cupids at right. Sig.: "Peter Maverick." NPL.

1222. $2. Top center, vign. of Gov. Cass treating with Indians, panels at ends, figure of deer in left. Panels line and lathe work. Sig.: "Peter Maverick." NPL.

1223. $3. Lower center, vign. of Indian and dog. Ends line and lathe patterns, agric. implements in left, ox in right. Two ports. of Cass at top. Sig.: "Peter Maverick." NPL.

Missouri

ST. LOUIS. MISSOURI EXCHANGE BANK. (Items 1231 through 1234.)

1231. 12½ cents. Simple rotary lathe panels at ends. Sig.: "P. Maverick, Durand & Co." Dated Oct. 1, 1819.

1232. 25 cents. Like preceding. Forms A and B seen.

1233. 50 cents. Like preceding. Forms A, B, and C reported.

1234. 75 cents. Like preceding.

ST. LOUIS LAND OFFICE. Copperplate, 7.8 x 3.11, on loan at Rutgers University Library, New Brunswick, N.J. (Items 1241 through 1244.)

1241. 50 cents. "Land Office" and "Post Office" in rotary lathe panels at ends; "Missouri" at top. Sig.: "P. Maverick, Durand & Co."

1242. 75 cents. Same desc.

1243. 25 cents. Same desc., except "N.Y." added to sig.

1244. 12½ cents. Like first two above.

New Jersey

CAMDEN. STATE BANK OF CAMDEN. (Item 1253.)

1253. $3. Upper center state seal, figures standing. Upper left canal boat, upper right merino sheep. Lower center eagle. Panels at ends. Sig. illegible, but this is almost surely part of a contract of March 3, 1812, for "two plates for notes of three dollars and one plate for notes of fifty dollars, one hundred dollars, and post notes" at $200 a plate.

ELIZABETH. STATE BANK OF ELIZABETH. (Item 1261.)

. . . . The contract noted in the preceding Camden item was made by the group of state banks at Camden, Trenton, New Brunswick, Elizabethtown, Newark, and Morristown, and banknotes of the denominations listed may be assumed for these banks. The award also stipulated that "Mr. Harrison of Philadelphia make three plates for notes of twenty, of ten, of five, and of four dollars" at the same price, all plates to bear the state seal near the center, an emblem of manufactures at the right, and one of commerce at the left.

1261. $1. State seal u. c. Moire panels at ends. Sig.: "Maverick, Leney, & Rollinson." Forms B and C seen.

JERSEY CITY. JERSEY BANK. (Items 1271 thru 1279.)

1271. $1. W303. Line. Center vign. of Commerce seated on river shore beside anchor. At ends, simple panels of regularly spaced wavy lines. No lathe work. Sig.: "P. Maverick." AAS, CNB.

1273. $2. W307. Line. Same general design as above, but embellished with simple rotary lathe work. Sig.: "P. Maverick & Durand." About 1818. AAS, CNB.

1275. $3. Straight-line panel, left only. Rosette upper right. Vign., upper left, woman seated on shore. Sig.: "P. Maverick sc." CNB counterfeit.

1277. $5. W313. Line, with simple lathe work. Center vign. a view of the banking house. Sig.: "P. Maverick & Durand." AAS.

1279. Blank post note. Lathe-work panels. In collection illustrating early lathe designs, given by the Durands to NYHS, and dated *ca.* 1819.

MORRISTOWN. STATE BANK AT MORRIS. (Item 1283.)

1283. $3. W425. Line. Center vign. of state seal flanked by standing figures. Left, canal barge under tow. Right, merino sheep. Line panel right, landscape panel left. Sig.: "P. Maverick. Newark."

MORRISTOWN. MORRIS COUNTY BANK. (Items 1291 and 1292.)

1291. $1. Upper center state arms, seated and standing figures. Straight-line panels. Sig.: "Maverick & Leney [sc?]"

1292. $1. Lower center state arms. Moire panels. Sig.: "Maverick Leney & Rollinson."

MOUNT HOLLY. FARMERS' BANK OF NEW JERSEY. (Item 1302.)

1302. . . . $2. Upper center state seal with seated figures. Rosettes upper left and right, straight-line panels at ends. Sig.: "Maverick & Leney."

NEWARK. NEWARK BANKING AND INSURANCE COMPANY. (Items 1311 through 1317.)

1311. $1.Vign. at left, horn of plenty leaning against tree. Man plowing, ship in distance. Panel at left, straight lines radiating from point. Sig., in arc: "P. Maverick s."

1312. $1. Upper center, coach and horses, plow (as in state seal) at bottom. Moire panels. Sig.: "P. Maverick s." AAS.

1313. $2. W486. Line, simple straight-ruled panels at end. Background of circles containing numerals consists of groups of horizontal lines so closely spaced that they print as a mass, like the black area in a woodcut. Center vign. of shoemaker at bench. Sig.: "P. Maverick." ANS, CNB, RU.

1316. $5. Line. Center vign. of state seal. Unsigned, but Peter Maverick had the contract for this.

1317. $10. Line. Center vign. of quarry with man, horse, and cart in foreground. Sig.: "P. Maverick sc."

NEWARK. STATE BANK AT NEWARK. (Items 1321 through 1326.)

1321. $1. Line. State seal upper center. Straight-line panels at ends. Figures beside seal seated and standing. Sig.: "Maverick & Leney." The words "State Bank" and "Newark" have been engraved over an erasure in the plate.

1322. $1. Upper center vign. of stone-cutter at work. Simple lathe panel at left. Sig.: "P. Maverick."

1325. $3. Line. Upper center state seal, standing figures. Canal boat, sheep. Straight-line panel at left, landscape panel at right. Payable at Mechanics Bank, N.Y. Sig.: "P. Maverick. Newark." CNB.

1326. $5. Line. At left, state seal flanked by seated and standing figures. Lathe-work panels at ends. Sig.: "P. Maverick."

NEW BRUNSWICK. BANK OF NEW BRUNSWICK. (Items 1333 through 1339.)

1333. $2. State seal upper center, seated figures. Rosettes. Moire panels at ends. Sig.: "Maverick, Leney & Rollinson."

1335. $3. Line. Vign. of sheaf of wheat, rake, etc. Sig.: "P. Maverick. N. York."

1336. $5. Line. Vign. upper left of thistle and extended hand. Straight-line panel at left end. Motto: "Sustine vel Abstine." Rosette with 5 superposed on V. Sig.: "P. Maverick s."

1339. $100. Line. Straight-line panel at left end. Rosette upper right. Vign. upper left, shield with ship and sheaves of wheat, leaning against tree. Sig.: "P. Maverick Sc." RU.

NEW BRUNSWICK. STATE BANK AT NEW BRUNSWICK. (Items 1343 through 1347.)

1343. . . . $2. W559. Line. Vign. of state seal, with seated figures. Moire-effect panels at ends. No lathe work. Sig.: "Maverick, Leney & Rollinson." ANS.

1346. . . . $5. W569. Like the two-dollar note above in design, work-manship, and sig. CNB.

1347. . . . $10. State seal lower center, standing figures. Straight-line panels. Sig.: "Maverick & Leney."

PATERSON. PATERSON BANK (FIRST). (Items 1351 through 1357.)

1351. . . . 6 cents. W653. Cross-hatched straight-line panels at ends, rosette upper center. Dated in plate July 20, 1815. Sig.: "P. Maverick sc." NYPL.

1352. . . . 12½ cents. Similar to the preceding in design. Same sig. CNB.

1353. . . . 25 cents. Similar to the preceding, rosette lower center. Sig. illegible.

1354. . . . 50 cents. Similar to the others of this series.

1355. . . . $2. Vign. of textile machine, upper center, wheel to right. Decorated rosettes and interwoven line panels. Sig.: "P. Maverick" at left of lower rosette, with possible mutilation of con-tinuation of sig. at right. CNB.

1356. . . . $3. Similar to the preceding, machine wheel at left. Sig.: "P. Maverick sc." CNB.

1357. . . . $5. W655. Similar to the two preceding. Sig.: "P. Maverick s." AAS, GC counterfeit.

PERTH AMBOY. COMMERCIAL BANK. (Items 1361 through 1368.)

1361. $1. Lower center, foreshore with church and trees, sailing vessel, others in distance. Lathe work. Sig.: "Peter Maverick."

1364. $3. W685. Upper center, vign. of city seen across water; full-rigged ship in foreground. Lathe-work panels and rosettes. Sig.: "Peter Maverick," in numeral, lower center.

1366. $5. Vign. of state seal, standing and sitting figures, ship in distance. Lathe-work panels and rosettes. Sig.: "Peter Maverick."

1367. $10. Rotary-lathe end panels, state seal at left, whaling scene at right. Sig.: "Peter Maverick, N.Y. NPL.

1368. $20. Rotary-lathe end panels, rose decorated numeral rosettes at top, state seal top center, vign. of sailing vessel and men clubbing seals below. Sig.: "Peter Maverick N. York." NPL.

SUSSEX. SUSSEX BANK. (Item 1375.)

1375. $5. Vign. of eagle perched on plow, upper center. Sheaves of wheat, etc., about. Lathe-work panels and rosettes. Sig.: "P. Maverick & Durand."

TRENTON. STATE BANK AT TRENTON. (Items 1381 through 1391.)

1381. $1. Line. State seal upper center, seated and standing figures. Rose-decorated rosettes, upper corners. Straight-line panels at ends. Sig.: "Maverick & Leney." See Farmers' Bank of Wantage, New Jersey. ANS, CNB.

1383. $2. Line. Upper center, vign. of state seal, flanked by seated figures of Liberty and Plenty. Panels as above. Sig.: "Maverick & Leney."

1385. $3. Line. State seal upper center, standing figures. Sheep upper right, canal boat upper left. One landscape and one straight-line panel. Lower center, eagle bearing figure *3*. CNB counterfeit, no sig.

1389. $100. W894. Lower center, state seal with standing figures. Upper right coach, left a dog, keys, etc. Sig.: "P. Maverick Newark." Blank one-hundred-dollar note, "Trenton" being inserted in ink.

WANTAGE. FARMERS' BANK OF WANTAGE. (Item 1391.)

1391. $1. Made from the Trenton State Bank plate, with the name of the bank and city engraved over erasure. The copy seen was used in 1850. CNB.

New York State

CATSKILL. CATSKILL BANK. (Item 1405.)

1405. $5. Center, vign. of hunter shooting wildcat, with sig. "Inman del." At ends, conventionalized leaf designs, line, with vigns. of Franklin at lower left and upper right, and of unrecognized worthy in upper left and lower right, with sig.: "Portraits by Longacre." Maverick's sig. on ribbon draping V, "Peter Maverick Engr. & Print." 1831 sale, plate $15. NPL.

HUDSON. BANK OF HUDSON. (Items 1411 through 1416.)

1411. $1. Line. Payable at Mechanics Bank, New York City. Moire end panels, spread-eagle vign. upper center, rosettes left and right. Sig.: "P. Maverick s." and across end: "Printed by L. Lemet, Alby." ANS, AAS, CNB.

1413. $2. Similar to the preceding. Ship in sail, upper center. Both sigs. same. ANS, GC, CNB.

1416. $5. Similar to the preceding, but left panel composed of concentric circles. Upper center, vign. of Justice seated beside river, with ship in distance. Sigs.: "P. Maverick s. Newark, N.J." and "Printed by L. Lemet, Alby." ANS, GC, CNB.

NEWBURGH. BANK OF NEWBURGH. (Item 1421.)

1421. In 1812, as shown by a letter of January 4, 1813 in the NJHS from

Maverick to J. S. Munn, cashier, Maverick restored plates for this bank. It seems likely, however, that he had not made them originally.

NEW YORK CITY. CITY BANK. (Items 1431 and 1439.)

1431. $100. Line. Upper center vign. of post-boy on horse. Moire panels at ends. Sig.: "P. Maverick sc."

1439. Post note, blank. Design, panels, and sig. as in preceding.

NEW YORK CITY. FRANKLIN BANK. (Items 1441 through 1445.)

1441. $1. CNB.

1443. $2. Vign. of Franklin, u. c. Rosettes, rotary lathe panels at ends. Vign. of arm and ax below center. Sig.: "Peter Maverick." ANS.

1444. $2. CNB.

1445. $3. Line. Vign. of bull, upper center, flanked by lathe-work rosettes. Lathe-work panels with ports., Franklin left and Washington right. Sig.: "Peter Maverick." CNB.

NEW YORK CITY. MANHATTAN COMPANY. (Items 1451 and 1453.)

1451. $1. Vign., center, bearded man pouring water from bucket. Below, "Public Health." Simple line-bordered panels at ends. Sig.: "P. Maverick."

1453. $2. Vign., upper left, of old man with water jug, viaduct in background. Upper right, child beside stone bearing figure 2. Sig.: "Peter Maverick." CNB.

NEW YORK CITY. MECHANICS BANK. (Items 1461 through 1468.)

1461. $1. Simple early work, no lathe work, unsigned or with sig. trimmed off, but very much resembling Maverick's work. AAS.

1462. $1. Moire panels, eagle u.c., rosettes upper r. and l. Sig.: "P. Maverick s." CNB.

1463. $2. Vign. of arm with hammer, in wreath, upper left. Number 2 in oval panel, upper right. Unsigned or with sig. worn off. NYHS Landauer.

1465. $5. Justice u.c. Panel of concentric circs. l., moire r. Ship in distance. Rosettes u.r. and l. Sig.: "P. Maverick s, Newark, N.J. MEHS.

1468. $50. Similar to 1463. Sig.: "P. Maverick sct." ANS.

NEW YORK CITY. INSURANCE COMPANY NOTES. (Items 1471 and 1481.)

1471. Dutchess Co. Ins. Co., New York, N.Y. Note form, 4 x 8.4 Top center, line vign. of fire fighting. At ends, rotary-lathe panels with port. of woman at left and military officer at right. Sig.: "Peter Maverick." NPL.

1481. The Life and Fire Ins. Co. New York, N.Y. Note form, 4.1 x 8.4. Top center, line vign. of ship in construction. At ends, rotary-lathe panels, ports. of Washington at left and Franklin at right. Sig.: "Peter Maverick." NPL.

NEW YORK CITY. MERCHANTS BANK (Probably two series here, the lathe work denoting the later contract). (Items 1491 through 1497.)

1491. $1. Two copies, CNB, probably both counterfeits. Simple early work, straight-line end panels. Sig.: "Maverick" in one copy, no sig. in other. CNB.

1493. $2. Straight-line panel at left. Center vign. of ship, with boxes and barrel in foreground, flanked by rosette on left and word *two* on right. Sig.: "P. Maverick sc." CNB.

1494. $2. Upper center vign. of ship in sail, flanked by simple lathe-work rosettes. Lathe-work panels at ends. Sig.: "P. Maverick." CNB.

1495. $3. Similar to the preceding in vign. and style. Sig.: "P. Maverick sc." and on vign.: "Inman del." ANS.

1497. $5. Straight-line panel at left, vign. of ship, boxes and barrels in foreground. Sig.: "P. Maverick r." RU.

NEW YORK CITY, PHENIX BANK. (Item 1509.)

1509. $100. Upper center, vign. of horse and rider, flanked by line rosettes. Moire panels at ends. Sig.: "P. Maverick sc." CNB.

NEW YORK CITY. UNION BANK. (Item 1511.)

1511. $1. Reported, with sig.: "Peter Maverick," the $3. denomination being by Leney and Rollinson.

1521. Potsdam. 1831 sale, Potsdam bank plate sold for $1.00.

POUGHKEEPSIE. MIDDLE DISTRICT BANK. (Items 1531 and 1536.)

1531. $1. Lathe numeral rosettes, vign. of horse in center. Line panels, cupids holding figure 1 at ends. Sig.: "Peter Maverick."

1536. $5. Simple lathe work. Sheep in upper center, agricultural implements, etc., in end panels. Sig.: "Peter Maverick." WMFA.

STEUBEN COUNTY. STEUBEN COUNTY BANK. (Item 1545.)

1545. $3. Upper center vign., a bull. Lathe-work panels with portraits, Franklin left and Washington right, and numerals above and below ports. Sig.: "Peter Maverick." CNB.

TROY. BANK OF TROY, WATERFORD BRANCH. (Item 1553.)

1553. $2. Upper center vign. of Justice. Rosettes, and flowered straight-lined end panels with the word *two* superposed. AAS.

Rhode Island

NEWPORT. MERCHANTS BANK. (Items 1561 through 1568.)

1561. $1. Center bottom, vign. of mill, with eagle and U.S. shield in foreground. Line panels at end, with view of vessel in sail in right panel, and stip. port. of Washington in left. Sig.: "Peter Maverick." NPL.

1563. $2. Center top, vign. of ruined tower. Rotary-lathe panels at ends. Sig.: "Peter Maverick." NPL.

1565. $5. Center, modern building. Rotary-lathe panels at ends. Sig.: "Peter Maverick." NPL.

1568. $50. Center, portrait of Perry with quotation, "We have met the enemy——," in vign. Rotary-lathe panels at ends. Sig.: "H. Inman del." probably referring to vignette, and "Peter Maverick sc. Broadway, N.Y." 1826–1829. NPL.

NEWPORT. RHODE ISLAND UNION BANK. (Items 1571 and 1577.)

1571. $1. Early simple work, vign. of clasped hands upper left, cow being milked upper right. Sig.: "P. Maverick sc. N. York." The copy seen was issued in 1804, and had been raised to $10. ANS.

1577. $10. Later work. Bank building upper center, two ports. of Franklin, lathe panels. Sig.: "Peter Maverick, N. York."

PROVIDENCE. EAGLE BANK. (Items 1586 through 1589.)

1586. $20. Vign. of sailing ship, rocky foreshore with anchor. Lathe-work end panels and rosettes. Sig.: "P. Maverick, Durand & Co." NYHS.

1587. $50. Vign. of ships, no foreshore, lighthouse in distance. Same rosettes, panels, and sig. NYHS.

1588. $100. Ship in distance, eagle and anchor on foreshore. Otherwise as described above. NYHS.

1589. Post note, blank. Rock, shield with anchor on it, water in distance. Otherwise as described. NYHS.

WESTERLEY. WASHINGTON BANK. (Items 1591 through 1596.)

1591. $1. Upper center, circ. port. of Washington, face slightly right, flanked by oval rosettes. Military gear behind port. Moire panels at ends. Sig.: "P. Maverick sc."

1593. $2. Similar to the preceding. Sig.: "P. Maverick." AAS.

1595. $3. Similar to the preceding. Sig.: "P. Maverick s." AAS, RU.

1596. $10. Similar to the preceding. Sig.: "P. Maverick sc."

D. Samuel Maverick

1701. ALBUM. F1066. Title-page line vign., Girl with basket and dog, in woods by bank of stream. Ins.: "Saml. Maverick Sc. / Philadelphia / Published by G. W. Mentz & Son." NYPL.

1702. ALMANAC. Line eng., colored, 7.14 x 5.14. Wheel to revolve behind slots to give perpetual calendar, with all usual almanac data. Sig.: "Saml. Maverick sc." WMFA.

1703. AMERICAN HOTEL. F1069. Trade card. Sig.: "Jas. Harris Dl. Saml. Maverick Sc."

1704. ANATOMICAL CHART. Male body from thorax to lower thighs, lettered indicators for genitals. Line rect., 5.8 x 4.2. Sig.: "Saml. Maverick." In *The New-York Medical and Physical Journal*, vol. V. N.Y.: E. Bliss & E. White, 1826.

1705. BURGOYNE, JOHN. St2269. Line rect., 6.9 x 8.12. Ins.: "Saml. Maverick Sc. / Capture of Burgoyne." In *American Military Biography*, Phila. 1831.

COFFIN, ROBERT S. *Oriental Harp, Poems of the Boston Bard*. Providence: 1826. AAS, BA. (Items 1706 and 1707.)

1706. Title page. Bibliog. data as given, seal of Maine, and quot.: "This is my own, my native land." Sig.: "S. Maverick Sc." WMFA.

1707. Portrait. F1063. Line rect., 2.15 x 2.6. Bust, seated, book in hand. One-line Latin quotation. WMFA.

COLDEN, CADWALLADER D. *Memoir Prepared . . . at . . . the Completion of the New York Canals*. N.Y.: Printed by order of the Corporation, 1825. NYHS, MMNY. (Though some of the following are unsigned, it seems likely that all are the work of Samuel. The volume contains many lithographs, but none by the Mavericks.) (Items 1708 through 1716.)

1708. Boat Builders' Association. Ball badge. Line vign., 3 x 1.12. Canal lock in orn. design. Sig.: "Sl. Maverick." NYPL.

1709. Hatters [?]. Line circ., diam. 1.10, enclosing a top hat. Sig.: "Sl. Maverick." NYPL.

1710. DeWitt Clinton. Ball badge. Line vign., 2.5 x 1.9, showing oval port. of Clinton above oval view of lock. Sig.: "Published by Samuel Maverick 73 Liberty St. / N.Y." NYPL.

1711. Saddlers. Line vign., 2.8 x 2.7. Heraldic design, shield with saddles, plumed horses. No sig.

1712. Chairmakers [?]. Line, 3.4 x 2.4. Foliage wreath enclosing chair. No sig.

1713. House painters. Heraldic, 2 x 2.4. Shield supported by leopards, crest a phoenix. No sig.

1714. Ticket. Canal Celebration Ball. Nov. 7th 1825. No sig.

1715. Whitehall. Line vign., 3.4 x 5. Rocky foreshore, long racing boat.

Title: "White-Hall Victorious May 20th 1825." Sig.: "Cummings Fecit. Eng. by S. Maverick & J. F. Morin." NYPL.

1716. Neptune. St2271. Line vign., 4.9 x 6.2. Neptune, with flags, in shell drawn by sea-horses. Sig.: "Sketch'd by Cummings From The Original. Eng. by S. Maverick & J. F. Morin." NYPL, GC, WMFA.

1717. COLUMBIAN FOUNDRY. F1070. Bus. card, line vign., 2.5 x 6.14. Sig.: "Saml. Maverick Sc. 73 Liberty St. N.Y."

1718. CULINARY. Mock armorial shield with kitchen implements, man and woman. Ins.: "Whilst we live, let us live. Published by S. Maverick, 73 Liberty St. N. York."

1719. DEAF & DUMB. Ticket for exhibition, line vign., 3 x 2.4. Hand making symbol for A. Only signatory ins. is the phrase: "Presented by Saml. Maverick."

1720. FRANKLIN. St2267. Line rect., orn. 2.13 x 2.4. Half-length, seated at table, face ¾ left. After Martin portrait. Sig.: "Sml. Maverick Sc."

1721. FORT GEORGE. F1068. Line rect., 8.6 x 13.14. Ins.: "Drawn during the Battle by an Officer of Come. Chauncey's Flag Ship Madison. Engd. by Saml. Maverick. N.Y. / [References, 3 lines] / Capture of Fort George U. C. May 27th 1813 / By / Major General Morgan Lewis & Commodore Chauncey. / Published & Sold By Samuel Maverick 35 Liberty St. New York." Illus. in *The Print Collector's Quarterly*, vol. 23, p. 41. Jan. 1936.

1722. JEFFERSON & JACKSON. Script, 11.8 x 9. Letter, 1824, from Thomas Jefferson to his namesake, T. J. Grotjan, and addition, 1833, by Andrew Jackson. Reproduced by Benj. O. Tyler, engr. by Samuel Maverick. Entered, etc., 1834. WMFA.

1723. LAFAYETTE. St2268. Line vign., 3.8 x 2.12. Bust, face left, civilian dress. Sig.: "Saml. Maverick."

1724. LAFAYETTE'S HOME. F1071. Line rect., 2.15 x 4.1. La Grange Bleneau. From *History of Marquis de La Fayette*, N.Y. 1826.

1725. LAFAYETTE. St2271. Line rect., 2.14 x 4.13. Ins.: "Imbert del. Saml. Maverick Sct. / Landing of Gen. Lafayette / at Castle Garden New York 16th August 1824." Used as front, to *A Complete History of the Marquis de Lafayette*, etc., N.Y.: R. Lowry, 1826 and with same title also, Hartford: S. Andrus & Son, 1845. Regarding this and the next, see I. N. Phelps-Stokes's *Iconography of Manhattan*, 3: 580–581, and Pl. 94. AAS, NYPL.

1726. LAFAYETTE. Line circ., diam. 3.1. View similar to the preceding. Entered, etc., Oct. 27, 1824, by Samuel Maverick. This print and its uses in other forms discussed in *Antiques*, 40: 106, Aug. 1941. NYPL.

MAPS. For *Ancient History*, by Charles Rollin, 4 vols., (N.Y.: George Long, 1827 and later editions). Samuel Maverick did a number of maps, signed uniformly "S. Maverick." All are in line rects, of the sizes given. (Items 1727 through 1733.)

1727. The city and port of Alexandria & Isle of Pharos, 5.6 x 8.4.

1728. Carthaginian Empire, 7 x 12.15. "Drawn by Mr. D'Anville."

1729. Syria et Assyria, 7.7 x 9.

1730. Plan of Babylon, 6 x 8.14.

1731. Syria, Phoenicia, and the Holy Land, 8.15 x 6.2.

1732. Plan of the City of Syracuse, 8 x 5.6.

1733. Egypt and Part of the Holy Land, 8.15 x 7.3.

1734. MAPS. Cover label, *A Series of Maps to* [Emma] *Willard's History of the United States*, etc. N.Y.: White, Gallagher & White, 1828. Engraved and printed by Samuel Maverick. UV, CU Plimpton. Many have added historical pictures. (Also items 1735 through 1746.)

1735. Plate 1. Wanderings of the Aborigines. 9.4 x 11.8.

1736. Plate 2. Map of 1578. 9.6 x 6.6.

1737. Plate 3. Map of 1620. 10.4 x 6.12.

1738. Plate 4. Map of 1645. 10.4 x 7.15.

1739. Plate 5. Map of 1692. 9.15 x 6.13.

1740. Plate 6. Map of 1733. 10.4 x 7.8.

1741. Plate 7. Map of 1763. 10.4 x 13.

1742. Plate 8. Map of 1776. 10 x 14.

1743. Plate 9. Map of 1789. 10.2 x 14.

1744. Plate 10. The Revolution in Southern United States. 9 x 6.11.

1745. Plate 11. Map of 1826. 9.12 x 13.15.

1746. Plate 12. Principal Seats of the War of 1812–1814. 9.12 x 7.8.

1747. MASONRY. Line rect., 13.10 x 10.12. Royal Arch Mason, Phoenix Chapter No. 2. Signed by Samuel Maverick, used Feb. 14, 1810.

1748. MASONRY. Line, 10.12 x 6.14. Seventh Degree. Signed by Samuel Maverick.

1749. MASONRY. Royal Arch Masonry cert., line rect., 10.4 x 6.11. Blanks for chap. number, etc. Sig.: "Published by Comn. S. Maverick, N. York." NYHS.

1750. MASONRY. Royal Arch Masonry cert., line vign., 13.6 x 10.8. Columns at either side, female figure above, Masonic symbols. Certification in both English and Spanish. Sig.: "Published and sold by Brother Samuel Maverick, New York." NYHS.

1751. MAVERICK. Trade card of Samuel Maverick in form of mock bank note. Rotary lathe work in end panels, steamboat at left, Franklin at right. Across center, "Maverick Bank," and above vign. of woman seated by seaside. Rosettes displaying number "5" flanked by words "Eighty" and "Liberty Street" to make Samuel's address after 1829.

1752. MAVERICK. Another similar trade card of Samuel Maverick. Panels of rosettes at ends, with port. of Franklin at left. Upper center vign. of seated figure, above which are the words "Franklin Office." Across center, "Maverick, Engraver & Printer." Rosettes as above.

1753. MAVERICK. Another similar card. Panels at ends, rosettes with number "3" followed by "doors west of Broadway." Center vign. of woman beside port. of Washington.

1754. MAVERICK. Trade card of Samuel Maverick, showing own card surrounded by other cards partially overlapped, obviously samples of his work. These samples reveal work for T. A. Ronalds, stationer; J. & L. Brewster, hatters; S. Crane; Munn, furrier; —erben, builder; Peter Ru— shipfitter (?); Jones of Charleston; E. Bliss, books; W. Pa—; Prime Ward & Co.; and Coffin, q. v., NYHS Landauer.

1755. MAVERICK. Like preceding, but instead of Ronalds it has D. Felt & Co.; instead of Bliss it has Carvil [l?] of 108 Broadway; instead of J. & L. Brewster it has Leary & Co., each in same business as the one replaced. AAS.

1756. MAVERICK. F1067. Trade card, Samuel Maverick. Three cupids, arch, Masonic pillars, etc. No separate signature. Address, 73 Liberty. MMNY.

1757. MAVERICK. F1065. Trade card, Samuel Maverick. Includes oval Franklin portrait 1 x .12 in design 4.1 x 2.10. Portrait leans at foot of blasted tree, with skull, swords, etc. at hand, hill and sea beyond. Ins.: "Franklin Office. / Samuel Maverick / Engraver / And Copper-Plate Printer, / No. 73 Liberty Strt. New York." AAS, MMNY.

THOMAS MOORE. Melodies. Bridgeport, Ct.: M. Sherman, 1828. (Items 1758 and 1759.)

1758. Title page. Line vign., 2 x 2.8 in design 3.8 x 2.8. Women with jug and stick, child in background, stile at left. Bibliog. data as given, sig.: "Saml. Maverick sc. N.Y." GC. See also 644.

1759. Front. Line rect., 3.4 x 2.4. Warriors in foreground, lightning over tower in background. Sig. like preceding. GC.

1760. VALENTINE MOTT, M.D. Lecture ticket, operative surgery, in the University of the State of New York. Vign., 1.2 x 1.10, of hand, in clouds, holding scalpel. Whole design 3.8 x 2.14. Sig.: "S. Maverick Sc." CU.

1761. PARKER. Ticket, Parker's Grand Ball, line vign., 1.11 x 1.8. Two girls in garden, skipping rose-woven rope. Sig.: "Saml. Maverick Sc." MCNY.

ALEXANDER POPE. PUBLICATION UNIDENTIFIED. (Items 1762 and 1763.)

1762. Rape of the Lock. Print reported but signed or authenticated copy not found. Possibly the trimmed print, line rect., 3 x 4, woman at toilet, man with shears, sylphs about, in NYPL Peter Maverick collection. No sig. or ins.

1763. January and May. Line rect., 4 x 2.9. Old man, young woman, young man kneeling behind her. Two-line quot. beginning, "Thus while she spoke . . ." Sig.: "S. Maverick Sc."

1764. PROVOOST. A bookplate done by Samuel Maverick for Bishop Samuel Provoost is reported, probably erroneously.

1765. RUINED CITY [?]. Line rect., 3.13 x 2.12. Man seated looking over ruins of tropical city. Dog at left. Three-line prose quot. beginning, "Here, said I, here once flourished an opulent city . . ." Sig.: "Saml. Maverick Sc." WMFA.

1766. RUTGERS. Original plate for badges of the Society of Natural History of Rutgers College. Line vign., 1.7 x 1.10, with rays extending farther. Center a book inscribed "Nature." Above a ribbon ins., "To Look Through Nature up to Nature's God." Below, "S. N. H. R. C." No sig., but container attributes it to Samuel Maverick. NYHS.

1767. COUNT DE SEGUR. *The Four Ages of Life.* N.Y., 1826. Engraving for this reported but not found.

1768. SIAMESE TWINS. F1072. Line rect., 7.8 x 4.8 in borders. Full length, at table. Sig.: "Saml. Maverick Sc. N.Y." Harvard Univ. Theater Collection.

1769. STEAMSHIPS. Line rect., 2.5 x 3.7. View of side-wheeler *Commerce* and barge *Lady Clinton* at top, and announcement of barges *Lady Clinton* and *Lady Van Rensselaer* in panel at bottom. Sig.: "Saml. Maverick Del & Sc." At head of letterpress form letter of New York Steam Navigation Company, reverse of which contains letter of Dec. 29, 1826, in Otis Collection, Mass. Hist. Soc.

1770. WEDDING CERTIFICATE. Line vign. of wedding group, 1.14 x 3.3, in lettered design 8.7 x 6, for general use by Reformed Protestant Dutch Church. Prior to 1831. Sig.: "Saml. Maverick Sc. N.Y."

1771. RUTGERS COMMENCEMENT BALL, BELL TAVERN, NEW BRUNSWICK. Line vign. and lettering, 2.14 x 4.4. "Rutgers College / 1829" in oak-leaf wreath, above invitation and names of 7 student managers. Sig.: "Sml. Maverick Sc." RU.

E. Emily Maverick Stoutenburgh

EYE, ANATOMY OF. Publication not identified. See also Peter and Maria A. Maverick for plates in this group. (Item 1801.)

1801. Plate III. Seven three-color three-copperplate line drawings of diseased eyes. Copperplate size 8.14 x 5.8. Sig.: "Drawn by H. Thomson. Engd. by Emily Maverick." NPL.

1802. MATERNAL AFFECTION. Lith, rect., 7.5 x 5.7. Mother and child. Sig.: "Peter Maverick Lithogr. Emily Maverick del." NPL.

NATURAL HISTORY. *Annals of the Lyceum of Natural History of New York*, N.Y.: The Lyceum, 1824. AAS, NYHS. (Items 1803 through 1805 from vol. I, part I (1824); items 1806 through 1808 from part II (1825); and item 1809 from vol. II (1826–1828).)

1803. Pl. V. Stip. vign., 6.10 x 4.6. Bilobites. Sig.: "Stansbury del. E. M. sc."

1804. Pl. VII. Stip., 2 x 4.8. Phoca Cristata. Sig.: "Inman del. Emily Maverick sct."

1805. Pl. II sic. Twenty colored stip. drawings of beetles. Sig.: "Leconte del. Emily Maverick sc."

1806. Pl. XIV. Four stip. vigns., 6.8 x 4.10 overall. Lychens. Sig.: "Inman del. Emily Maverick sc."

1807. Pl. XVI. Stip. vign., 2.8 x 5.12. Drawing of lizard, Menobranchus Lateralis. Sig.: "T. R. Peale ad viv. del. Emily Maverick sc."

1808. Pl. XXI. Stip. vigns., 7.4 x 4.2 overall. Details of Chlamyphorus. Sig.: "W. W. Wood del. Emily Maverick sc."

1809. Pl. I. Stip. vign., 8 x 4. Siren Intermedia. Sig.: "I Le Conte delin. Peter Maverick dir. / Emily M. sc."

SHAKESPEARE. *Works*. Edition not found. (HU Theatre Collection data not correct.)

1810. Portrait design. St2179. Stip. vign., 7.1 x 4.13. Shakespeare leaning against tree, above him a circle showing Edmund Kean as Richard III. Eight smaller circles with scenes from plays. Sig.: "H. Heath del. Emily Maverick sculp." NYPL, WMFA.

F. Maria Ann Maverick Townsend

1901. CHRIST, FROM GUIDO. Lith. vign., 3.12 x 4. Head crowned with thorns, staff at left. Title as given. Sig.: "Maria A. Maverick del. Peter Maverick's Lith. pr. 149 Broadway, N.Y. 1826." NPL.

EYE, ANATOMY OF. Publication not identified. See also Peter and Emily Maverick for plates in this group. (Item 1902.)

1902. Plate II. Six three-color three-copperplate line drawings of diseased eyes. Copperplate size 8 x 5.8. Sig.: "H. Thomson del. Maria A. Maverick sc." NPL.

1903. a. EXCURSION. Lith. circ., diam. 7.12. Woman in boat, boy with parasol at side. Steps and balustrade at right. Sig.: "M. A. Townsend Del." 1828–1832. NPL.

   b. Same, hand colored. NPL.

1904. ITALIAN PEASANT GIRL. Lith. vign., 6.4 x 3.13. Half length, flowers on shoulder and head-dress, necklace with heart-shaped locket and cross, laced bodice. Sig.: "Maria A. Maverick." NPL.

1905. MATHILDE AND MALEK-ADEHL. Lith. vign., 9 x 5.8. Woman, hands clasped, kneels beside turbaned man on desert. Cert. in family scrapbook as work of Maria Maverick. NPL.

NATURAL HISTORY. *Annals of the Lyceum of Natural History of New York*. N.Y.: The Lyceum, 1824. AAS, NYHS. (Items 1906 through 1908 from vol. I, part I (1824); items 1909 through 1911 from part II (1825); and item 1912 from vol. II (1826–1828).)

1906. Pl. VIII. Megatherium, four drawings. Stip., 6.12 x 4.4 Sig.: "Inman del. Maria Maverick sc."

1907. Pl. IX. Shells, 8 stip. vigns., 6.8 x 4.6 overall. Sig.: "Maria A. Maverick del & sc."

1908. Pl. XIII. Stip. vign., 6.14 x 2.5. Trilobites. Sig.: "M. A. M. sc."

1909. Pl. Stip. vign., 2.8 x 6.4. Abranchus Alleghaniensis. Sig.: "T. R. Peale ad viv. del. Maria A. Maverick sc."

1910. Pl. XVIII. Details of preceding. Sig.: "T. R. Peale del. M. A. Maverick sc."

1911. Pl. XXIX. Eurypterus Remipes. Sig.: "I. I. Graves del. Maria A. Maverick sc."

1912. Pl. VI. Utricularia, 11 line drawings; and Megatherium, 2 stip. drawings, 6 x 4.12 overall. Sig.: "Inman del. M. M. sc."

1913. ORIGINAL DRAWING. Pencil vign., 2.8 x 2.8. Seated woman at Gothic doorway. Sig.: "Maria Ann Maverick del." Below, 13 lines of blank verse signed "Maria" and dated New York, Dec. 20, 1827. NPL.

SHAKESPEARE. Works, edition not found. (HU Theatre Collection data not correct.) (Item 1914.)

1914. Portrait. St2180. Stip. vig., 7.2 x 4.14. Bust, face slightly left, drapery at side, figure with crown above, Tragedy and Comedy below. Sig.: "Heath del. Maria A. Maverick sculp." NYPL, WMFA.

G. Catharine Maverick

2001. BIRDS. Lith. vign.: 8.6 x 5.10. Songbirds billing on blossoming apple bough. Sig.: "C. M. del. Peter Maverick, Lithr." 1831 sale, 300 for $3, though this notation might refer to another print. NPL.

2002. CHILDREN AND DOG. Lith. vign., 8 x 6.8. Five grimacing or crying children, one holding struggling dog. In family scrapbook, signed in pencil "Catharine Maverick." NPL.

H. Octavia Maverick Spafard

2101. ORIGINAL WATER COLOR. Apple and cherry blossoms, certified in family scrapbook as done by Octavia Maverick Spafard at Cooperstown, May 27, 1843. NPL.

2102. ORIGINAL WATER COLOR. Peach and cherry, as above. May 24, 1843. NPL.

2103. UNIDENTIFIED MAN. Lith. vign., 9.6 x 9. Man in pad-arm chair, right hand hooked in vest, left holding pamphlet. Spectacles on chair-arm. Face forward, hair loose, shaggy burnsides. Sig.: O. M. S." NPL.

I. Peter Maverick, Jr.

2201. THE ONLY IMPORTANT PRINT as yet attributed with certainty to young Peter Maverick, 1809–1845, is the lithograph of Wall Street, made three years after the death of the more important Peter. The design is a view looking down Wall Street from Broadway, size 14 x 18.12, set in an ornamental design which includes a front elevation of the buildings along each side of the street; and it is the knowledge of the business changes on the street that makes possible the 1834 dating. The work is of no distinction, but the print is so rare that one brought a price of $3950 at the Anderson Galleries in November, 1916. Four copies are reported, all in private hands except the NYHS copy. The work is signed "H. R. [Hugh Reinagle?] P. Maverick Lithy. New York." It was reproduced as a Christmas card, size overall 7.10 x 9.9, for the Metropolitan Trust Company of New York. It is found in I. N. Phelps-Stokes's *Iconography of Manhattan*, 3: 615, Plate III. Reprod. also in *Antiques*, 39: 304, June, 1941. See also *Art News* for Jan. 11, 1936, regarding sale of the Robert Goelet copy.

2202. ENGLISH & CLASSICAL SCHOOL cert. of merit. Lith. 2.15 x 6.12 (to borders) imitating currency. Portrait of Franklin and another, with American eagle in center. School under Richard J. Smith and R. Carter, 459 Broadway. Sig.: "Peter Maverick's Lithography." Circa 1833. AAS.

2203. WAVERLEY. Lith. rect., 8 x 6.1. Woman, children, dog, soldier— man in tartans at rear. Flora's song in Glen of Glennaquoich. Sig.: "P. Maverick's Lithogy. N.Y. fr. W. Allan." NPL.

2204. PALM—SOAP (Part of name cut away). Lith. soap label, 4 x 5.10. Two women, in adjacent panels, with ornate dresses and hats. At ends, currency-like rect. panels, and at bottom oval panel, inscribed "1" and "one" as if for a premium coupon. Inscription: "Palm [excision] Soap. / Lithography by Peter Maverick / Six Dozen Assorted." Probably early 1830's, resembling both sartorial and pictorial style of Maria Ann Maverick in No. 1903 of this list. Possibly the work of the older Peter Maverick. NYHS Landauer.

179

J. Ann Maverick, née Anderson

2301. GARDEN PARTY GROUP. Relief cut, in border 4.15 x 7.12. Nine young people, fairies and elves about. Sig.: "Ann Maverick." NYPL.

2302. ST. CHRISTOPHER. Relief cut, vign., 4.13 x 3.4. Saint with infant Jesus on shoulder. Lantern on staff. Sig.: "Ann Maverick." NYPL.

2303. ST. PAUL'S CATHEDRAL in Calcutta. Relief cut. Ref. to Bishop Wilson. WMFA.

Appendices

A. MAVERICK ADDRESSES

Peter Rushton Maverick, 1755–1811:

1775 . . . . Batteau [Dey] Street.

1784–1794 . . . . . 3 Crown Street, except possibly 5 Crown Street for a time about 1786–1787.

1794–1802 . . . . . 65 Liberty Street.

1803–1811 . . . . . . 73 Liberty Street.

Peter Maverick, 1780–1831:

To 1802 . . . . Same as father's address, above, (found on some early engravings).

1802 . . . . 68 Beekman Street.

1803–1804 . . . . . . 26 Nassau Street, except possibly a short stay at 20 Nassau in 1803.

1805–1806 . . . . . . 92 Nassau Street.

1806 (also) . . . . . 84 Nassau Street.

1807 . . . . 85 Nassau Street.

1808–1809 . . . . . . 29 Frankfort Street.

1809–1820 . . . . . . Home and shop in Newark, New Jersey; in the New York directories, however, he kept addresses as follows, and sometimes, though rarely, used these on his work.

1810 . . . . 34 Liberty Street; this was the address also of Andrew Maverick and Francis Kearny.

1811 . . . . 231 Duane Street.

1812 . . . . 115 Liberty Street.

1813 . . . . 49 Walker Street.

1814–1815 . . . . . . 27 & 110 Liberty Street, Andrew's shop and home.

1816 . . . . 114 Broadway.

1817 . . . . 21 Liberty Street, Andrew's shop.

1818 . . . . 2 Cedar Street; this was apparently Durand's New York lodging, 1817–1820.

1819 . . . . 2 Pine Street; the listed name is that of the firm, P. Maverick, Durand & Co.

1820 . . . . 2 Pine Street, 64 Pine Street, 84 Maiden Lane, and 342 Broadway; this was the year of the return to New York.

1821–1826 . . . . . . 342 Broadway, except that the shop was at 1 Murray Street in 1822.

1826–1827 . . . . . . Shop 149 Broadway; residence 5 Carlisle Street.

1828 . . . . Shop 149 Broadway; residence 505 Broome Street.

1829 . . . . Shop 149 Broadway; residence 61 Grand Street.

1830–1831 . . . . . Shop 59 Grand Street, residence 61 Grand Street.

Peter Maverick, Junior, 1809–1845:

To 1831 . . . . . . With father.

1832–1833 . . . . . . 409 Broadway.

1835–1836 . . . . . . 29 Sullivan Street.

1836–1837 . . . . . . 60 Sullivan Street.

1843–1844 . . . . . . 60 Thompson Street.

1845 . . . . 67 Laurens Street.

Andrew Maverick, 1782–1826:

To 1805 . . . . In his father's shop, with residence at 13 Fair (Fulton) Street after his marriage in 1804.

1806 . . . . Shop 27 Liberty Street; residence 13 Fair Street.

1807 . . . . 27 Liberty Street.

1808–1810 . . . . . . 34 Liberty Street.

1811 . . . . 58 Gold Street.

1812 . . . . 9 Cedar Street.

1813 . . . . 5 Cedar Street.

1814–1815 . . . . . . 27 Liberty Street.

1816–1826 . . . . . . Shop 21 Liberty Street, with separate residence addresses.

Samuel Maverick, 1789–1845:

To 1809 . . . . In his father's shop.

1810–1811 . . . . . . 10 Liberty Street.

1811 (also) . . . . . 36 Lumber Street.

1811 (also) . . . . . 73 Liberty Street, A. & S. Maverick; this is the year of the death of their father at this address, the initials of this entry probably standing for Andrew and Samuel.

1812–1829 . . . . . . 73 Liberty Street.

1829–1845 . . . . . . 85 Liberty Street, not a change of address from the preceding, but a change in the house numbering.

Andrew Rushton Maverick, ca. 1809– ca. 1835:

1829–1830 . . . . . . Andrew Maverick, engraver and copperplate printer, is listed at 122 Fulton Street in this period; this must be the son of the Andrew listed above, and the husband of Ann Anderson Maverick; see pages 73–74 for her engraving career after his early death.

Aaron Howell Maverick, 1809–1846:

1830 . . . . Called "engraver of Liberty Street" in record of fire company; Samuel's son.

B. NOTES ON SOURCES, AND SELECTED BIBLIOGRAPHY

Notes on Sources

The comments of William Dunlap in his diary and his history of the arts of design, of T. S. Cummings in his account of the National Academy, and of W. H. Sumner in his account of East Boston (see bibliography), constitute just about all the printed primary source material, and in part these accounts do not appear to be correct.

A few family letters and papers are to be found indexed under the Maverick name in NYHS, NJHS, MHS, NYPL, and WMFA. The Durand Collection in NYPL contains more of Peter Maverick's letters than all the other lots combined, and gives information about the partnership with Durand and its dissolution. The items in the NYHS collection, which deal chiefly with Samuel's family, were sent to me by Samuel's great-granddaughters with instructions to give them to some institution when I had finished with them. Use of church records of marriages, baptisms, and burials, of militia records, polling lists, rosters of freemen or citizens, and census tabulations, is obvious.

County records of deeds, wills, and mortgages in Newark, New York, and Brooklyn will be recognized by the reader as the sources for many facts here related. Two items were especially rich mines of information. One is the detailed inventory in the New York County probate records of Peter Maverick's estate after he died without a will in 1831, from which we can reconstruct not only the picture of his shop, with its presses, raw materials, and its stock of prints for sale, but also the living quarters, the pictures on the walls, the silver spoons, the wine glasses, and even the frying pan which sold for three cents. The other, also in New York County, is the record of the long hearing throughout the winter of 1853–1854 on the probate of the will of Rebecca, P. R. Maverick's widow. The testimony of relatives and friends, both by what was said and the manner of its saying, indicated much of the character and temperament of people who would otherwise be mere names in a genealogical chart.

Genealogical data about the family have been published by NEHG, and I have supplemented and corrected these by many other records. I have made no attempt to record any genealogical data on the Mavericks not related to the lives of the engraving group.

Other bibliographic resources will be evident to the reader. City directories, membership lists of organizations, and newspaper files have been of much help. Such manuscript material as the diary of Alexander Anderson (CU, copy NYHS) has yielded much of the atmosphere of the time. The life of Asher B. Durand, by his son John, though it almost ignores Asher's teacher, gives us, along with the Maverick-Durand correspondence in NYPL, the only glimpse we have of Peter Maverick's Newark shop. C. C. Hine's *Woodside*, with its vague reminiscence of "a Maverick" on the bank of the Passaic before 1820, is, aside from land records, our only evidence for Peter's third Newark home. And in like fashion Grant Thorburn's copious and repetitious New York reminiscences (published variously; copies in NYPL) give me, with other evidence, reason for believing that Peter was the hero and sufferer in the incident of the yellow-fever epidemic.

Selected Bibliography

ALLEN, CHARLES DEXTER. (A with number.) *American Book-Plates.* N.Y.: Macmillan, 1894.

CRESSWELL, BEATRIX F. *The Mavericks of Devonshire and Massachusetts.* Exeter, Eng.: James G. Commin, 1929.

CUMMINGS, T. S. *Historic Annals of the National Academy of Design.* Phil.: Childs, 1865.

DUNLAP, WILLIAM. *History of the Rise and Progress of the Arts of Design in the United States,* 2 vols., N.Y.: George P. Scott Co., 1834. Rev. and enlarged, Boston: Goodspeed, 1918.

DURAND, JOHN. *Life and Times of A. B. Durand.* N.Y.: Chas. Scribner's Sons, 1894.

EVANS, CHARLES. (Evans with number.) *The American Bibliography.* Chicago: Priv. printed, 1903–1934. N.Y.: Peter Smith, 1941– .

FIELDING, MANTLE. (F with number.) *Dictionary of American Painters, Sculptors, and Engravers.* Phil.: Printed for Subscribers, [1917].

FINCHAM, HENRY W. (Fm.) *Artists and Engravers of British and American Bookplates.* London: Kegan Paul, 1897.

PETERS, HARRY T. *America on Stone.* Garden City, N.Y.: Doubleday, Doran & Co., 1931.

———. *Currier and Ives,* 2 vols. Same pub., 1929–1931.

STAUFFER, DAVID MCNEELY. (St with number.) *American Engravers upon Copper and Steel.* N.Y.: Grolier, 1907.

ST. MEMIN, CHARLES B. J. FEVRET DE. (St. M. with number.) *St. Memin Collection of Portraits.* N.Y.: Elias Dexter, 1862.

SUMNER, WILLIAM H. *History of East Boston.* Boston: William H. Piper Co., 1869. (Earlier ed., 1858.)

TITCOMB, SARAH E. *Early New England People.* Boston: W. B. Clarke & Carruth, 1882.

WISMER, DAVID CASSEL. (W with number.) *Descriptive List of Obsolete Paper Money Issued in New Jersey.* Federalsburg, Md.: J. W. Stowell, 1928.

Index to Text

Munn, Ann Maverick, 9, 18, 30, 31, 36, 69
Munn, Patrick, 31, 36, 69

National Academy of Design, 55, 59, 67, 68, 76, 79
Neagle, John, ix, 68 and n.
Neal (Mr.), 56
Neal, John, 68
Newark in 1809, 38
Newark Centinel of Freedom, 40, 43
Newman, Harry Shaw, x
New York Society Library, bookplates, 85

Otis, Bass, 65
Owen, Robert, port., 66

Packer Institute, 76
Paine, Thomas, 29
Palmer, Elihu, 28
Paper mill, 56
Parkes, Grace E., ix, 29, 75 n.
Parkes, Harriet M., ix, 29, 75 n.
Parkes, Harriet Matilda Maverick, 75 n.
Parkes, Mary Louise, 75 n.
Parkes, Smith A., 75 n.
Parkes, Woodworth M., 75 n.
Pattee, Grace M., 77 n., 78
Payne, Eloisa R., 58
Perfect Felicity, print, 67
Perkins-Durand firm, 64 n.
Peters, Harry T., 185
Peyton, Col., 63
Pintard, John, bookplate, 85
Pompey, Maverick's servant, 43
Potts, William S., 42
Prior and Dunning, 44
Provoost, Samuel, bookplate, 85
Puppies, lithograph, 67
Pursell, Henry, 16

Rabbits, print, 67
Republicans, 28

Reynolds, Ann, *see* Ann R. Maverick
Reynolds, Clara, *see* Clara R. Maverick
Reynolds, Rebecca, *see* Rebecca R. Maverick
Reynoldses, copperplate printers, 27
Riley, Joseph, 74
Rise and Progress of the Arts of Design, 76, 184–185
Robertson, Alexander, 45
Rollinson, William, 50
Rowe, Elizabeth, 85
Rudiments of Drawing, 62
Rushton, Bethiah, 14
Rushton, Peter, 13, 14
Rushton, Sarah, *see* Sarah R. Maverick
Ruskin, John, xix-xx
Rutgers College, diploma, 86
Ruth and Boaz, engraving, 59

St. John's Burying Ground, 71, 78 n.; Park, 72
St. Memin, Charles B. J., 185
Sayre, Isaac, 32
Scott, John M., 14
Shipman, Charles, 16
Signatures on Maverick prints, 84–85
Silversmith work, 16, 18
Simons, Joseph, 16
Smith, Enos, 48, 49
Smith, Jemimah, *see* Jemimah S. Maverick
Smith, William, 17
Smith, William D., 42
Snipes, lithograph of, 66
Society of Mechanics and Tradesman, 17
Sources, biographical, 9, 10, 183–185
South American trade, 64–65
Spafard, Edwin, 76
Spafard, Octavia M., vii, 44, 46, 66, 76, 79
Spanish editions of prints, 64, 65
Spiro, J. N., ix, 87
Stakes, Barthalemus, 17

Index to Check List

(References are to item numbers in check list)

Holy Land, 1731, 1733
Homer, 32, 552, 553, 555, 791; port., 554
Hooker, William, 1118
Hooker, W. & Blount, E., 1116
Hoole, John, port., 332
The Hope of Israel, 724
Hopkins & Baird, 478
Hopkins, George F., 478
Hopper, Edward, 547
Horanian Society Library, bookplate, 141
Hosford, E. E., 738
Hotel, trade card, 1703
House painters' association, 1713
Hudson, Henry (publisher), 332
Hudson, New York, Bank, 1411
Hudson River, 686
Human Heart, A View of, 724
Humphreys, D., 37
Humphreys, David, 556
Humphreys, F. L., 556
Hunter shooting wildcat, 1405
Hunter, Dard, 492
Hunter, William J., bookplate, 142
Huntington, David, 465, 467, 588
The Hyacinth, 377, 378, 472, 475, 635

Ice-house garden, trade card, 13
Illinois River, 681
Imbert, [Antoine?], 1725
Indian chief, 668
Indian presents, 33
Indolence, The Castle of, 753
Industry, 486
Inglesby & Stokes, trade card, 1014
Ingham, Charles, 449
Inland Voyage, Travels on, 686
Inman, Henry, 124, 433, 455, 493, 510, 535, 547, 590, 654, 681, 685, 909, 1405, 1495, 1568, 1804, 1806, 1906, 1912
Innes, John, 557 to 573
Innocence, 410

Insurance Co., see Assurance Company
Insurance Company, Newark Banking and, 1311; Jefferson, 581; Life & Fire, 1481
Insurance Company notes, 1471, 1481
Insurance policy, 1026
Isaac, 591
Israel, The Hope of, 724
Italian alphabet, 482
Italian Peasant Girl, 1904
Italy, 362
Ives & White, trade card, 1016
Ives, see Currier & Ives
Ives, I., 1016

Jackall and Fox, 411
Jack Halyard, 433
Jackson and Palm Tree, 574
Jackson, Andrew, History of, 577
Jackson, Andrew, 1722; port., 575, 576, 577, 578
Jackson, James, port., 579
Jacob, 355
Jadon, 592
James, T., 906
January & May, 1763
Jarvis, J. W., 337, 367, 370
Jay, John, 67; port., 580
Jefferson Insurance Company, 581
Jefferson, Thomas, 766, 1722; port., 581, 582, 583
Jenkins, John, 491, 584; port., 585
Jeroboam, 592
Jersey Bank of Jersey City, New Jersey, 1271
Jersey Bank building, Jersey City, New Jersey, 1277
Jesus, Sepulchre of, 421, 422
Jewel mark, Masonic, 70
Jeweler, trade card, 1003, 1004, 1007, 1010
Jewett, see Waldo & Jewett
John the Baptist, 498

218